MOORE
than a legend

Published by Goal! Publications
PO Box 2268, Romford, Essex, RM2 6BW

First published in the UK, November 1997

© Copyright Goal! Publications and Phil Daniels

ISBN 0-9529641-9-8

Designed by Andy Smith
Printed by Butler & Tanner Ltd, Frome, Somerset

Contents

Dedication

For Bobby's Grandchildren – so that one day you may know your Grandad.

Acknowledgments

I would like to thank everyone who has contributed in any way to the completion of this book. Particular thanks go to the interviewees, all of whom kindly spared their time and co-operation to talk about Bobby Moore, which, for many, was a very upsetting and difficult experience. Special thanks go to Bobby's children, Roberta and Dean, whose initial encouragement was vital and whose on-going friendship is valued more than they will know; to Tina, for all her help and memories; and to Stephanie for her co-operation.

My thanks also go to Stuart Allen for compiling the statistics and to Debbie Lambert for transcribing the tapes. I would also like to express my appreciation to everyone who offered contact numbers and the army of secretaries, press officers and agents out there who passed on faxes and helped organise interviews. My thanks also go to the following people for their help which was above and beyond what could possibly be hoped for, in no particular order: Peter Storrie and Lorraine Gunn at West Ham; Mike Newlin; Helmut Lenz and Franz Beckenbauer; David Taylor; Sue Ball and David Barber at the Football Association; Debbie Josefson, Ian McLaurin and Martin Protheroe at Umbro; Pele; Chris Hull; John Pawsey; Rob Steen; Dennis Selinger; Michael Caine; Gary Firmager; Kenny Lynch; Noel Cantwell; John Mitchell; Jeff Powell; Chris Lightbown; Nigel Clarke; Rob Jenkins; Geoff Hurst, Nobby Stiles and George Cohen; Vic Jobson; Martin Tyler; Terry O'Neill; Michael Hart; Rose Robertson; Ricky Dalton; Kam Shafqat; Chris Richardson; John Hardie; Tony McDonald, Steve Blowers and Danny Francis; Andy Smith, John and Robert Bollé. Also the people who kindly contributed photographs, including Bobby Moore's family and friends, Alan Jacobs, Sporting Pictures, Allsport, Colorsport, Richard Austin and Les Gold; everyone who willingly gave support at the offices of *The Sunday Times*; and the girls from Goal! We have been unable to trace the sources of all these pictures but any photographer involved is invited to contact the publishers in writing providing proof of copyright. If I have excluded anybody, please accept my apologies – your help was no less appreciated, but make sure you let me know I've missed you off the list!

Without all these people, this book would not have been possible.
Phil Daniels

The Bobby Moore Fund For Imperial Cancer Research

Bobby Moore died of bowel cancer in February 1993.

It is the second highest cancer killer in the UK today.

Nearly 30,000 people a year get it and 20,000 of them die. The death rates have barely changed in 30 years.

The Bobby Moore Fund is dedicated solely to improving these dismal statistics.

This is a synopsis of the work carried out by the Fund with the money that has been raised so far:

The Bobby Moore Research Fellow at the Western General, Edinburgh

Since 1993, Dr Jill Gardiner, the Bobby Moore Research Fellow at the Medical Oncology Unit in Edinburgh has been carrying out research on a new approach which involves treating the spread of colon cancer to the liver by loading tiny balls, known as microspheres, with an anti-cancer drug called EO-9, which is delivered to the cancer without affecting the rest of the body.

Pre-clinical trials will lead to full clinical trials involving patients.

The Computer Data Base System at St. Marks Hospital, London

This new system allows accurate and precise conclusions to be drawn from the clinical details of bowel cancer patients, in relation to particular features of their individual clinical history or pathological findings. This information will allow the examination of a huge variety of factors and relationships that may increase an individual's risk of developing bowel cancer, thus allowing prediction and therefore a high rate of prevention.

The Bobby Moore Research Competitive Fellowship

This project was selected from a number of applications and has been deemed the best bowel cancer related study by Imperial Cancer Research Fund and is to be conducted by Professor Roland Wolf of the Molecular Pharmacology Unit at Ninewells Hospital, Dundee.

It is the aim of this project to gain a deeper understanding of how dietary factors, as well as specific types of drugs, effect the cancer progress. This will allow new ways of increasing the protective effects of drugs or preventing the harmful effects of certain dietary components. Initially research work is carried out scientifically but will lead to trials with cancer patients.

It is hoped that these studies will rapidly lead to new approaches for the prevention and treatments of this disease.

Sources of research and tributes

Recommended further reading: Books

Jeff Powell: Bobby Moore - The Life and Times of a Sporting Legend (Robson Books, 1993); David Emery, Christopher Hilton, Steve Curry and James Lawton: The Illustrated Guide of a Footballing Legend (Headline, 1993); Roger Hutchinson: It Is Now! (Mainstream Publishing, 1995); Bobby Moore: England! England! (Stanley Paul, 1970); Harold Shepherdson: The Magic Sponge (Pelham, 1968); Geoff Hurst: The World Game (Stanley Paul, 1967); Rogan Taylor and Andrew Ward: Kicking and Screaming - An Oral History of Football in England (Robson Books, 1995); Martin Tyler: Boys Of '66 (Hamlyn, 1981); David Miller: Boys of '66 - England's Last Glory (Pavillion 1986 & 1996); Kenneth Wolstenholme: They Think It's All Over (Robson, 1996); John Northcutt and Roy Shoesmith: West Ham United - A Complete Record (Breedon, 1993); Dave Hill: England's Glory - 1966 and all that (Pan 1996); Andy Pringle and Neil Fissler: Where Are They Now (Two Heads Publishing, 1996).

Recommended further viewing: Videos

Goal! - Official FIFA film of 1966 World Cup (Polygram Video 632 368-3); Tribute to Bobby Moore (VSI Sports Video VHS WHBM93); Bobby Moore: Tribute to a Legend (Independent Television News Ltd VHS VC2221); The Bobby Moore Story (Watershed WSP 1130)

TRIBUTE ACKNOWLEDGMENTS

Apart from the books and videos above, the short tributes in this book were extracted from the following sources: The Sunday Times and The Sunday Times Magazine; World Cup 30th Anniversary Tour official souvenir programme (published by Underworld Ltd, London E1); The Times and The Times Magazine; The Sun; The Independent and Independent on Sunday; Route 66 Magazine (Independent Magazines UK Ltd); When Saturday Comes; Total Sport Magazine; FourFourTwo Magazine; The Observer; England Magazine; Daily Mail; Mail on Sunday's You Magazine; The People; Ilford Recorder; Barking and Dagenham Post; Hammer - West Ham United programme; The Official Souvenir Programme for the Bobby Moore Memorial Match; Daily Mirror; Daily Express; News of the World and Sunday Telegraph.

Foreword

by Stephanie Moore

Everyone who is old enough remembers where he, or she, was when England won the World Cup in 1966. It has become one of the most memorable moments of our lives.

As a young teenager, I watched the match in monochrome in the kitchen, while doing the ironing, little realising that one day Bobby Moore would have such an all-consuming impact on my life.

From the moment he held the Jules Rimet Trophy aloft, Bobby Moore became a British hero. And Bobby the man was a hero, too, to his large and lovely family, to his friends, to everyone who knew him.

Bobby came from Barking in the East End of London, growing up in a very close and supportive family. They were warm, funny, stoic, disciplined, with a tremendous sense of integrity which he inherited.

As an only child, he had a very happy childhood. To his dad Robert (Big Bob) and his mum Doris, he was the most important thing in their lives.

He had a great support system in his aunts and uncles, Ena, Dora, Beattie and Fred, and an army of cousins who always valued Bobby for what he was, not the World Cup hero he became. To them he was just 'Robert', one of the family. They have their own memories of him, too numerous to be included in this book.

Representing the family, you'll be reading the memories of Tina and Bobby's children, Dean and Roberta, whom he adored, from his cousin, Graham, who, out of all his cousins, spent the most time in the Moore household when he was growing up, and his aunt Ena. Their warm recollections are echoed by all the family.

Bobby and Stephanie at home, 1992.

Bobby was a wonderful human being as this book will reveal. He was warm, selfless, affectionate, with his father's dry sense of humour and his mother's stoic determination to do what was right in life. Sadly I never knew Big Bob, his father, but his mother was a wonderful lady and I had the greatest respect and love for her.

Bobby epitomised everything I could possibly have wanted. He was my soulmate. He had a tremendous thirst for life and new experiences and he treasured his family above all else. He had amazingly few faults. One of the few I can now recall was his uncanny ability to always be on the golf course the day that we moved house!

When Bobby was diagnosed with cancer he was very strong. He never allowed himself the luxury of self-pity, bitterness nor anger. He worked and played even harder than before and so fought the disease the way he's lived his life.

Roberta and Dean had lived with us at different times over the years but after Bobby's illness was diagnosed, they became even more involved and spent a lot of time with him. They were also a tremendous strength to me.

When Bobby's first granchild, Poppy was born to to Dean's partner Sara, they came to live with us too.

When Bobby realised that the disease had spread, and that there was no hope, he tried to live the last two years of his life as normally as he could. He ran daily with Sophie, the Dobermann we'd found as a stray and been allowed to keep. He played squash, golf, tennis. He continued his commitments to his company MMA, which he ran with his great friend John Mitchell, his radio work with Capital which he loved and his involvement with the different charities he'd always supported. He looked so amazingly fit it was hard to believe that he was going to die. They were two bitter-sweet years.

Bobby had bowel cancer, the second worst cancer in the UK today. 30,000 people get the disease every year and most of them die. Yet if caught early enough, this is one of the most curable cancers and most people should survive.

By buying this book, you are helping people to survive. The Bobby Moore fund for Imperial Cancer is dedicated to research into this common disease and is undoubtedly saving lives by raising the profile of this neglected, un-talked about cancer.

Bobby lost the battle against bowel cancer but there is still a war to be won. And if you can help further, the address of the Bobby Moore Fund is 61, Lincoln's Inn Fields, London WC2A 3PX.

Bobby and I were very happily married, very much in love and I miss him everyday. It has been very emotional for me to read this book. There have been moments where I have cried at people's memories of Bobby, but also many moments where I have laughed out loud. Many of the memories have helped me, some have been painful, but I would like to thank everyone who has made this book possible.

What shines out from every page is the tremendous pleasure Bobby gave people, both on and off the pitch. We are all better for having known him.

Stephanie Moore, October 1997

Bobby and Stephanie with Bobby's mum, Doris, in December 1991.

Introduction

by Phil Daniels

never knew Bobby Moore. He was my hero as a kid and I had forgotten how much he meant to me until the phone rang at 6.45pm on Wednesday, February 24, 1993. It was someone who broke the news of Moore's death. I had heard some vague rumour about him being ill but had dismissed it as the usual nonsense – so many of these nasty stories do the rounds. It did not register, for once, the rumour might be valid and that Bobby Moore might die. He was solid and dependable. He couldn't die. But it was true.

I wasn't immediately sure how I felt. Stunned, certainly. My first response, however, was to get in the car and drive straight to Upton Park. A rather daft notion, perhaps, but I guess I suddenly needed familiarity. When I arrived at the ground, I found I wasn't the only one with that same silly notion.

Even though it was a bitterly cold night, there were already a dozen faces there, some I recognised from West Ham games. I felt better the moment I arrived on the old manor where I'd seen Bobby play, surrounded by these familiar faces. 'It's like losing someone in the family,' one of them commented. That was it, I thought, one of the family. Bobby Moore was ours. The rest of the country only had him on loan.

At this stage, there were only a few isolated items put on the main gates by the early arrivals. The number six shirt, photographed so much that week, hung in the middle surrounded by a couple of scarves and two small bunches of flowers. They looked a bit sparse up there on their own, but they formed a wholly genuine and spontaneous tribute.

We began swopping memories of Moore; things we had seen him do; how we'd heard the news; which tribute the club would pay. All the standard stuff, but it served its purpose. We watched as fan after fan arrived to pay their homage and lay a personal tribute. Even passing cars and buses either deliberately slowed down, dimmed their headlights or their drivers simply acknowledged the mourners.

I saw many people turn up to pay their respects, go home, only to return an hour later. Sadness and restlessness, it seems, brought them back. For my part, I just couldn't leave. Something kept me there and I kept making excuses to stay a little longer. In the end, I left at 1am. Had it not been for the cold, I could've stayed all night. On reflection, it seemed barmy to spend all that time there but it helped in some strange way. When I saw recently on TV the vigils of so many people at various venues in London following the tragic death of Princess Diana, I understand now that my actions that night weren't so barmy after all. The close proximity of the ground, and the closeness of the people who were suffering in the same way, helped ease the pain. This need for familiar surroundings is nothing new, of course, but it was new for me and many of the people at the ground that night.

Oddly enough, it wasn't until the following morning that the full impact, the horror, of Bobby's death really hit me. Bobby Moore, my first hero, was dead. His era was a very special time for many of us and it is Bobby's era, the rock 'n' roll years, that activated my emotions as much as the man himself and his achievements. He was an embodiment of the '66 and '70 World Cups and an era that we remember as a better time, regardless of how accurate that is.

All the '66 team were giants but no one commanded more standing in the country's hearts than Robert Frederick Moore. He brought discipline, standards and values from his upbringing in the austere 50s and carried them into the swinging 60s. Where others were affected sooner by the youth culture – George Best was the Fifth Beatle, the hippy who often failed to deliver or turn up – Moore was still the clean-cut Golden Boy, smart, chivalrous, reliable, who wouldn't let you down when the going got tough. And he looked good, too. When Bobby Moore got the ball, no one looked away. He was the coolest bloke who ever laced up football boots. They called Steve McQueen the King of Cool – if that's true, then Moore was the Emperor of Cool.

Everyone goes on about Bobby's leadership, the calmness, the passing, the physical retributions on players who took liberties, but what sticks in my mind more than anything from watching him play is the way he looked – his style. It's a cliche, but Bobby did cut a dashing figure with that blond hair. He swept up and down, back and forth across the back of the West Ham defence with that odd, bow-legged gait of his as gently and unconcerned as a tide drifting in and out, while permanently holding down the cuffs of his long-sleeve shirt with his fingers. That was a peculiar habit, wasn't it? Just like the way he held the ball on his hip as he came out the tunnel and knocked it up in the air with the back of his hand before starting a jog once he'd emerged from the tunnel. Peculiar, but undoubtedly stylish.

One recollection that stays vividly in my mind was how, when playing, he never seemed to need to look at the ball. This can't be right but I seem to recall him with his head up throughout 90 minutes.

Another thing Bobby Moore did so well, which few players have understood since, let alone mastered, was the way he 'marked space'. Invariably, when you looked, Bobby seemed to be guarding a larger area of space than any of his teammates. This is partly explained by the requirement of the semi-sweeper role Bobby played, picking up the pieces from the centre-half. But even taking that into account, the area he used to dominate was far greater than it should have been. I have a vision of Moore filling this huge area of space and, no matter what, always winning 99 per cent of encounters in that space, frequently against much faster players. If an opponent was 15 yards ahead and running with the ball towards

MOORE **than a legend**

Bobby's space, you just knew Bobby would win the tackle. Or, if he didn't win it, he would always do enough, get a toe in, push the ball 18 inches away so it couldn't be retrieved by the forward or slip it neatly to a West Ham team-mate. By whatever tactic, he somehow snuffed out the attack altogether or, at the very least, held up the momentum of the move, which is often effectively the same thing. That was one part of it.

His magnetism, a kind of force-field he honed over the years, took up this big open area and he filled it entirely. In truth, what we were witnessing was his presence frightening people away – maybe without them even realising it. Possibly it might be one reason why he encouraged the detachment in his manner? Perhaps he realised it helped give him the distant aura that aided his football presence on the field?

It always amazed me that as a much slower man, he got to tackles first. Even when players were considerably faster than him. Not only that, but he never tore into tackles. In fact, he won tackles by actually slowing down. Literally, he backed off an opponent, started to jog, then nipped the ball away. The only other person in British football that comes anywhere near him is Paul McGrath. But he never brought with him onto the field the same presence and clout that comes with being a world champion and a legend, something which frightens opponents.

Something else Moore did effortlessly was to lure unsuspecting forwards into places they didn't want to go. He knew instinctively where the danger area would be in any move, so he often let the opponent slip into the space where he wanted him, sometimes near the byline. He would trap him and dispossess him on his own terms. Somehow, the forward lost the ball or was forced into turning away and relinquishing it hurriedly. Bobby led people into alleyways and then sealed them off.

His tidying up at the back was a joy to watch. There was one hairy moment I recall in the '70 World Cup, which isn't an obvious example of Moore's class, but one that sticks out for me. Brazil were attacking, there was a loose ball and what seemed like a million Brazilians in our box. The ball rolled into a pocket of space and you expected one of Pele or Jairzinho or Rivelino or Tostao to pounce and score. But with yellow shirts on all sides, Bobby was the first to react and move in. Except you couldn't see how he was going to get the ball out. He was boxed in. Yet, somehow, he played a sidefoot pass through a gap no one else could see to the edge of the box. It wasn't to anyone in particular, but that was the genius of it. He passed to space and by the time people had realised what he'd done, the danger was gone and England eventually got the ball away. I laughed when I saw it. It was so funny how he outwitted the 1970 Brazilian team single-handed – a team who were widely acknowledged as the greatest team in the history of the game.

But the interception was only part of it. He used that same presence when he had the ball as well. I adored the way, when coming out of defence, he used to push the ball out a long way in front of him while he looked upfield for the right pass. Even though he was usually in space between midfield and defence, rarely did anyone seem to attempt to close him down or make him rush. If they did, Moore just seemed to slow down yet again, use his body to shield the ball, let the forward come in close, therefore momentarily taking the opponent out of the play, before he laid it off and switched the attack. And the stuff with the outside of the foot, the little chips and the weighted passes were as good as anyone else's in the world. It wasn't accurate just some of the time either – his passes *never* went astray. If Bobby Moore made a bad pass in a match, the crowd would gasp. If he made two in the same game it made headlines.

But what came through to me in the days following his death were those wonderful memories of Moore and the 60s and 70s. I was six when I got my first West Ham strip for Christmas. It was hanging in the sportshop stall in East Ham market and, as kids are want to do, I had pointed it out to my mum every time we had passed it for weeks beforehand. A proper number six, Bobby's number, was extra money, so mum cut up my old white pyjamas, created a six and sewed it on for me. It was still an age where it didn't matter what you wore and if you couldn't afford the pukka stuff, anything, home-made or otherwise, would do.

There were other memories, too: I had the first edition of *Shoot!* magazine with "Bobby Moore writes for you" on it that I foolishly swopped later for an Airfix model; the monstrously-long woollen scarf and bobble hat my grandma knitted for me and the first time my father had taken me to Upton Park and we'd watched from the Chicken Run. He took me several times and in later years I recall standing with him at the back of the North Bank the day Bobby Moore scored against Stoke when he hit a shot from outside the area. It struck a defender's back and sailed over the top of Gordon Banks' head into the net.

There was silly stuff, as well. You know, the daft, embarrassing things you do when you're a kid? When I was very young, maybe eight years-old, I wrote to Bobby and invited him and his family over for tea. My dad took the letter and handed it in at Upton Park. 'Don't worry,' they said, 'we'll see Bob gets it.' For a week I was going around telling my neighbours, kids at school, the milkman, anyone who would listen, that Bobby Moore was coming to tea. I cringe now, but at the time it was magical. I never got a reply, although, of course, there is no way of proving my invite ever reached him. But it never bothered me one bit. In fact, it only added to my worship. When you're a kid, it's too unreal to think your hero would bother with you, right? In some respects, my child logic said he wouldn't be a proper hero if he did.

Once, I queued up for two hours just to get his autograph at the opening of a petrol station in the Barking Road. When I got it – and this was the closest I ever got to meeting him – I promptly went outside and rejoined the back of the queue. Then there were times I used to make the pilgrimage on my bike to Green Street, just to look through the glass of his sports shop in the hope of catching a glimpse of him serving behind the counter. I cannot describe the disappointment when, having pedalled all the way from East Ham to Upton Park – no mean feat on a small bike – I found a woman serving instead. Because I wasn't supposed to cycle that far, I didn't tell my parents. It was some while before I discovered footballers trained in the mornings, a fact which soon prompted more bike rides in the afternoons.

My favourite Moore-related memory stretches back to a holiday camp trip when I was about nine years-old. As a footballer, I was slightly tubby, had white blond hair, no pace, and played all my kickabouts in my claret and blue strip with the number six on the back. Sound a tad familiar? Anyway, at this camp – a place called Gunton Hall – all the kids under 14 years-old played a local team made up entirely of huge kids all aged 14. It doesn't sound a big difference but when you're nine, 14 year-olds look like basketball players from the NBA. Unfortunately, our lot were mixed ages and I was easily the youngest. The biggest kid on our side appointed himself captain and organised positions. As is always the way, all the little kids and nerds got stuck at the back and all the big kids, including this captain, played as strikers to get all the glory. We really were raggedy-arse rovers. I was at the back with all the usual suspects: a fat kid, a girl, a ginger kid, a kid with glasses, the only black kid on the camp and a smelly kid with messy hair who was playing in shoes. A mob of mums and dads were lined up on the touchline but I couldn't take my eyes off all these giants up the other end of the pitch – it looked something like that Nike TV advert where Cantona and Wright play the team of monsters and winged serpents.

The game kicked off and a kid with long hair put his head down and started dribbling toward me with the ball. He carried the ball past the girl and the kid with glasses so I stuck out my foot in the path of the ball, the way my dad had taught me, and this long-haired kid tripped over the ball and went flying. The campers on the touchline went potty. I looked up and managed to toe-poke the ball upfield as hard as I could before any of the other big kids could get near me. Consequently, because the local kids had pushed up expecting to get a goal, one of our team ran on to the pass and scored. 'Well done Bobby Moore!' shouted one of the dads. 'Give the ball to Mooro!' shouted another. It all sounds extremely silly now but I cannot describe the feeling it gave me to have all those people cheer for me in that way. I was always pretty ordinary at football, second team at school, all that, but the buzz I got from doing so well and hearing grown-ups call me 'Bobby Moore' was like a fantastic dream come true. I was filled with pride.

From that moment, my confidence soared and, for a nine year-old, my game was out of this world. It turned into one of those rare games that come along once or twice in your life where you can't do anything wrong. I was tackling kids twice my size and coming away with the ball time and again. Better than that, I found myself pointing to the others, telling them where to play, bringing the urchins up to the half way line to play off-side. Our back row of nerdy misfits became a disciplined, fighting unit – not even Tony Adams and the Arsenal off-side robots ever moved up in such a tight unit. I can't recall exactly, but I suspect I may even have started running funny and pulling the sleeves of my shirt down past my wrists. We won, somehow, but it didn't stop there. For the rest of the holiday, everyone at Gunton Hall, campers and staff, called me Bobby Moore. I got 'Oi, Bobby!' and 'All right, Mooro?' everywhere I went. It may sound insignificant, but when you're a kid you take your limited experience of life on holiday with you and for two weeks each summer, that camp becomes your world. In those two weeks at Gunton Hall, I was a star. And, my hero, Bobby Moore, had been responsible for that brief fame.

On the Sunday after Moore died, I returned to the gates of Upton Park. I'd seen the tributes building up on the TV news and in newspaper pictures but I wasn't prepared for what I found. I was overwhelmed by the honesty and wholeheartedness of people's gestures.

The first thing that struck me was the immense sacrifice of the items fans had left on the railings. Aside from the flowers and candles, it was stuff that had been salvaged from lofts and attics across East London and Essex, much of it faded and worn. There were flags, teddies, cushions, bobble hats, towels, rosettes, signed photographs and every single style of West Ham shirt since the dawn of time. Personal messages and poems were scrawled on paper, there were programmes from important matches, World Cup final tickets, pennants covered in autographs, a Munich 1860 flag and plenty of those montrously-long hand-knitted scarves, just like the one my grandma knitted for me all those years ago. The scene was like some giant vandal had come along and tipped the entire contents of the club shop into the street.

Everything was so priceless, so irreplaceable. All given away free without a second thought. The slightly-mad logic of such sacrifice is that by giving something up in that way, it is more likely to stay with you. And people were giving so much up without bothering to ask why. It was the natural thing to do. It was wonderful. And I was so proud of the people that follow my football team.

"I was at the back with all the usuals suspects: a fat kid, a girl, a ginger kid, a kid with glasses, the only black kid on the camp and a smelly kid with messy hair who was playing in shoes"

I was holding up quite well working my way through all the tributes but a series of things I spotted hit a raw nerve. Firstly, and this may sound daft, but there was an old hand-knitted jumper tied to the fence in claret and blue patches. All stretched and out of shape and it looked like such an old rag that if you dug it out of the bottom of your wardrobe you would be embarrassed to offer it to Oxfam. And given we live in a far more profit-orientated world of Adidas, Reebok, Umbro and the vast range of club merchandise, it looked especially sorry and pathetic. But it reminded me of my mum's number six and my grandma's scarf: It was part of a bygone age when people were poorer but no less passionate and no one really gave a toss about designer gear. And somewhere, somebody's auntie or mother or nan had taken the care to knit this jumper in all good faith for someone they cared about. I was, perhaps, being a bit over-emotional, but a lump had appeared in my throat nevertheless.

The snow was beginning to fall on the carpet of memorabilia now. I moved along with the crowd, reading the tributes. One read: 'This scarf was swopped with an Anderlecht supporter. May it go with you wherever you are – Clive, Hornchurch.'

At that point, I spotted something which made me shiver. It was a poster pull-out of Moore from an issue of *Shoot!* just before the 1970 World Cup in Mexico. It was in colour, with Bobby dressed in the white England strip with three lions in the centre of his chest, holding an orange ball. I remember the picture vividly because at the time it came out I had tried to sketch that same photograph for a drawing competition. It had taken me days and when I finished the ball wasn't round and the arm was wonky, but when you've drawn something you never forget each line and angle. It was an eerie experience coming face to face with something I had completely forgotten about. The combination of happy childhood memories and my acute sadness over the loss of Bobby, was becoming too much for me.

I was cold and on my way out of the gates when I read one last tribute and, in some ways, I wished I hadn't. It read: "Bobby, we didn't know you but we know all about you from our Grandad. God Bless - Hayley (6 years) and Tina (5 years)." To me, that said it all. How the tales of true talent can be passed from generation to generation and still mean something.

I walked away from the gates with tears streaming down my face. When I got to the car I cried in a way I hadn't done for years. This sounds a bit over-the-top in the cold light of day, but I know why I wept and it was a good cry for many reasons. I cried for Bobby Moore. For '66 and '70. For the passing of my own childhood. For fond memories of a better time, and for the caring innocence of Hayley, six, and Tina, five. I think most people out there will know exactly what I mean.

After Bobby Moore died I wanted to find out more about my first hero. I began reading the other literature available, and, although helpful, I wanted to know more. So I contacted his daughter, Roberta, to do an interview for the West Ham fanzine, *Over Land And Sea*. After that, someone who saw the piece suggested I take it a stage further and write a book. To begin with, I couldn't see a fresh way to approach another book on Moore, given that the traditional biographies had been done. However, I felt that interviews from a wide cross-section of people from all areas of Moore's life might work. I started the interviews way back in May 1995 and the project has taken me on a journey of discovery. The task was, essentially, a labour of love for me. Each person I spoke to offered a different view or anecdote about Bobby. Slowly, the pieces of the jigsaw unfolded.

Many interviewees pointed me in the direction of new ones and I realised I was starting to uncover an army of people who had been touched by this incredible man. I was pleasantly surprised to find that absolutely no one had a bad word to say about Bobby – which in over 100 interviews from a sport not known for its decorum, is breathtaking. At times, I worried that the finished article would be so utterly positive that it would seem unnatural and I would be accused of writing a book that showed just one false side. But, as the work went on, I realised it wasn't fake at all. It was the true Bobby Moore.

I hope you find the journey through the life of Bobby Moore as enthralling and moving as I did.
Phil Daniels, October 1997

Chapter 1
Family: the early days

Tina Moore

Tina met Bobby in 1958 and they were married in Ilford in 1962. Their first child, Roberta, was born in 1965 and their second, Dean, in 1968. They were divorced in 1986 after 24 years of marriage

I met Bobby just before my 16th birthday. He asked me to dance at the Ilford Palais and we made arrangements to meet somewhere. I can't remember where, but I didn't turn up. Something happened, I think I overlooked an engagement I'd made with some girlfriends.

I bumped into him again and he asked to see me. I agreed, but suggested we should make arrangements next time I saw him. Then my mother and I were driving past a coffee bar, saw Bobby and I said: 'That's the boy who asked me out'. She liked the look of him and said: 'He looks lovely. You really should go.'

The next time I saw him – third time lucky – he asked me again and I went out with him. From then on, we saw each other more or less six days a week. Friday nights used to be a girls' night for me, where we would chat, but then Bobby would be on the phone all night long anyway. From then on it was very intense and quick and we didn't have much time apart, except for when he went on football trips around the world.

At that age, he was shy and unsure of himself, but he was a very determined young man. He showed that in all aspects of his life. He was determined with his football, and he was determined to have me. He always put a lot into whatever he did – like our relationship. Every hour he wasn't at football was devoted to us going out. He was wonderful. Very generous, thoughtful and considerate.

I went away once with my mother and when I came back, unbeknown to me, he'd been around and redecorated my bedroom, reupholstered a chair and kitted out a sort of filing cabinet with green felt compartments and made it into a jewellery box for me. He was quite handy like that and it was such a pleasant surprise. The first time he went on a trip he came back with a tortoise shell powder compact for me, which I still have to this day. I'd only known him a short while at that stage.

Bobby's dad was a really nice man. His mother took longer to warm to but I got on well with her eventually. To start with she was wary of me because Bobby and I were both so young. She was proud of him, naturally so, and I think she found it difficult getting used to Bobby having a girlfriend. When Bobby got involved with someone or something it was all or nothing and I was the first serious girlfriend he'd had. His mother and I were both very strong women, so occasionally we had our differences, but nothing terribly serious. She was very kind but I realised she was a different type of person to me, but his father was an absolute gem. We really got on right from the word go.

One of the reasons I wasn't that keen to go out with Bobby initially was that I wasn't interested in football. I'd been to a match with another boyfriend and, to me, it was cold and damp and there were people screaming and shouting. It didn't appeal to me at all.

My father left when I was two and I was brought up in a very woman-orientated

*Bobby and Tina
with baby
Roberta.*

environment with my mother, my grandmother and spent a lot of time with my aunt so I didn't understand the magnitude of football's popularity then. To me, it was just a game. At that time, players hardly got a fortune – Bobby earned about £8 a week and the most you could get was £16 a week, so I wasn't terribly impressed by the fact he was a footballer. Once Bobby's mum realised I wasn't some kind of football groupie and I wasn't interested in her son for the fame, she accepted me and everything was fine.

Bobby adored my mother and she thought he was the absolute bees-knees and she found him to be handsome, clean-cut and saw really admirable qualities in him. In fact, she pushed me towards him. I was more outgoing than Bobby and she felt he was the perfect man for me. She thought Bobby was steady, reliable and very gentlemanly and she sensed he had an inner quality.

When she was dying with a brain tumour, Bobby came and stayed on a bed at the hospital. She was in St John's hospital for nervous disorders and died at three o'clock in the morning. He insisted on staying with me the whole time. Bobby was very in tune with her. I can't remember if it was one or two nights, but he cancelled all his appointments and stayed with us. He was with her when she died. They were really close.

She was manageress of a shop with a large staff working for her, but she gave it up because Bobby started the sports shop business in Upton Park and she worked there for us. It was very successful. They had a lot of contact because of the business. Bobby was good to her.

MOORE **than a legend**

Bobby and I married in 1962 and he was beginning to get famous because he'd been picked for England. We were both from very ordinary backgrounds and to be catapulted into the eye of the media was strange at first. I was a young girl working for the Prudential and suddenly I was thrown into the limelight because of Bobby. It took some getting used to.

He and I had been together for three years and, all of a sudden, everywhere we went, people wanted to speak to him, invite him to loads of places, drag him off to do different things. I hung back initially until I got used to it.

The wedding and the birth of the children was covered by the press. Eventually we had journalist friends and it became easier, more personal, but it was quite traumatic to go from living a normal, quiet life to getting such attention. Being in the spotlight wasn't something I'd lusted after and I didn't know what all the fuss was about.

But it wasn't just the media. It was also the beginnings of the hangers-on realising Bobby was on his way up and they started demanding his time. The husband who was with me one hundred per cent of the time was suddenly being lured here, there and everywhere. But Bobby would insist I be included and I remember him refusing to go if I wasn't invited. Twice, we were both invited to Buckingham Palace, to cocktail parties, but both times I fell ill, which was really unfortunate, but he didn't go. He stayed to make sure I was okay and I always appreciated him for doing that.

Bobby was untouched and unspoiled by his fame. He was aware of everything, but eventually he got swept away a bit by some of these people. Bobby had a bit of a blind spot on certain types, because he was shy and reserved, he was actually drawn to very extrovert characters with style and flair. I think he was sometimes attracted to people who were not the right influences.

Bobby didn't like confrontation. He found it difficult if someone upset him so he would withdraw and try to dismiss it. He hated confrontation of any type, whether it be rude people or totally over-the-top intrusiveness, or whether it was battling with a problem in business. On many occasions when things actually had to be confronted he would say: 'Tina, you're better at dealing with people than me', and I had to fight battles for him.

He was very neat and tidy with everything in life. He tended to put things nicely away in compartments. If something couldn't be easily compartmentalised, he was thrown. He liked order and disliked disruption. He found it offensive.

As his career grew, life was a double-edged sword. Initially, it was very flattering being in the public eye but, as I said, that constant publicity was also a bit scary. But as Bobby grew, so did I. I realised a long way back in the marriage that he was going upwards and onwards into celebrity stardom and I decided I better go with him.

We did some TV advertisements. We did one with Martin and Kathy Peters called 'Pop down to your local', where Bobby and Martin came in and we were playing darts in the pub. Then we did another one for Bisto gravy. I was making the gravy for Bobby to come home to and I had to say: 'Ah, Bisto'. That was fun, although I found it nerve-racking. Looking back, I wouldn't change one day. When it's happening you don't appreciate it. It's like the fame rolled along and carried us with it. It was too fast to take in. I did so many things most of us don't get the opportunity of doing and I'm very grateful for that.

The 60s were different. It was one big breakthrough. Ordinary, everyday man was coming to the forefront. I don't think it was the class system breaking down so much as people were crossing lines they had never crossed before. Society was changing, football heroes started making money. In fact, before the maximum wage was abolished, I earned more than Bobby. When I got married and finished work, I earned £20 a week and he earned £16, something like that. I went to Ilford County High, spent my teens studying and met Bobby about three weeks after I left school. So most of my life has been with this man. Basically, I went from a very sheltered childhood into a very sheltered marriage. If you're married to a celebrity, when you go out, you're cloistered and everyone tends to look after you. It becomes another form of sheltering. It was only when I was on my own, when Bobby and I were divorced, I learnt what the real world was all about. It was an unusual existence.

"The whole kidnap threat business was very terrifying and shortly after there came a call threatening Bobby's life. I answered the phone and was told Bobby was going to be shot during the game that day"

Bobby and I got a kidnap threat once and the police took it very seriously. The letter said they were going to kidnap either myself or the two children and they wanted £10,000. Bobby came straight home and we had three detectives living with us for two weeks. Bobby bought crates of beer for these detectives and they would sit and have a few drinks. They got to be good buddies. At the time we had a young nanny called Pauline living with us and I had this strange feeling she would marry one of the detectives - a guy called Geoff. I said to Pauline: 'See that detective in the garden? I think you're going to marry him.' The really odd thing was that she did. I just had this feeling.

The whole kidnap threat business was very terrifying and shortly after there came a call threatening Bobby's life. I answered the phone and was told Bobby was going to be shot during the game that day. I rang the police and he was escorted off the pitch after the match by a ring of officers.

We had a very strange life. I did an interview once and said: 'It had been a hard life as well as a good life,' and the interviewer took the mickey, saying: 'Yeah, such a hard life'. But it wasn't a normal life. With the good things, you also get bad, like attracting these crank letters and people who were envious or jealous or were sick in some aspect. It made me very protective towards my family. It was a horrible thing to have gone through.

Bobby had some pubs with a partner. There were five pubs altogether: 'Mooro's' at Stratford was first, then 'Tipples' and 'Champers', 'The Blind Beggar' at Whitcchapel and one at Sawbridgeworth in Hertfordhsire called 'The Three Horseshoes'. Mooro's was an absolute winner, but the others never really lifted off.

Harrison-Moore, the leather goods firm that Bobby had, was so unlucky. It was successful when it started but was ruined by the three-day working week. They decided to open a factory in Cyprus but, unbelievably, Turkey invaded Cyprus and the factory finished up on the wrong side of the border and that was the end of that.

Bobby also opened up the shirt business called Bobby Moore Shirts, but it just didn't take off, which was a shame, because they were nice shirts. Then Bobby had Bobby Moore Jewellery with some aquaintance of his but there was little or no profit.

He was very unlucky with his businesses. He certainly wasn't lucky with some of his business partners and, unfortunately, I think he trusted some of the wrong people. He was swayed a lot by vibrant personalities. It's no secret he relaxed when he'd had a drink, he was a different person, and I think he was liable to be too easily taken in. He wasn't a very good judge of character in business and he was unlucky. Then there was Woolston Hall.

It was a country club in Chigwell that turned into a financial disaster. When Woolston Hall opened we had the most wonderful party involving every celebrity you could possibly imagine, including Gene Barry who played *The Adventurer.* Everyone was there and we gave away champagne, caviar, the works. It must have cost thousands. We tried to create a wonderful country club, but we had more kitchen staff than The Dorchester.

We had a women's club that went on outings to Pinewood Studios to meet stars. We even had a Vidal Sassoon hairdresser there. It was a fabulous place but, in hindsight, if we'd all been a bit older and wiser, it would have been a successful project. People still talk about it, but it was before its time. It was too expensive, too over-staffed and some of the staff were pilfering. We had it for almost two years – wonderful concept, great fun while it lasted, but not enough planning. Not one person on the board knew what they were doing yet all of them were grandiose in their schemes and their thinking. It was a case of no expense spared and very little expertise.

The place didn't work, the bank eventually called in the loan and Bobby got caught to pay an enormous amount, something in the region of £100,000. His face went grey when he was told he had to pay it. It cost us all our savings and he worked for God knows how long to pay that debt back.

It was devastating for Bobby. That sort of money was a fortune in the 70s. I remember when he finished the payments we opened a bottle of the finest champagne. Bobby was always very stylish and he wanted to celebrate the end of a very unhappy experience. I don't think he ever recovered financially from that loss.

I went to watch him make *Escape to Victory* in Budapest. It was unbelievable. They used to play tricks on Michael Caine, Bobby especially. Michael would lead the team out and Bobby would take great delight in leading them out the opposite way. We went out for dinner with Michael and I asked him to remove his glasses. Michael looked puzzled and said: 'Why?' and I explained that he and Bobby looked alike, they had similar hair and same shape bone structure. We had lots of fun.

The reaction Bobby provoked from people never failed to astound me. I remember being with him at the FA Cup final in 1975 and people were shouting: 'Bobby!'

and holding up their babies for him to touch. You could see the reverence in people's eyes. We could be in the middle of Africa and people would simply stare or call out his name. His effect on people was amazing. So much admiration. It was like he was a God.

Bobby was lucky - he was blessed with a talent, but most people had no idea how hard he worked to develop that talent. Bobby also had an indefinable quality. Some special people have that star quality - the really big stars like Bobby and Sean Connery and Michael Caine seem to retain a humility that lesser people perhaps feel is not necessary.

One thing I felt very sad about is that Bobby was not at Roberta's wedding. I know it was his dearest wish she should be married in the OBE chapel at St Paul's and I know how very proud he would have been to see Dean take his place and give Roberta away. It was such a great sorrow for us all that he was not there.

Roberta Moore

Since the death of her father, Roberta has married Matthew Hobbis. While living in New York, their son, Frederick Robert, was born — Bobby was christened Robert Frederick

Too many people misunderstood my father. Some accused him of being aloof, but that was because they didn't really know him. He was special, and I'm not saying that because I'm his daughter. He did what he did, and you don't do that if you're not special, do you?

My father was his own man, very independent. He had an inner strength that some people couldn't understand. He never followed the pack - the pack followed him. Some people mistook him as a loner, but he wasn't. He was just a private man who was relaxed with people he knew but reserved with strangers.

There were times when people would stare at him in the street or in other public places and say: 'It is, isn't it?' That's a strange thing to be asked, isn't it? How do you answer that?: 'Yes, I'm Bobby Moore.' I felt dad kept them at bay very well, but was always polite and courteous, never rude.

He was such a kind man. He had time for everyone and he hardly ever talked about himself, even when he was very ill. 'How are you?' people would ask. 'I'm fine, but how are you?' he'd always say. When he sensed people might be a uncomfortable around him, he went out of his way to make them feel at ease.

One of his most special qualities was his wit. His sense of humour was so dry and he was very funny. He often poked fun but always in a playful, harmless way. Once, he took the turkey West Ham gave to each player as a Christmas present into a pub, put it on the bar and said: 'I'll have half a lager and the turkey will have a gin and tonic!' Imagine what the barman must have thought!

According to my mother, another Christmas Eve he came home with some of the West Ham team and found our Christmas dinner in the fridge. There wasn't much left the next day!

He was exceptionally disciplined when it came to his fitness and he always trained incredibly hard. When I was little, I would go with him on my bike when he went running. We'd go from Chigwell to Gants Hill to Woodford - a long way - but I always gave up half way and he would end up practically carrying me and pushing the bike up the hill. Even when he was ill with cancer, he still went running every morning and when I managed to go with him, he'd always be yards ahead of me.

He was very tidy and loved things to be in order and just so. He always wore smart clothes – even his casual clothes were smart. He kept his clothes neatly in the wardrobe, almost like it had

Roberta gets a close-up view of Bobby's winners' medal and the Jules Rimet replica two days after the '66 final.

been prepared for inspection. His jumpers were even hung in order of dark to light. At night, on his bedside table, everything would be lined up neatly. Watch, money, credit cards and keys would be evenly spaced apart. Even the change would be stacked going from big coins to little coins. He was the same at work. Whereas I wrote my office diary in biro and scribbled out changes, dad used a pencil for everything, just so he could rub it out and keep it tidy. I've inherited some of his traits but, unfortunately, my diary still looks a mess.

He was great to work with – very polite and he never stood on ceremony. Some of the bosses I've worked with in the past used to buzz through and say:'Get me a coffee, will you?' Dad always made tea and coffee for us all. If he was on his way to the office from a meeting he would call in and ask:'Does anyone want a sandwich or anything brought in?' He was considerate and generous.

When we were young and dad was still playing football, we would go to training with him. I distinctly remember sweeping the terraces at West Ham one Christmas morning in my new dress. Mum wasn't too pleased. At home games mum, Dean and I always sat in the same seats. At some point during the match, dad would have this secret wave for us. He used to waggle the fingers of his right hand under his left arm as he ran past.

I found my father a very easy man to be around. He was caring, and wasn't afraid of being affectionate. He didn't like confrontations much and we hardly ever argued. When Dean and I were little you knew there was a problem if dad told us off. I think he was embarrassed by tension or squabbling. Dad would put on a pleasant appearance for people who had offended him - not that he would tell you he had been offended, that is. I don't know how he did it - he was always nice. A lesson from which we should all learn.

I believe my father had to deal with many disappointments in his life but always chose to keep the pain of those to himself. He never let the hurt show, but I could always tell – he was more sensitive than he'd let you believe. Like the time dad had agreed with Elton John to become coach at Watford. While we were on our family holiday in Majorca, he saw the newspapers saying Graham Taylor had been appointed instead. He never uttered a word about that, but it must have had such an impact on him. I don't know why Watford changed their mind but, in dad's eyes, he felt they had shaken hands and that was that.

Dad handled the news of the cancer very bravely. The day after he had been told he needed chemotherapy treatment, I got up in the morning to find a note saying: 'Gone for a run'. He played his illness down. When asked about it, he would say: 'Oh, I'm fine'. Sometimes, only sometimes, he would pass on bad news from the doctor so not to get our hopes up. He was the one who was ill, yet he still thought of us and protected us.

I had to go away shortly before he died and during one of my phone calls home to check on him, dad came on the phone. He was very weak and his voice was strained. 'How are you?' he asked. 'I'm fine,' I said, chatting away with my news, so dad didn't have to talk. He suddenly said: 'You enjoy yourself . . . don't worry about me. . . I'm not doing anything special.' Despite his illness, he was still trying to ensure I didn't worry. He was just so incredibly brave.

Just a few days before he died, he was commentating for Capital Radio at Wembley. Two days earlier it had been made public that he had terminal cancer. In the lift a couple of journalists said to him: 'We could do with you out there tonight, Bobby.' Dad replied: 'I think I might need a late fitness test!'

After he died, I went to say goodbye to him and he had that same old cheeky Mooro smile of his. I like to think that he knew he was getting all the accolades and the admiration that he so deserved.

I don't think I'll come across anyone like dad again and I'm not surprised so many people feel the same way. He was a very, very special man with an unbelievably big heart and a giving, generous nature. I'm so very proud to say he was my father. I loved him so much and miss him every day.

I'm very sad that Freddie, my son, will never get to see his grandad; and that dad could never hold him like he did Poppy, Dean's daughter. But I can't wait for Freddie to grow a little so I can start showing him all the videos and tell him all about how his grandad won the World Cup for England.

I'm sure Freddie will be as proud of him as I am. Who knows, perhaps one day he will even follow is his footsteps?

Bobby's grandson, Freddie.

Dean Moore

Dean had spells at The Sun as a layout artist and also with his Dad at the Sunday Sport, when Bobby was sports editor. After parting with Sara Day, the mother of his daughter Poppy in 1992, Dean trained as publican with his girlfriend Sue Janeway. They have been managing a pub in Chelsea since 1996.

People say I've taken my dad's death well, but I don't think I've even started to come to terms with it yet. He's been gone five years and I still miss him. I want to speak to him. I want to ring him up, just like I used to. I've grieved for him but I've tried to put the grieving off by filling up my life with other things.

Dad suffered a lot of discomfort with his illness but he never complained. What do you do when someone tells you you're going to die? It was heartbreaking for him, but he never showed it. He would say: 'I'll be all right, son. Don't worry.' He was upset, but he never wanted us to see that.

He never mentioned the word cancer. It was always: 'We'll get over this thing if we stick together.' And we did stick together. Even my mum. They had been apart ten years but the moment she heard about his illness she was on the phone from America. Some people are bitter after divorce but dad had such an impact on her that she still cared.

If he was going to Scotland for treatment or away with Stephanie for a holiday, he would ring me and say: 'Deano' – he always called me that – 'I've got to go away.' I was always afraid something might happen and I hadn't said what I wanted to say to him. When he got back I would ask: 'How did it go in Edinburgh? How are you?' and he would say: 'Yeah, fine, lovely, no problems.' That was it. There was no 'Has it got worse?', 'Is it getting better?' He always maintained things were okay, regardless of the truth.

Dad went to America for a last holiday and I met up with him out there. We spent a lovely couple of days together in Palm Beach, playing golf, had a few talks. We got back ten days before he died. I stayed at the house during his last week and the doctor wanted to take dad away and I said: 'No, let him stay, whatever it takes, we can look after him.' Hopefully he would have been proud of the way I handled it.

I believe that the decision to split with mum was the hardest he ever had to make. I think dad had a lot of guilt over the split, for hurting all three of us, and with mum, he was embarrassed by it almost. I guess only he could say how he really felt.

I'll never forget when he told me they were splitting up. Southend had lost 6-4 to Wimbledon and as we were driving home, he said: 'Dean, I've got something to tell you.' I knew something was up. 'I know what it is,' I replied. He said: 'Your mum and I aren't getting on. It's nothing to do with her, I just think we need a break.' Typical kid, I said: 'That's fine, but who's going to pay my pocket money?' He sorted out everything with mum in the next few days. I still never got my pocket money, though!

I was at school at the time. Their marriage break-up was in the papers, on the news, it was a bit too public. I was upset and I went a bit off the rails, so to speak.

It was hard for my mum and sister and it didn't help with me playing up. Mum said: 'Go and spend a few days with dad and sort yourself out.' I went down to Southend where he was living and had a talk with him for a couple of hours, man to man. He was a good shoulder to cry on. We finished up going to a pub with Brian Dear, left about seven o'clock, half-cut, and he sent me back to mum. She wasn't impressed.

I was about 13 when I realised other kids couldn't believe who my dad was. He was clearly different but he was still just my dad. Everybody's dad is special at something and so was mine.

Mum and dad were always having parties. I returned from a golfing weekend with my friend and his dad once and dad invited them in. When we came through the door of the lounge, Alan Ball was on a stool singing, everyone was drinking and rolling about, having a wild time. My friend's dad said: 'No, it's all right, it's not my scene, thanks all the same,' and backed out the door like the house was on fire!

Dad had a group of mates he would drink with: Terry Creasey, John Brain, Patsy and Jimmy Quill, Ernie Felgate. There was always a party at someone's house. One summer we had our friends and neighbours round. It was pretty lively and one of the neighbours said: 'Let's go and use our swimming pool.' So everyone set off for their house. As I walked up the road I came across drunken stragglers everywhere, some collapsed on lawns, others resting on lampposts. Out of the twenty-odd people who left our house only about ten reached the pool. Dad made it, looking sober as a judge, even though he wasn't.

Dad was exceptionally tolerant. He was always so composed and easy-going with Roberta and me, especially when I did things wrong as a kid. On my eighth birthday he bought me a motorised go-kart for about £100, a lot of money then, and a mate and I took it to bits in my bedroom. But dad didn't say a word. If he was pushed that much, you knew when he was going to snap, but when I look back at some of the things I did, I wonder how he didn't snap more often.

I was eleven when I went to the launch party for *Escape To Victory* at Stringfellows. Mum and dad wanted me to dress up in a jacket and tie and I said: 'I don't want to wear it!' In the end, dad said: 'Put them on!' and I did. Dad introduced me to Sylvester Stallone and Michael Caine and afterwards I was thinking, did I *really* talk to Sylvester Stallone? I was privileged to meet such people through dad.

When I was a kid, dad would always bring me back something from countries he visited. As I got older he started bringing me hats. I do love a hat. The best was a hat from Russia which he bartered off a soldier as he was getting on the plane. On the same flight he had a bag full of caviar confiscated – but he still got some through in his pockets!

We went skiing as a family for the first time when dad finished playing football. He couldn't ski before then because of players' insurance. On the slopes I needed the toilet so dad and I skied off and found a quiet spot behind a tree. I undid all my clothing, the suit, the thermals, and I started to go to the toilet when the snow gave way beneath me and I fell down this little crevice and got stuck, legs over my head, skis sticking out. No chance to zip up my outfit. Dad was looking down laughing and he said: 'I'll make sure the rest of the party ski on then I'll come and help you.' But I looked up and he'd brought the whole class – women

Bobby, the proud grandad, with Dean's daughter, Poppy.

as well – to the edge of this crevice to laugh at me. Dad was mischievious like that, but good fun.

We had some great times out on the town. He took me to Mortons in Berkley Square and to Tramp for my nineteenth birthday. I was proud of being with my dad and hopefully he was proud of being with me. He would introduce me to all sorts of people, then leave me to fend for myself. He liked to put me in it. We had a different relationship to some fathers and sons because living apart made it easier for us to be friends as well.

When he first came over to watch me play Sunday morning football, the match turned into a farce, with punch-ups and everything, and I remember seeing him walking off bewildered by it all.

Whether it was shopping down Oxford Street or walking down the red carpet in Westminster Abbey, it somehow came easily to him. It inspired me as a kid, but unfortunately it didn't rub off on me enough. I get worked up when I'm driving yet dad stayed calm with 100,000 South American fans abusing him. He was cool but he had a firm side if people needled him. He would quietly smoulder or blank them, but he wouldn't explode.

Dad, myself and a mate hired out a fishing boat along the Thames for a few days. I don't think he loved fishing, he just wanted to spend a bit of time with me. He did the cooking, we had a black and white telly on the boat so we sat with the rods out, had a few beers and watched England cricket matches. We even had little wagers like whoever caught the first fish won a tenner. After mum and dad split up, he was always taking me on things like that.

Towards the end I helped him with the driving for his Capital Gold work. Jonathan Pearce sat in the back and dad alongside me in the front, so he could have a rest on the way to the game.

In his last week, I was sitting by his bed looking after him and we were watching telly. He was slipping in and out of sleep but occasionally we got a comment out of him. My drink of vodka, grapefruit and cranberry juice was on the bedside table and one of the visiting nurses came in to check a few things and she picked up my drink, which looked like fruit juice, and was about to stick it in dad's mouth. Stephanie noticed and said: 'Don't give him that, it's vodka. It's Dean's drink.' I looked down at dad and he had that cheeky grin on his face, as if to say: 'Yeah, I wouldn't mind some of that.'

I can't deny it, he hurt us all by leaving mum, but we still love him. And the hurt never outweighed our love for him or the great memories of our time with him. We know how much pleasure he gave to the country and we're proud of him.

After dad's first operation, my daughter Poppy was born. When she was about three months-old a Sunday paper took some pictures of Poppy and dad together. He was really chuffed. It's a nice picture for Poppy to treasure.

Poppy is six now and she knows all about Grandad Bobby. She went in to see him a few times in his last week. She would kiss him and a give him a little nuzzle. He always had a grin for her. She has been to Grandad Bobby's grave with me and she can pick him out in photos and on video. She loves him still.

Poppy thinks Grandad Bobby is up in heaven. She asks when she will see Grandad again. The other day she said 'Will I see Grandad Bobby next year?'

Bobby and Poppy with Sophie, the Doberman who used to join Bobby on his regular morning run.

my Grandad Bobby.
I Love you very much
He lives up in heaven he is is a
with the angels
famous grandad and he
loves me lots and lots.
Love poppy grace
moore

Poppy remembers her grandad.

Ena Herbert

Bobby's aunt – Doris's sister – who lives in Worcester, aged 88.

I was at work the day Doris went into labour with little Robert. Our mother, Beatrice Buckle, and Big Bob's mother, Mrs Cooper, were with her during the afternoon and the midwife was popping in and out. But Doris couldn't give birth to the baby so they called an ambulance to take her to Upney hospital. I was doing war work with a building society in Ilford and I left work at 4.30pm. When I got to Waverley Gardens, Doris was on a stretcher in the hall and Bob's mother popped across the road to her house to collect her coat and got in the ambulance with Doris. Little Robert was delivered in Upney hospital. I'm pretty certain she stayed in the hospital that night and came home to Waverley Gardens the next day. Bob's family had brought the bed down from upstairs and made a bedroom downstairs for Doris. But that night there was a very heavy German bombing raid and an explosion in the neighbourhood blasted ceilings down and blew windows in. Naturally, Doris was very upset by this, after all, she was holding a new-born baby and Bob's mother and Bob laid across the baby and Doris to protect them from injury. The raid was so bad they had to evacuate Doris and little Robert from Waverley Gardens, which was near the industrial area, close to the power station on the river, which was a target for the German bombs.

Because of the heavy raid I was unable to get back to my own home in Ilford so I stayed at my parents at Faircross Avenue – which is the other side of Barking, beyond the park, which is not so near the industrial area. About midnight I was getting a hot water bottle ready to take down to the shelter when there was a crash at the front door. I wondered what the hell had hit it. I went to the door and Big Bob said to me: 'Take this!' and he thrust a bundle into my arms. I said: 'What is it?' and he said: 'The baby!' So I asked: 'Where's Doris?' He replied: 'In the Mayor's car over the road!' When I looked across the road, sure enough, the car that had brought little Robert and Doris across Barking was the Mayor's limosine. On his first day in this world, the man who was to lead England to win the World Cup had certainly travelled in style.

When my father, Fred Buckle, heard this, he dashed out into the street, went to the car and picked Doris up in his arms and carried her into the house like a baby, straight into the middle room downstairs which we had converted into a bedroom for my parents. I had the hot water bottle which I had prepared and I put that into the bed with Doris as well. We didn't have a cot that night so we improvised and took a drawer out of the chest and turned it into a makeshift cot with a pillow and blanket and wrapped little Robert up in there. Doris and little Robert stayed with our mother and father for six weeks. And for those six weeks I washed his nappies.

Graham Hardwick

Bobby's cousin. Graham's mother, Beattie, was Bobby's mum's sister.

Bobby was always 'Robert' to the family. Bob was his father, also known as 'Big Bob,' and Doris, his mother, was known as Doss. It was only the media, I guess, who named him Bobby. There were eight years difference between Robert and I, so when I was ten he was eighteen. It would not be right for me to suggest we were close, because we were a generation apart. At eighteen, he was existing in a different world from us altogether. It wasn't until later years that we became a lot closer.

Like many families in the East End, we lived 'over the road' and 'round the corner' to each other. People didn't move very far then. Good, stable family traditions. I was particularly close to Robert's parents. My aunt Doss was unbelievably generous and she would give away things that she didn't have, let alone things she did! She was totally supportive of everything Robert did, loyal and even protective of him.

Uncle Bob had come from a difficult background – his father was killed in the first world war. He had a brother called George Moore and a stepbrother called Bill. They all worked at the local power station, doing lagging work for the boilers. Uncle Bob was an absolute gentleman, one of the most humourous people you could wish to meet. Fun to be with and often poking fun at his own expense and making jokes about the fact he was prematurely bald. He was a real scream. We regularly went on holidays with them to Devon when I was in my teens. They were super people: warm, welcoming, kind and incredibly modest. They would never, in any circumstances, enjoy reflected glory from Robert's fame. They were almost paranoid about it. I remember just after West Ham won the European Cup Winners' Cup, there was a film of the final being shown at a local community centre and Big Bob and Doss were invited. I went along with them and recall how annoyed they were when somebody announced that Bobby's parents were there. They really hated it.

I can also remember sitting with them at Wembley among the players' relatives one day watching a match – Bobby had won some 60 caps by then and had been captain a long time – and there was this chap who kept standing up in front of us. Uncle Bob politely said: 'Do you think you could sit in your seat because we're missing all the important bits of the game here?' And this guy whirled around and snapped: 'Do you know who I am? I'm so and so's father!' It was a player winning his third cap. Uncle Bob just smiled but said absolutely nothing. That was typical of their nature. Regardless of the provocation, they never used Robert's status to make a point.

Aunt Doss and uncle Bob were similarly modest when it came to having their photo taken. Considering that, in her younger days, Doss was, by all accounts, an extremely attractive lady, she was always reluctant to have her photograph taken, and you'd be lucky to find a photo of uncle Bob where he wasn't messing about, pulling a funny face or wearing a silly hat. Both of them were brimming with qualities that were reflected in their son.

When it came to the '66 World Cup, I was staying with Doss and Bob because my parents were on holiday. We went to two of the early games but Doss was always very supersticious and she would be inwardly tense about the most important games. She was a private worrier at the best of times but it was worse with watching Robert. In the latter stages of the tournament she wouldn't go to Wembley, so uncle Bob went off to the games and I stayed at home with Doss. But the further Robert and his team got, the less she could watch. She didn't watch any of the Portugal semi-final. She was pottering around the house and I had to keep her updated from the TV. When it came to the final, she spent the whole afternoon in the back garden, just messing about, keeping busy. She didn't come into the house once and, at the end, when they'd won, she permitted herself to watch the presentation. She sat there trying to hold back a tear and not show any emotion. It was all held inside. She would not allow herself to celebrate and when the tension had lifted, she would make some excuse like 'let's go for a walk' or 'let's walk into town and do some shopping.' Her way was to keep busy.

Robert was every bit as enigmatic to me as he was to others. You would be hard pressed to get him to discuss a football match. When he was playing, it was: 'I'm home from the office and the last thing I want to do is talk about work.' It was different when he retired from playing.

In later years, uncle Bob's health deteriorated. He suffered two strokes and became incapable of looking after himself, and for many years sat around staring into space and just muttering. There were many adverse effects that made him a totally different person to the gentle man we had known. He was a tremendously difficult patient and Doss nursed him on her own without a murmur of complaint.

I recall one occasion when uncle Bob's health worsened and he was taken to hospital. Robert was playing out in San Antonio at the time and we had difficulty getting him home because of flights. He flew back from the States and I met him outside the hospital. Between the car park and the ward I needed to brief him about uncle Bob's condition but fans who recognised him kept coming over and interrupting, wanting autographs. Yet Robert dealt with them placidly and politely and signed their autograph books. He must have been tired and tense yet he didn't show it. It is the lasting impression I have of Robert.

Uncle Bob died a year or so later, in '78, and aunt Doss died on June 13, '92, some eight months before Bobby. Ironically, she also died of cancer. She lived in the family home in Waverley Gardens right up until her last few days, when she was admitted into the Dury Falls Court nursing home in Romford. Officially, I don't think she was told by Robert about his own cancer but I wonder if she suspected. At the time, we found it mysterious because when we visited Doss two days before she died, we were surprised to find Robert was away in Scotland on business. Of course, afterwards we found out that the 'business' was in fact treatment for his own cancer.

I was an executor to aunt Doss's will and I got a phone call from Robert, where he started going over old ground that we'd previously covered. I thought this was strange. Then he checked on how we all were and asked where we were going for our summer holidays. It was not until afterwards I realised it was his last call to check up on us all.

Moore tributes: the early days

I remember the night after Bobby was born – April 12, 1941 – very well because the German bombs blasted down the largest shop in Barking, at Blakes corner. At that time we were mostly living in bomb shelters at the end of the garden. At six in the morning I went across the road to see Doris Moore and her new baby, but there was no answer. Bobby's father came home from his night shift and it turned out he had taken them to her mother's house for safekeeping. Bobby was a dear soul. I remember him always kicking a ball in the road as a child. It came into my garden often enough and I'd tell him to take the ball somewhere else, but he was really no trouble. He was a good boy, but then most kids were in those days – with air raids going on, night and day, they weren't allowed to stray very far from home. If he saw me he'd politely say: 'Hello, how are you?'. I remember, too, how he seemed to glide when he walked down the street. Naturally athletic people do that. In later years, he was always in bed before 10pm, even when he was at West Ham. His mum would call him and he would go at once.

Doris Frome, neighbour, Waverley Gardens, Barking

As a young lad Bobby was a bit on the tubby side. He said he could remember going into a cafe after a school game and there were some boys in there from another school. One of them asked his mates: 'Is that Bobby Moore, the fat one?' When he changed to go to the Tom Hood school, the journey was no joyride. Bobby recalled: 'My mother had to get me up at 7.15, then I had to catch the bus to Barking Station, a train to Wanstead Park and another bus to the school.' All this journeying gave Bobby travel sickness and led him to obtain a doctor's certificate telling his headmaster that a transfer to another school would be in the pupil's best interests. However, Bobby said: 'On the day I returned with the letter, I got the news I'd been picked for the Leyton District Under-13s. Thinking fast, I decided to suppress the letter. My travel sickness suddenly felt much better!'

Tony Hogg, *Hammers News Magazine*

My over-riding memory of Bobby when we were kids was his great physical size. He was only aged twelve but he was always easily the best player out of us all.

While we played in our boots he used to play with no shoes to make it easier for us. He used to practice football for hours on end every night after school. In the winter he would kick a tennis ball up the stairs, let it bounce down and trap it.

Clive Elmore, childhood friend, Waverley Gardens, Barking

We used to play football in the streets because there were no cars around. Bobby was a great cricketer, too, and was offered a job with Essex County Cricket Club but he chose to play for West Ham instead. We used to pick our teams and took turns in goal, but Bobby was always a bit of a leader. He was the most dedicated of us all.

Brian Moore, Bobby's cousin, Glenmore Way, Barking.

MOORE **than a legend**

I was really proud when we saw him on the telly. Not everyone had a relative who captained England. The last time I saw him was at his mother's funeral the year before he died. He always looked after his mum. He used to come and see her all the time and if he couldn't, then he would phone. His mother was very keen on football and encouraged him all the way. He started kicking a ball around when he was about four. My recollection of him as a boy was that he always had a football at his feet. His mum and dad were always taking him to football matches but, despite his fame, he still visited the area and looked after his mother. You always knew when he was round because there was a nice car parked out the front. The local kids used to go up to the door to ask for his autograph and if they didn't get it, then his mum would always get it for them later.
June Cooper, Bobby's aunt, Barking

He was very respectful to everyone and I never heard anyone ever complain about him. The '66 final was the first time that I was interested in football and watched it on telly. And it was only because our Bobby Moore was in the team. Everybody in the street was thrilled for him that day. He used to come along every Sunday morning and knock on the door for my son. He had a football but Bobby didn't, so he used to come along here to borrow it.
Catherine Godfrey, former Borough Magistrate, Barking

At school, he was a prefect, but never Head Boy. He was very popular. It was a technical and commercial school and Bobby passed the equivalent of nearly half a dozen 'O' levels in one go. Whenever there were pupils who wanted to become footballers and thought they didn't have to try at academic work, I'd point out Bobby Moore as an example to show it is possible to do both.
Joan Wright, teacher, Tom Hood Technical High School, Leyton

In 1952, Bob and I started at Tom Hood Technical School in Leytonstone together and we remained friends until we left five years later. He was always well into football and all sports and his father never missed supporting him when he was representing the school. On Wednesday afternoons our first lesson was History. I sat next to Bob for this subject and in those days all the England internationals were played on Wednesday afternoons, so whenever there was a game I'd have to say he'd been taken sick so he could go home and watch the match. It worked every time! Later, I remember when we met the careers officer, Bob told them he was going to be a footballer and they said he should look at his options in case he didn't make it! In our final year we were both made prefects and like everybody else were looking forward to the end-of-schooldays dance. It was cancelled, however, because the teachers said it would interfere with our studies as our O levels were going to be held a little bit later than usual. Disappointed, we all went on strike. However, Bob's duty that week was to take the teachers' lunches to the staff room – which he didn't do - and he was duly suspended from school. Eventually, though, the staff had to get in touch with Bob for prize giving because he'd won the Sportsman's Cup. When he came back to school for the presentation, the teachers cheered just as loudly as the pupils!
Mrs U. A. Preston (nee Foy), Norwich

Chapter 2
Boleyn boys
(part 1: 1958-66)

Malcolm Allison

Played for West Ham from 1950-58. Won League titles as coach of Manchester City and Sporting Lisbon, and also managed Crystal Palace and Middlesbrough.

Ted Fenton asked me to coach the local kids and Bobby was twelve when I first saw him. After training one day we were standing at the bus stop together – I was going to Barkingside and he was heading for Barking. He asked if he could sit next to me on the bus and he was always asking questions. He was very inquisitive. Even then I had spotted his awareness for the game, his ability to recognise things so easily. He had a clever memory and he was very bright. At twelve years of age, those aspects of his play, the things he was famous for, were showing up already.

After a month, Ted asked which of the young players I'd been impressed with. 'Well,' I said, 'I like this young lad, Bobby Moore.' Ted replied: 'What about the kid, George Fenn?' Fenn was a player most of the other clubs in the country were after because he scored six goals in an England Schoolboys game. 'Everyone is after him,' continued Ted, 'what do you think?' I said: 'Well, the only one I'm really interested in is Moore'. Ted couldn't understand it at the time.

I got tuberculosis before Bobby was seventeen and I went into hospital. On one of Bobby's visits to see me, he walked straight in and said: 'Malcolm, I've got some news. I've been picked to play for the England youth team.' So I replied: 'That's great, Bob, you must be the captain'. He said: 'No, I'm not captain, I'm just in the team'. 'No,' I said, 'you must *be* the captain. When you are centre-half, you've *got* to be the captain.'

'What do you mean, Malcolm?' he asked. I explained further: 'You can read the game, you know what to do, so when you are a centre-half, you tell everyone else what to do. It doesn't matter who goes up to flip the coin, you be the captain in your own mind. Be in control of yourself. Take control of everything around you. Look big. Think big. Tell people what to do. Be in command.' I knew he'd taken it in because he laughed. Sure enough, he was outstanding in that game. He was good like that – quiet, but a good leader. Sometimes, he was amazed at his own ability.

One day on the bus he asked: 'What is the most important thing in football?' So I replied: 'Knowing what you're going to do with the ball when you get it.' That was a strength he used all over the world. He knew who he was going to pass it to before the ball arrived. I sat watching

Bobby with his god-daughter, Gina, on New Year's eve 1992 – just two months before he died.

MOORE **than a legend**

West Ham captains and great friends together: Bobby, Malcolm Allison and Noel Cantwell at the christening of Malcolm and Lyn's daughter, Gina.

him play in an under-23 game against Hungary at Tottenham with Raymond Kopa, the French player. Bobby made over 100 passes and only one failed to find a team-mate. Kopa said: 'If Bobby hadn't made that bad pass, I wouldn't have known he was playing.' But even then, at under-23 level, Bobby's percentage of passing without relinquishing possession was fantastic.

Noel Cantwell, Bobby and I were very great friends. Very close. Noel was captain of Ireland, Bobby was captain of England and we were all captains of West Ham. We had some great times together. Bobby had many natural strengths he didn't learn from anyone: the charisma, his leadership instinct, the distancing from others. I went to games with him and he would avoid people. He had his head down and he would duck out of the limelight. He didn't particularly want to be in the public eye and he didn't want to be recognised. I found that very unusual but it was just the way with him. He was so famous, I suppose, and people didn't realise just how famous he was.

He came with Stephanie to stay with my wife Lyn and I in Portugal. He went into a restaurant one night with us and the owner was so overwhelmed that Bobby Moore had come into his place to eat. He kept plying Bob with different ports, saying: 'Try this one!' and 'try that one!' and Bobby was sipping away. When we got home, at about 2am, I said: 'Did you have a great time, Bob?' and he said: 'Marvellous! It could've been anywhere in the world!' I asked Steph why he was so happy and she said it might have something to do with the fact he had sampled two dozen ports! But he really loved Portugal. And that night he was treated like he would be in a restaurant in the East End. I think he was surprised they admired him so much.

Shortly after my daughter Gina was born, Bobby and Steph invited us down for Christmas for a few days. We had a great time and afterwards both Lyn and I agreed we would ask them to be godparents to Gina. They said they were hoping we would ask. Steph and Lyn have a close friendship now, albeit from long-distance, and Steph thinks the world of Gina.

Bobby was terribly important to the English people. With England winning the World Cup, he got the emotions of the whole nation. He was adored by the people. Terry Venables said at the time they had a minute's silence at football matches all over the country for Bobby, that there should have been a minute's silence for Bobby by the whole country. He deserved it.

He is easily the most famous English footballer of all-time, and I'd say he is one of the most famous Englishmen of all-time.

Noel Cantwell

Republic of Ireland defender who spent eight years with West Ham until 1960, when he was transferred to Manchester United. Cantwell's managerial career took in spells at Coventry City, Peterborough United and the New England Tea Men in the North American Soccer League.

I phoned Bobby's house on the Sunday before he died. I spoke to Steph and asked how he was. She told me he wasn't good but she was sure he would want to speak me. Bobby came on the phone and I said: 'I'll be down next week to see you, Bobby.' He excused himself to have a glass of water. He came back and his voice was very weak and he said: 'Come down *this* week.' But, sadly, I didn't take in the significance of what he meant. That Wednesday, I was on the way back from racing and I stopped in an hotel bar for a drink with some friends. At the bar a fellow said: 'Isn't it sad about Bobby Moore?' and I replied: 'Don't you worry about Bobby. He's a fighter. He'll get over this.' I'd known for sometime he'd got cancer. Bobby told me that he 'had a fight on his hands', that he 'had to have treatment,' everything except saying the actual word 'cancer'.

But the fellow in the bar said: 'You haven't heard? He died today.' I said: 'I don't believe you!' Straight away I phoned Maggie, my wife, and she said: 'Yes, it's true. It's been on the television.' It was a sad day. He was such a kind-hearted, very lovely guy.

I rang Steph and asked if it would be wrong of me to go and see Bobby and pay my respects, wherever he was resting, and she said she would let me know. She phoned back next morning and said: 'If you want to come down and see him, you can. But Noel, you can't come to the house in Putney because the world's press are outside and everybody wants to know where Bobby is and they all want to take pictures of the coffin and things like that. But if you and Maggie want to come down, I'll meet you at East Putney station at five o'clock and I'll take you to see him.'

So Maggie and I got the train and we went to London. We got to East Putney station and Roberta was there in the car with Steph to meet us. It was a cold, wintry night and we went off to the undertakers. It wasn't very far. We knocked at the door, the undertaker let us in and we went in to see Bobby. A terrible tragedy for such a young man. I had known Bobby nearly forty years, I was best man at his first wedding and godfather to his son, Dean.

Bobby's first game for West Ham was an unusual experience. It was the beginning of the 1958-59 season and we were about to play Manchester United in only our third home match after being promoted from the Second Division. Ted Fenton, the West Ham manager, had a selection problem and he summoned me to the office the day before the game, as it was usual practice at West Ham to ask the captain for his opinion.

Ted said: 'The left-half position? Man United have got that lovely player Ernie Taylor playing on that side, what do you think?' The choice was between Malcolm Allison, my best friend, and the young lad, Bobby Moore. Malcolm and I were very close and he was a big influence on my career. Ted had got the idea of coaching the youngsters around Dagenham and Barking on Tuesdays and Thursdays and Malcolm was given the job because he was a Football Association coach, but he was taken ill in 1957 – he had part of a lung removed through tuberculosis – and I took over the captaincy of West Ham and the coaching duties with the kids.

Bobby didn't have exceptional ability as an apprentice, although he was always immaculate. He never said very much but was a great listener and a dedicated trainer, always a very curious, inquisitive guy who wanted answers. He fastened on to Malcolm and myself because we talked football all the time. Everything was geared around how we were going to achieve success and if we sat down somewhere Bobby was there, always listening, never imposing his viewpoint or interrupting. We even used to go back to train at West Ham in the afternoons. The ground was always open and Malcolm instilled it into us that you had to practice to improve.

Bobby, Noel Cantwell and Geoff Hurst at the christening of Bobby's daughter, Roberta.

We were only on twelve quid a week so Ted did a deal with Phil Cassettari that we could spend vouchers for our lunch in his cafe around the corner from the ground. Every day after training about a dozen of us would march down there. Phil said we were disrupting his regular clientele so he gave us the upstairs room. Malcolm would usually hold court. Jimmy Andrews would be there, Frank O'Farrell, John Bond, Dave Sexton, mostly the guys who lived a fair way away. I lived in digs and would have a great big mug of tea, a big fry-up or dinner with huge doorsteps of bread and butter. Fantastic. I ate as much as I wanted because there were no diets then and I wouldn't be likely to get another meal that day. Ernie Gregory and Dick Walker would go home for lunch but John Dick would change his voucher and bloody starve himself so he could get a half crown to go dog racing! We hatched our plans and tactics in that cafe and all the salt and pepper pots became players. We filmed a couple of TV programmes at the cafe – one for an FA coaching thing in 1990 and another for the BBC series *Kicking and Screaming* with Malcolm and I. But the cafe was an important part of it all.

When he got TB, Malcolm spent some time in London Hospital and at Midhurst in Sussex, where I visited him at least once a week. Bobby asked me if I would take him along to see Malcolm, so I took Bobby in the car the next time I went, which, strangely enough, just happended to be 6th February 1958 - the day of the Munich air disaster. We heard the news of the Manchester United crash on the radio. You never forget something like that. All three of us were very upset.

Malcolm came out of hospital and trained while Bobby was cruising along in the reserves. Malcolm was ready for that United game but the vacancy was for left-half. Malcolm was more of a stopper and it needed someone more mobile.

When Ted asked me who to pick, it was a hard decision. The sorcerer or his apprentice? I deliberated then said: 'I would play Bobby Moore.' He seemed sur-

prised I picked Bobby over my closest friend, Malcolm. 'All right', he said, 'thank you.' The team sheet went up and Bobby was there, number six, playing left-half. Everybody was excited for him because it was his first game and he went home to tell his mother and father he was playing against the great Manchester United.

We were outstanding and beat United 3-2. We were delighted because United's scalp was a big achievement. Bobby did a good job on Ernie Taylor but after the game Malcolm stormed into the dressing room and called me for everything. 'You bastard!' he said. 'I could've played against Ernie Taylor with my ankles tied!' How he got to know I had influenced Ted's decision for Bobby to play, I'll never know. I didn't say any more. It was an embarrassing position for me and it soured the night, although I had answered Ted's question with the right choice for that particular match. Later, Malcolm admitted I was right to choose Bobby. That was Bobby's first game for West Ham.

Once he asked me if it was possible for him to be a great player without being fast. He was concious that no matter how much he practised sprinting, he was still the slowest player in the squad. I didn't want to shatter his dreams, so I told him Johnny Haynes had got no pace but had a quick brain and was a wonderful passer and if he can be a great player there is no reason why anyone else can't. Bobby seemed to accept this.

Bobby had a wonderful temperament, he never got flustered and he became a two-footed player – he was a natural right-footer and he practised on his left. He liked to impose himself on a game but he was never a man-for-man marker because he wasn't a quick or severe tackler like Nobby Stiles or Norman Hunter. When Bobby made a good tackle he loved it, it was like him winning the pools. He never got too close to people who might beat him for pace – he merely gave them a bit of room in front. But in a congested area he didn't like heading. I can't recall him getting his head cut. Leave that to the uglies, he thought, the rough school – he was too pretty to get cut. We laughed together when he said: 'I can't head, can't tackle and I've got no pace, yet I was voted the best player in the World Cup?' He was a most modest man and I never heard him brag. He didn't say 'I' all the time, it was always 'We' or 'Us' or 'The team'.

Bobby could be criticised for being a better international captain than a club one. There were times when he played like he was strolling around and could've given greater leadership at West Ham. When we talked about it he felt Ron Greeenwood should've bought some harder players. I said: 'You need a player like Maurice Setters, someone who is going to win the ball and not just play pretty and get beaten.' Bobby said: 'You're right.' He went to Ron but he said: 'No, we don't want players like that at West Ham'. Bobby felt he could do no more and I think he became a bit complacent on trying to change things, but only as a captain – his playing contribution was oustanding.

Ron was a purist who saw the beauty of football, the passing and the angles. In fact, Ted had a tougher view of how to play. West Ham could beat anybody at home, but there was always a suspicion they bottled it outside Upton Park. We put it right in the mid-50s because we won promotion to the First Division and you had to stand up and be counted when you went to places like Bolton and Burnley. One or two of us would kick people – we had a fellow called Andy Malcolm who could border on being a dirty bastard. Nice players are okay, but nice doesn't often win you much.

Ron and Walter Winterbottom were in the group of English coaches who went abroad and discovered new methods and training became more interesting than just running around. West Ham didn't do the usual stamina work and Ron thought weight-training was a waste of time. It was all very revolutionary and a pleasure to watch, but I think it could've been mixed in with stamina work. Malcolm had gone on courses and came back with folders of coaching ideas. Ted gave Malcolm licence to work and try out his ideas. Malcolm started the revolution at West Ham, then Ron introduced his own ideas that culminated in the success of '66 where Bobby and Martin and Geoff used some of Ron's teachings to great effect, like the late near-post run. Funnily enough, John Bond and I used to do a similar thing in the late-50s at corners and free-kicks. Bondie was a great chipper of the ball and I would lose my marker, arrive in the hole in front of the goalkeeper and there was nothing else to do but head it in. We got six goals a season doing that. But it was all stuff we worked on in training with Malcolm.

> **"He was conscious that no matter how much he practised sprinting, he was still the slowest player in the squad"**

Malcolm was a big influence at West Ham. Once we were due to play this game and it was very hot, about 80 degrees, and Malcolm got these scissors and cut the long sleeves off our strip. Brand new shirts. 'We're not playing in them!' snip, snip, snip. Another time we were playing in a cup match at Spurs and we were only getting four tickets for our family so Malcolm went to see Ted and said: 'If we don't get twenty tickets each, we're not playing and that's it!' He was so adamant, I think Ted relented and we got some extra tickets.

When Bobby went on honeymoon with Tina to Spain it was nearby where Malcolm and I were going to be on holiday with our wives, Beth and Maggie. On the wedding day, Tina's mother said to us: 'I don't want you two contacting Bobby while they're on honeymoon. They are two young, innocent people and they don't need you and Malcolm's interference,' and we had to promise her we wouldn't contact Bobby and Tina. But we were sitting on the beach about a week after Bobby's wedding and who came along the beach but Bobby and Tina – they had decided to find us. We had a good few drinks, a right skinful, and they stayed overnight, but Bobby and Tina had an argument and Bobby finished sleeping in my room and Tina slept in Maggie's room. I thought if Tina's mum got to know we were all together she wouldn't be too pleased! She would've blamed Malcolm and I. They stayed a few days and we had a great time.

We always invited Bobby to any parties. He came up to visit our pub several times with Tina and, of course, with Steph, his second wife. I went to his 50th birthday party which was a lovely occasion at the house in Putney with just his good friends. There were about forty people: Malcolm, Budgie Byrne and I remember the rugby player, Peter Winterbottom, was there. Terry Venables and George Graham sang, and they can both sing well. So we had a good laugh. Bobby seemed to have many good friends, but didn't have really close friends. He kept things to himself a lot.

The international scene suited Bobby. He loved the glory, the glamour and when he walked out at Wembley he grew in stature. Walking out at Upton Park was one thing, but international matches are rare and inexperienced players can freeze, but Bobby would want the ball immediately and take the game by the scruff of the neck to show the others. When he put on that white shirt with three lions on his chest and his blond hair, he seemed to grow into a giant.

For Bobby to hold up the World Cup, play against the greatest in the world and have the likes of Pele and Beckenbauer hold him in such great esteem, was beyond the wildest dreams of the boy from Barking. It couldn't have happened to a nicer fellow.

We had some good times, Bobby and I, playing golf and things. He was the only man I know who looked tidy in a training sweatshirt. A good man, a good professional and such a very kind person.

Dave Sexton

Joined West Ham in March 1953. His career ended with a knee injury while at Crystal Palace, however this sparked an illustrious managerial career at Chelsea, QPR, Manchester United and Coventry City.

Bobby was a talented but modest person and always had a welcoming smile on his face. He was a schoolboy at West Ham United when I left in 1956. I was very disappointed to leave West Ham, I liked it more than any of my subsequent clubs and I left behind some good friends. In October '57 I went to Brighton and Hove Albion and shortly after we played a friendly with West Ham. Noel Cantwell and Malcolm Allison were very enthusiastic about the lad, Bobby Moore, and when I played against him that day I could see why. He was so composed for such a young man.

Tommy Docherty offered me my first coaching job at Chelsea and around that time, Bobby played in a testimonial at Brighton. After the match we retired to a friend's flat for a drink. Ron Greenwood had just gone to West Ham as manager and I quizzed Bobby about Ron's wonderful new ideas: movement off the ball, supporting the man, making two against one where possible, that sort of thing. It was pretty revolutionary at the time and Bobby was very helpful. A lot of my early coaching knowledge came from the conversation with Bobby that evening. I've never forgotten it.

I can sympathise with Bob's plight in football management. I bombed in my first job at Leyton Orient, couldn't make any impact at all, so I resigned. I was out of work for several months. My wife and I had a couple of kids and we were worried sick, but I got a job as coach at Fulham – they were bottom of the League and thankfully they stayed up. I was lucky after failure. I got another chance.

I saw all our games in the '66 World Cup and in '70 I went to Mexico with 12 other managers. I was manager of Chelsea by then, we had just won the FA Cup and two of my players, Peter Osgood and Peter Bonetti, were in the squad. Bobby Moore was stupendous against Brazil. They were a great team but if you could out-think them, as Bobby did that day, you stood a chance. I had great pleasure in seeing Bobby at his peak.

Bobby was a thoughtful person, a thoughtful player and, given a bit of luck and the right opportunity, he could have been a thoughtful coach or manager as well. I failed in my first job. I only wished Bob could have had another chance too. He had a lot to offer.

Ron Greenwood

Played for four clubs before starting in management at Eastbourne United. He became manager of England's youth team, Arsenal and then England's Under-23 side before managing West Ham from 1961-1974. In 1977 he was appointed manager of England until 1982.

Bobby was a hard person to get to know and didn't open up easily. He kept his own countenance and that's probably why there wasn't much written about his personality. But, above all, he was a very dignified football hero.

I saw Bobby play for London Schoolboys against Glasgow at Stamford Bridge. Even at 16 he had stature, a certain appearance, an awareness of the game others did not possess. When I became England youth manager he came on one of our courses and our relationship started from there.

I made him captain of the youth side and the under-23s. He was thirsty for knowledge and I spent hours talking to him about the game, whenever there was a free moment. When we had trips away he almost raided you for knowledge.

When I went to West Ham Bobby was struggling. Ironically, Geoff Hurst was playing in Bobby's left-half position but Geoff wasn't a very good defender, so I made him a forward and Bobby settled in his natural role. Once again, I made him captain and the relationship grew stronger. We got very close through football and we had a great respect for each other. However, I was never involved with him on any personal level.

He was exceptional on the training ground, a coach's dream. Whatever you asked him to do, he could do it. Football came easy to him. It wasn't a question of teaching him, merely a question of honing his considerable abilities. I made him captain because he was such a natural leader and had everyone's respect. West Ham had a few fruitful years with Bobby leading us, winning the FA Cup and the European Cup Winners' Cup. He was desperate to succeed and was a good captain because he didn't ask anybody to do anything he couldn't do.

41

I always felt he was destined for greatness. He had a tremendous awareness of everything happening on a football field. He could read the runs of his teammates, could ping balls about all over the place without thinking, always so composed, never in a hurry, streets ahead of everyone else. I used him at West Ham as a sweeper, which was then an unknown position. He played loose behind the defence and he thrived there. He was a football genius, but not in the mould of the usual ball players like Pele.

He was a gentlemen on the field and the only time Bobby got ruffled was when we were playing at Manchester City. There was an incident, he stepped in to help a team-mate and got sent off. But he was rarely in trouble with referees.

Later on, Bobby and I had some differences of opinion. When we reached the stage where West Ham had won everything, after the European final, Bobby was ambitious and felt we weren't a big enough club and didn't spend the right money. We had a good Cup side but fell short in the League. That irked him. He wanted to be the best, win a championship, and we never quite made it.

After that period, people were speculating that Bobby should go to another club. Bill Nicholson, at Tottenham, showed an interest in him – there was talk of a swop with Jimmy Greaves – and Manchester United were keen to sign him and Geoff as well.

It's never easy when a long-serving favourite has to be dropped, but in Bobby's case it wasn't as difficult as it might have been because he was injured and we had signed Mick McGiven. Mick played well – in the mould of Bobby, funnily enough – although not with the same awareness or skill.

> **"Bobby was ambitious and felt that we weren't a big enough club and didn't spend the right money. We had a good Cup side but fell short in the League"**

After the injury, Bobby asked to try somewhere else and when I transferred him to Fulham the arrangement was quite a good one for him. I was sad when he left, especially when he played against us in the FA Cup final the following year, although I probably would have felt more sad if Fulham had won. But, despite the move, Bobby and I retained a great respect for each other.

In the 60s at West Ham we wanted to play with flair, something which Bobby felt very strongly about. We had Martin and Geoff and other good players and we were a joy to watch. We had some disasters but in the main we wanted to please. We had big crowds during that period because people wanted to watch us. I don't think they cared whether we won or not at that stage because winning hadn't become that important. Winning at all costs grew into the game later on and some teams didn't care how they did it, as long as they won and were up to all sorts of tricks. But I couldn't condone entering into that sort of thing.

My philosophy was to play pure football. Having been involved with England youth and under-23s, I had mixed with foreign coaches, seen games all over the

Mutual respect as Ron Greenwood thanks Bobby for his service to West Ham just before he joined Fulham.

world and experienced different types of play, so I had an advantage over most managers. I was intrigued by European styles and wanted to achieve that with an English club and compete with the European teams, which we did. By winning the European Cup Winners' Cup and getting to the semi-final the next year, I felt vindicated by our approach. Not necessarily having cups on the sideboard but having a status recognised all over the world.

When I first went to West Ham they employed inside-forwards and wing-halves, but eventually we changed our system to a flat back four to encourage Bobby to play – he was the lynchpin. We set standards because we had players capable of it and other teams tried to copy us without having the players.

Our full-backs would push up and get forward. In fact, they were more attacking than some present-day wingers. But we believed in wingers as well like Johnny Sissons, Peter Brabrook, Harry Redknapp and Alan Sealey. We had Geoff up front and Ronnie Boyce, who was a workhorse in the middle of the field, and Martin Peters. At the back, Bobby could read along the line and cover the whole area. Everyone was tight going forward and Bobby played loose, free, behind everyone else, and the team could go forward with the confidence Bobby was always behind them, reading anything coming through, mopping up. It was a joy to watch him play.

Basically, we didn't really have a system, merely that we were all involved and we all went up together and went back together. It was a very loose system – how Liverpool and one or two other teams play now, with three at the back and two wide wing-backs.

We almost attained total football – what the Germans and other countries have achieved with inter-changing positions where forwards came back if required and defenders went forward.

Such was the interest in the way West Ham played, people actually came to watch us train, which was unheard of then. They were amazed at the amount of work we did with the ball. In those days players ran around a track and did sprints, but we did ball work all the time. It was all quite revolutionary. In actual fact, I don't think we ever did any real training.

Bobby's greatest game under my management was our European Cup Winners' Cup final when we beat Munich 1860 and, to my mind, his greatest performance for England was not in the '66 or '70 World Cups but in a tour match against Brazil in Rio de Janeiro, in the summer of 1969. His performance that day was something special.

When he died, Martin, Geoff and I laid a wreath of his number six shirt made of flowers at the Wolves match. We had a minute's silence and everybody in the ground seemed to feel as if they knew him. It was a very touching moment. Sadly, I was unable to attend the memorial service at Westminster Abbey because I was laid up in hospital with my leg in plaster.

I only knew him as a footballer. I didn't know him as a person. His life was private. Perhaps that's how it should be in football.

But when you see him in your mind, holding up that World Cup statue, it is something that befits the man.

John Cartwright

Played for West Ham from 1959 to 1961. In 1962 John quit to begin coaching. He is now Technical Director of the PFA's coaching department.

Bobby and I were at West Ham at the same time. We started out as groundstaff. There were a few of us who would go to parties: Bobby Keetch, Tony Scott, we did things as a group. It's amazing how so many of that batch went on to become top class footballers and, in Bobby's case, scale the world stage. Our duties in those days were sweeping the terraces, painting the stands and working on the pitch. I remember in the winter, when the pitch was a quagmire, there was no way we could use a roller as it would sink, so the groundsman would hitch Bobby and I up to this board with weights on it and we used to pull it across the pitch like plough horses, just to flatten the mud. We played in the FA Youth Cup final two years running and Bobby was captain the second time.

I recall a time when the first team came back from Czechoslovakia in pre-season and they had seen, for the first time, the 4-4-2 system, with a flat back four and a semi-sweeper. Ted Fenton was the manager and the players, led by Noel Cantwell, Phil Woosnam and Malcolm Musgrove, felt they could

(Left) Examining his European Cup Winners' Cup medal in '65.

(Right) Seconds after lifting the FA Cup for West Ham for the first time in '64, an interview for the BBC's David Coleman.

employ it. So the first team tried it, long before Bobby got his debut. Bobby was unable to play a role dashing forward from midfield, but eventually there was a spot for someone to play the sweep-up position alongside the centre-half. Bobby played it superbly and it was his spot forever more. There have probably been players physically and technically better than Bobby but few tackled as astutely as he did.

Sadly I lost regular contact with those lads over the years in the way you always do, but I bumped into Bobby a couple of times at games. Once or twice I had a bite to eat with him and his wife. He was good company and we always talked about the old times.

Ronnie Boyce

'Ticker' Boyce made his League debut in 1960 and was a regular until 1973, having played 339 first team games. Subsequently joined the coaching staff at Upton Park and now scouts for Millwall.

It was so unfortunate Bobby went at such an early age. There might be the odd player whose death might get a similar response, but no one would've held as much respect as Bobby did. When I first joined the groundstaff Bobby was in his second season in the first team but even then, as a youngster, you looked up to him because he stood out, you knew he was going a long way.

His greatest technical strengths were knowing when to tackle and when not to tackle and when to hold opponents up. His passing with either foot was spectacular. Of course, the pass was the second product – his first touch was always so faultless. That first touch gave him an opportunity to put the ball where it mattered. Mooro also had the ability to play the ball first time, and I'm not just talking about a ten-yard pass, but up to fifty yards first time, no problem. And, just as importantly, his passes would always be a dream to receive and always in the right path.

His positional judgement was second to none. He would put himself in the right spot for anyone hitting a thirty-yard ball in his direction, he knew where it was going to fall and he'd be there before anyone, picking the ball off.

He was quiet when he was playing. He would never yell but he might say: 'Try this', 'Try that', 'I'm always available', that sort of thing. He was forceful when he suggested ideas, without shouting. He spoke quietly and you couldn't do anything but admire him and do what he suggested.

He had immense discipline and he expected it from others. I think inwardly it disappointed him that others didn't have the same level of discipline. He knew if you didn't show that sort of discipline off the field, you wouldn't show it on it. He would look at some of the youngsters and think: 'All the billing in the world, son, but I'm not sure you're going to make it.'

Even after getting all his caps for England, he still worked as hard as anyone else and would always give himself 15 minutes extra training, on his own, with the ball in the gym, while everyone else was getting changed. He'd clip little balls against the wall, short volleys, headers, whatever, going round the gym, brushing up his first touch. It was that little bit more effort than everyone else. It made a difference. He demanded a lot of himself but he knew the demands kept him a good player.

Bobby was accepted in showbusiness circles, but he would never come back after a night in the West End and say: 'I was out with such and such last night'. He wouldn't brag, certainly not about himself, that's for sure. His feet stayed firmly on the ground – he knew you're only as good as your last game.

He would always listen to anybody, even if it was a supporter. He might not agree with them, but he would take it in. As much as people had a lot of respect for Bobby, Bobby had a lot of respect for people.

I tell you what, I miss him even now. I sit down and sometimes I think about the old days and Bobby is the first thing that comes into my mind. I don't think I'm the only one who feels like that. Bobby was a different class.

Ken Brown

Signed professionally for the Hammers in October 1951. Ken's first appearance in the 1952-53 season came while he was still serving in the army. Eventually he had spells managing Torquay, Hereford United, Bournemouth and Norwich City between 1980-88.

We were centre-halves for West Ham. I was the stopper and Bobby was the play-maker. My strength was heading and safety first, his strength was control and weighted passing. He could volley or one-touch a pass without looking and you wouldn't struggle to reach it, it would drop at your feet. You'd think, bloody hell, he didn't know where that was going. But he knew.

My natural instinct was to cover him in case he missed a ball but I can't remember him ever bloody missing it. He was so consistent. The only time I remember him making a mistake was in the international against Poland where the ball ran under his feet. I remember thinking: 'Ain't it marvellous, the one time I'm not there to cover him, he makes a mistake!'

The week before the FA Cup semi-final with Manchester United we played them in the League and they put out a lot of reserves and beat us 2-0. They were saying: 'You wait till next week, we'll put our first team out.' But, typical West Ham, we beat them 3-1 in the semi-final. The pitch up at Hillsborough was thick, heavy mud. We were winning 2-0 and got a free-kick, which John Bond lined up to take. I got some mud and built up a tee to put the ball on, like a golf shot. He mis-kicked it and the ball dribbled a few feet. United broke away and scored their only goal.

Not long after we beat TSV Munich 1860 in the European Cup Winners' Cup final we went to America and beat them again in a tournament. They said: 'You lot are coming out drinking with us,' and they took us to the German beer garden. Not surprisingly, neither team won another game after that.

I went to Wembley in '66 with Dick Walker and Andy Malcolm and I didn't want the match to finish. Afterwards we got invited into this big tent for drinks. I

Reunited in memory of their captain and inspiration: West Ham's cup-winners from 1964 and '65 together again for the Bobby Moore Memorial match at Upton Park on March 7, 1994 – the night the new South Stand was officially opened in Bobby's honour.

can't remember going home.

About a dozen of us did a pools syndicate for a season and because Mooro was a lucky bugger we said 'Let Golden Bollocks pick the numbers.' We didn't win anything and it stopped the following year. Percy, the commissionaire at West Ham, was the pools agent and one morning he looked like he'd seen a ghost. He said that even though he couldn't afford to continue with Mooro's numbers, he had saved them and that week we would have had eight draws come up. We were sick as parrots, especially Mooro. We missed out on a fortune.

The West Ham team nearly all became fathers at the same time: Geoff Hurst, Peter Brabrook, Ronnie Boyce and Jim Standen. We almost had a team of babies. My wife Joan gave birth to our first baby, Amanda, two weeks after Bobby's Roberta was born. I've got a load of black and white cine film of Tina playing in the garden with Roberta and Amanda when they were kids.

I couldn't go to Bobby's memorial because Joan died of cancer two weeks after Bobby.

Eddie Bovington

Made his debut for West Ham against Manchester United in 1961 and his final match was against Sheffield Wednesday in 1967.

Bobby Moore was a powerful figure on the field. I don't mean by his build, but by what he did. Whatever you could do, he could do it better, so you had to respect him.

Bobby had played for the first team since 1958 when I got my first game. I played right-half and Bobby was always there to help if you needed any advice. His guidance was very good because he was very wise.

Bobby was a good fellow to be out with. Although some people might think 'England captain', to us he was just plain old 'Bob from Barking.' - a workmate.

There were a lot of comedians in the squad. Bobby wasn't a joke-teller but he would come back with a quip. He was sharp at observing things, same as his strength on the field. He wasn't a great communicator, not one to instigate a conversation. Shy people don't communicate very well with strangers.

Bobby got me tickets for every game in '66, including the final where I sat among all the players' wives. I was next to Peter Bonetti's wife. The atmosphere, the spectacle, is difficult to describe. I didn't get home until 1am, having met Johnny Byrne and a few others in The Valentine at Gants Hill afterwards, but everbody was out that night.

Bobby was a great player but he was also good company.

Peter Brabrook

Signed for Chelsea in 1955 and was chosen for the England World Cup squad for Sweden in 1958. Peter cost West Ham £35,000 when he signed in 1962. In 1968, he joined Leyton Orient. After retiring he ran a butcher's shop but has since returned to Upton Park to help with youth coaching.

When we played West Ham, I always roasted Noel Cantwell, the left-back, who was probably the best left-back in the country. But I could never seem to get past Bobby. He was nowhere near as quick as Noel or me, but he never let you get in a position to beat him – he led you into a trap and caught you by the byline or the corner flag. He read your brain before you could. The Chelsea manager, Ted Drake, would say: 'You haven't got past Moore, what's wrong with you? He can't run!' I'd reply: 'I know, but you bloody well try it! He just makes me run out of space.'

In one game, Bobby had to go in goal and I cut in from the wing, jinked past Noel and only had Mooro to beat. I smashed it right in the corner but, to my amazement, he stuck out a boot and knocked it round the post. I couldn't believe it, and he looked at me and said: 'You still haven't beaten me, have you?'

I remember West Ham's FA Cup victory over Preston in '64 quite vividly. We were odds-on favourites because Preston were in the division lower. We didn't settle to start with but once we got our passing rhythm going, we won it. For me it was more nerve-racking than when I got my first England cap.

We all had a feel of the Cup during our lap of honour – Kenny Brown and John Bond put the lid on their heads and were dancing. Strangely enough, as we were running around the pitch, I noticed two of my cousins at the front of the terrace, so I went and showed them my medal. There was a team photograph taken with the Cup and I'm missing because I was talking to my cousins!

Afterwards we had a huge function in Soho with wives, ex-players, the lot – we packed the place out and stayed up all night drinking at our hotel. We were a happy group. That was a big part of our success. The team often had a meal together, usually with the wives. It helped to keep us close.

Before every match Bobby laid his handkerchief out on the bench and placed his rings, watch and money inside and folded it up and put it away safely.

Bobby didn't do silly things or imitate people, although he regularly came out with humourous little quips. He was quick like that. People never laughed at the way he played though. They just admired his dedication.

John Lyall

Between 1959-62, John played 31 League games at West Ham but later made his name in management. He was appointed assistant manager to Ron Greenwood in 1971, team manager in 1974 and manager in 1977. He departed in 1989 and finished his football career with Ipswich Town.

Most of the West Ham lads came from what I call solid backgrounds, our parents had been through the war and were grateful for being alive. They were proud we had become footballers. My father was a policeman and he would say: 'You earn more in three months than I do in a year'. We had it drummed into us: don't do anything to let football down because you are privileged.

Quite a few of us had been given grammar school educations: myself, Geoff Hurst and Ronnie Boyce and we'd been taught some good values. Bobby had gone to a technical high school in Leyton but he had an academic understanding of football. He was a shining example of how a young player should be: married, settled, with a house and a car. Most of us were married by 21. Beyond that, football became our only goal.

Parental discipline put Bobby in good stead. His mother and father idolised him but in a way that helped him. They discouraged him from being arrogant but people of that generation had much the same lessons instilled into them. The 40s and 50s weren't easy years and money didn't influence anything because there wasn't any. On Wednesday when you asked mum for a lolly, and she had no money, you didn't get any 'till Friday. That was it. You learned.

Bobby was, however, more disciplined than any of us. He and I used to go to the Ilford Palais dancehall and one night we got back real late, about 12.30am, and I was

Bobby (standing, far left) in West Germany on one of his first overseas tours, with West Ham Youth in 1957. John Lyall is standing, far right, in the line-up.

staying at his house. I put my suit on a hanger but Bobby got his clothes brush out and brushed his whole suit down. Years later, Bobby would use one pair of tie-ups for his socks all season because he would religiously put them in his boots after every game. Albert Walker, the old boy who laid out the kit, would say: 'It's amazing, the captain of England uses the same tie-ups all season yet the rest of them need new ones every week.'

Bobby first saw Tina down at the Ilford Palais. They made a smashing couple. I had to give up playing and went in the office, doing the wages and youth football, so I felt alienated because I was apart from the players, but Bobby and Tina never worried about such barriers. They went out of their way to retain our friendship.

Although the lads were in competition for places they were still a close bunch. It was like having brothers. At night, we'd go together to see games at Tottenham or Arsenal – Bobby and I would go on the bus before we had cars. In the end, Bobby bought a Triumph Herald Convertible and I can remember sitting in it listening to that offshore radio station – Radio Caroline – with him.

We were students of the game. We sat for hours talking football, reviewing games, talking tactics, discussing training. England's defeat at the hands of Hungary in '53 started it all. Walter Winterbottom, the England manager, realised the Hungarians were light years ahead so he developed a group of coaches and they pursued new tactics and thinking. Malcolm Allison went on some courses in the late 50s and got inspired by it all. He persuaded Ted Fenton, the manager, to let him try out a few things at West Ham and Ted was shrewd enough to let Malcolm have a go.

> ## "Bobby was like a good, steady car and Ron tuned him up to Formula One standard"

Ron Greenwood arrived at the club, saying: 'Outside of the foot, flick it here and pass it there.' We could do it, but Ron taught us why we were doing it. Ron looked at football in a different way. It would frighten you what Ron could see that no one else could. 'Did you notice what he did there?' he'd say. We had trouble seeing it even after he had explained it.

If you played alongside Bobby he was always encouraging. He'd say: 'There's one on your outside, hold it, you're all right now, no hurry, okay, give it to me now', that sort of thing. He was only 18 or 19 years-old then, he was already an accomplished player, but Ron gave him a bit extra. Bobby was like a good, steady car and Ron tuned him up to Formula One standard.

Ron did a lot for everyone. One day we were doing some one-touch circuits around the pitch and it was in groups of threes and they had to run the full length of the pitch, pass it along the line and score. Bobby, Martin and Geoff were doing it rather lazily because it was so easy for them and I said: 'Okay, you think you're such great players. Let's see how good you are. Try it off the ground.' They did it first time. They went 'bonk, bonk, bonk, wallop' and it was in the net. To show it wasn't a fluke, they went around a few times and it was 'bosh', in the net every time. That wasn't luck. It was the talent they had.

Often in training, as the ball would come to them, they would shout: 'Corner flag!' or whatever and hit the ball against it with incredible accuracy. I remember watching Harry Redknapp crossing for Martin Peters after training once. I was watching from the dug-out and Martin said to Harry: 'Stick one over' and as it came over he shouted: 'Bar!' and volleyed it against the bar. Harry shouted something like: 'Bet you a quid you can't do that again!' So Martin said: 'Yeah, okay.' Harry sent it over and Martin volleyed it against the bar. 'Just lucky,' said Harry. 'One more, double or quits?' and Martin said: 'Sure, if you want to lose more money.' Harry's corner came over, Martin whacked it against the bar. As they were coming off, Martin called to me: 'John, put your hands up!' A little sceptical, I put my hands up and Martin chipped it from the six-yard box right into my hands and I didn't have to move an inch. The place was buzzing because of the sort of unbelievable talent Ron had at the club. Ted had the ability to recognise talent and Ron had the ability to nurture it.

In one match, Bobby pulled a ball down on his chest, came out of the area, beat one player, got caught by a second player, lost the ball and the opposition scored. The press asked Ron: 'Have you told Mooro off?' and Ron replied: 'Why? What he did was right but the moment wasn't. Qualities like Bobby's should be nurtured, not destroyed.' Bobby was lucky Ron believed in skill so much.

Mooro was so good he could dictate matches from the back. One trick he used

West Ham's most famous three making it all look so easy in training at Chadwell Heath.

to start attacks was by passing the ball back to the 'keeper. He'd draw people over, then release it, creating space over the other side of the pitch. Some teams tried to stop Mooro from running the show by putting someone on him, but Bobby would go for a trot, away from his usual left side, and drag the marker all over the place. He loved playing cat and mouse. He might go wider against the touchline or over to the right side of the pitch, opening up the space he vacated for others to play in. Sometimes, Bobby would move into midfield instead and Ronnie Boyce would just drop back. No matter what they tried, they couldn't stop Bobby playing.

Ron's philosophy was goals come from anyone who arrives in the right place at the right time and he taught the players when to make a run and when to stay, about cutting off angles, closing people down, areas of supply. Some of them asked Ron to explain it again, but Bobby got it first time.

If something had gone wrong on the pitch, Bobby waited for a quiet moment and would say: 'We didn't do such and such right.' He had honest opinions, good and bad. Ron mostly left discussion of games 'till Mondays because he believed emotions were high after a game. Personally, I am a great believer in hitting things when they happen: Talk now before players think you don't care.

Bobby always rose to a challenge or criticism. If you read in the paper some-body's six-foot four centre-forward saying Mooro was poor in the air, Bobby would respond in the match by nipping in front of him every time and nicking the ball. Heading is as much about timing as it is about height.

Ron gave me more and more responsibility and in the early 70s he put me in charge of a tour to the States. Bobby and Geoff hadn't had a break after interna-tional duty and Ron had said they only need play half the games. On the plane, Bobby said: 'John, I'll do all I can for you. If you want me to play every game, I will.' I thought that was a lovely gesture. I had Ron's support from above but it was heart-ening to get such help from Bobby. Mooro would do anything you asked and I could say to the rest of them: 'If he does it, the rest of you do it.'

On the trip I asked Mooro to keep an eye on the young lads in the squad and he replied: 'Don't worry, John, I will.' The first night he asked them to join him for a drink at the bar. Four hours drinking later, Bob was saying: 'Put it all on my tab.' I said: 'Bob, you don't have to do this. They've all got spending money.' But he replied: 'I've been lucky, John, you know that, and if the lads can take home some dollars, it won't do them any harm.'

At the time of the '66 final I was on holiday in Clacton with my in-laws and we watched it on TV. I had great pride whenever West Ham lads played internationals, even later with Trevor Brooking. Geoff's goal from Bobby's free-kick: a quick look, ball down, play it into space, nod down, goal! At that moment, we were watching the genius of Ron.

The England team's achievements in football were comparable to the achieve-ments of The Beatles in music. Before their success, the great singers were Americans like Elvis and Little Richard, but with The Beatles you felt our music was suddenly as good as America's. That's what happened when we won the World Cup: we could say: 'Hey, our lads are the best in the world.'

My wife has never been involved in football because we like to keep the family separate, but she always liked Bob. She believed he was a good man because he never failed to say: 'Hello.' You don't forget manners and kindness like that. An insignificant thing, some might say, but not to us.

Bobby Moore. He always said and did the right thing at the right time.

 ## Moore tributes

I heard the terrible news the day after he died. I was very distressed, especially as I had spoken to Bobby on the phone only a week before. Despite being so far apart, we kept in regular contact. Things will never be the same. In the days when Bobby and I used to play together there were some great wags in the Chicken Run and they would shout: 'See you in the Retreat after the match'. Bobby and I regularly drank in there.
Johnny 'Budgie' Byrne

People will have only good memories of Bobby. He set fine standards, as you would expect from a player brought up the West Ham way. His use of the ball was uncanny and, as Pele said, he was the greatest defender in the world.
Frank O'Farrell

I heard the news of Bobby's death on my car radio. I was shocked and saddened. I helped to coach Bobby along with Noel Cantwell and Malcolm Allison and other senior pro's on Tuesdays and Thursdays at the ground. It was a great loss to the club and an even greater one for world football.
Malcolm Musgrove

Bobby's untimely death came as a great surprise. He was the leader of the pack.
Jimmy Andrews

I knew Bobby like the back of my hand. He deserved so much more in life. I consider myself very lucky to have played with him. He made the rest of us look second rate.
John Bond

Bobby with Budgie Byrne blowing bubbles to the South Bank as they parade the FA Cup in '64.

53

Saturday 30th July 1966

World Cup Final

Empire Stadium, Wembley
96,924

ENGLAND *(1)* 4   W GERMANY *(1)* 2 *(aet, 2-2 at 90 mins)*

Hurst 19, 100, 120   *Haller 13*
Peters 78   *Weber 90*

Referee: *Gottfried Dienst (Switzerland)*
Linesmen: *Tofik Bakhramov (USSR) & Harol Galba (Czechoslovakia)*

ENGLAND	WEST GERMANY
Gordon Banks *Leicester City*	**Hans Tilkowski** *Borussia Dortmund*
George Cohen *Fulham*	**Horst Dieter Hottges** *Werder Bremen*
Ray Wilson *Everton*	**Karl-Heinz Schnellinger** *Milan*
Nobby Stiles *Manchester Utd*	**Franz Beckenbauer** *Bayern Munich*
Jack Charlton *Leeds Utd*	**Wolfgang Weber** *Cologne*
Bobby Moore *(capt) West Ham Utd*	**Willi Schulz** *Hamburg*
Alan Ball *Blackpool*	**Sigi Held** *Borussia Dortmund*
Geoff Hurst *West Ham Utd*	**Helmut Haller** *Bologna*
Bobby Charlton *Manchester Utd*	**Uwe Seeler** *(capt) Hamburg*
Roger Hunt *Liverpool*	**Wolfgang Overath** *Cologne*
Martin Peters *West Ham Utd*	**Lothar Emmerich** *Borussia Dortmund*
Manager: **Alf Ramsey**	*Manager:* **Helmut Schoen**

Chapter 3

Boys of '66

Geoff Hurst

Made 499 appearances for West Ham United between 1959-1972 scoring 248 goals. He also won 49 England caps netting 24 times for his country. Geoff remains the only player to score a hat-trick in a World Cup final.

Mooro was six months older than me and he started at West Ham before I did. Immediately I noticed Bobby's tremendous willpower. For example, in training, the whole squad – professionals and juniors – would do the six-inch raises exercise where you lie on your back and lift your legs no more than a foot off the ground. In our test, the last one to lower them down would be the winner. Inevitably, Mooro would always be the last to lower his legs. He wasn't necessarily stronger or bigger or better than anybody else, but he had such willpower to be the best, in anything he did, even then.

In 1969 England were going on a pre-World Cup trip to play Mexico, Uruguay and Brazil to familiarise ourselves with the conditions. On the flight over the players were in end-of-season mode, relaxing with a few drinks. We weren't playing for another week. The stewardesses asked around the lads what drinks they wanted: 'lager,' 'gin and tonic,' they were saying. When they asked Mooro he said: 'Orange juice.' A couple of the players looked surprised but they knew Mooro had switched into 'work' mode. He was going to make sure nothing prevented him from playing well, impressing Alf and securing his place for the World Cup. It was the willpower again.

The six months age gap meant Bobby had a year's development on me and he got in the first team before I did. That gap was quite significant and it somehow seemed to separate us. At the training ground, one of the groundstaff would sort the fan mail. A pile for Mooro and Johnny Byrne, and a pile for the rest of us. Nearly all my letters said: 'Dear Geoff. You played okay against Wanderers last week. P.S. Could you get me Bobby Moore's autograph?'

We were friends but we didn't socialise that much. Mooro had a different circle of social friends, but we did have a strong bond between us from working together all those years. I had huge respect for him as a person and a player, but I was never totally sure it was a mutual appreciation. Saying that, though, we beat Sunderland one year and I had one of those days where I couldn't do anything wrong – I'm not sure if I scored, but I certainly made a couple of goals. After the game I was soaking down in one of the small slipper baths and Mooro walked over. He wasn't a person for saying a lot. In truth, he never said much about anything, but he said: 'Today, you were f****** brilliant!' It's a compliment that I will never forget.

Our wives were friends and we lived near the Moore's house in Chigwell for about five years. We would go for meals to the steakhouse in Gants Hill on a fairly regular basis and seven or eight of the players and wives would often go to the Moby Dick in Chadwell Heath. This would usually be on the Saturday night after a game. I may have gone out once early in the week, but we were fairly disciplined. We certainly wouldn't be out the night before games or any of that nonsense.

One evening Mooro and I went out with Kenny Lynch to a club in London and although Lynchy is a well-known celebrity on the circuit, that night he had trouble getting in. We were laughing because in the end he had to say: 'I'm with Geoff Hurst and Bobby Moore,' and they said: 'Well, why didn't you say so?' and promptly let him in. We ribbed him something rotten about that.

At West Ham, the era under Ron Greenwood was a great time. Ron was one of the greatest coaches ever and he had a bunch of keen youngsters who all peaked at the same time. It was no surprise he took three players, with basic ability initially, and transformed them into nigh on world-class players. Certainly Bobby was world class, Martin probably was and although I wouldn't put myself in that category, I could handle playing in world-class competitions.

Mooro just kept on raising his game. He played for West Ham at a level, he played for England at another level and if he had represented planet Earth against Mars, he would have risen to an even higher level.

When Ron first came over from Arsenal we were all a bit uneasy but Bobby Moore reassured us when he said: 'I've played under Ron at England Under-23 level. Things are going to change around here, this chap is incredible on the game.' And he was right. Ron taught us that space is only space until you move into it. Stuff like that.

West Ham were the pioneers of the style known as 4-2-4 and later 4-3-3 and they were among the first to get forwards to defend and defenders to attack, abandoning conventional fixed positions. For years we operated a sys-

> **"Bobby never said much about anything, but he said: 'Today, you were f****** brilliant!' It's a compliment that I will never forget"**

tem where we had an extra man at the back, but it meant we were short up front. So at the start of the 1966-67 season the defence played one-on-one and we pushed a man up. We got some terrible results initially, and we were getting beaten in matches where we had 80 per cent of the ball. The plan was no matter how many goals we gave away, we'd score more. It also meant the goalkeeper, Jim Standen, had to become an extra sweeper, forced to come out of his goal and use his feet. After a few months of getting beaten, it started to work. In three games in one week we scored 17 goals. But, slowly, any chance of winning the League slipped away. I think we attempted too much too soon, but the approach was exciting.

I remember West Ham once went, as a squad, to New York for a cup tournament there. We stayed in apartments that had their own kitchen and we would take it in turns to make the tea and breakfast. The best apartment of all was the top-floor penthouse flat and Johnny Byrne and Mooro bagged it before the rest of us could blink. It didn't do them a great deal of good because all the players kept dropping by to borrow sugar and suchlike and would flop into one of the best chairs to sunbathe on the roof garden. When the wives came over to watch us they caught on to the penthouse attraction so there was hardly any room for Mooro and Budgie to stand, let alone sit.

In the FA Cup semi-final in '64 we had to face Manchester United at Hillsborough. The press gave us no chance. One writer even suggested we hadn't got the right to be on the same pitch as United. Far from depressing us, it made

MOORE **than a legend**

Bobby meeting The Queen on October 26, 1992, in honour of Her Majesty's 40th anniversary of ascension. Bobby Charlton, Geoff Hurst, George Cohen and Jack Charlton are also in view.

the squad hopping mad. The weather was miserable and the pitch was a sea of mud, but we won because of Ron's planning. He claimed that no matter how good United were, what could Law and Charlton accomplish without the ball? Their constant source of passes came from the wing-halves, particularly Pat Crerand, so our wingers closed them down and it worked like a dream. The other thing I remember about that game was my goal and how Bobby Moore made it for me. He made a bold run down the wing and I made up twenty yards to whack it in. It was, as far as I was concerned, the best goal I ever scored. The press described Bobby's run in glorious detail and finished with '...and Hurst scored'. Bobby laughed about that.

In West Ham's second year in Europe, we played Olympiakos. Having beaten them 4-0 at home we went out to Athens. The Greek fans were fanatics. There were less than 40,000 but they made so much din it made the Wembley roar seem like a whisper. Also, we came out onto the pitch to a shower of fruit, stones and fireworks aimed at our heads and every time there was a dull moment in the match, the barrage started up again. The Greek players flew at us, tackling, screaming like madmen. Somehow we managed to earn a 2-2 draw but Bobby proved himself a great captain that day. Not only was he everywhere in defence, he was all over the pitch as a troubleshooter. In every team you get one player with a short fuse under provocation, and had Bobby not been so quick to step in at any tense moment, someone would have been goaded into thumping a Greek – in which case, none of us would have got out of that cauldron alive.

1966 was an event you can't really put into words. If someone had written the story, you would say it was a fairytale. It's the biggest day of joy we've had in this country for a long time, sporting or otherwise. Like many things, you didn't realise at the time what a momentous day it was. It brings it home when people still talk about it, telling me what they were doing that day. I've heard fantastic stories. I get more pleasure from the stories now than I did at the time.

It was only twenty years after the Second World War finished and my late father-in-law had been a paratrooper and he was very emotional, crying after the game. It was an especially significant day for people who had fought the Germans or suffered in the war.

The build-up beforehand was a difficult period, because I was waiting, not knowing if I'd play in the final. Card-playing with the other players helped to pass the time, but often I found it best to be alone. I used to go to the shops in Hendon to buy toothpaste or shampoo – my room ended up looking like a salesman's sample bag, full of stuff I didn't want and would never use. But it used up time. Eventually the big game arrived.

My second goal has been much-discussed. Although the consultation with the linesman took only a few seconds, it seemed to take forever before the referee gave it the nod. I've said it for thirty years now, Roger Hunt made no attempt to put it in, instead he shouted: 'It's there!' and wheeled away. The film is inconclusive so Roger's reaction was good enough for me. For my third goal, I was in two minds whether to run towards the corner flag and use up some time, but everything opened up and I got within striking distance. I was very weary and decided to hit it with everything I had left. If it had gone over, precious seconds would have been wasted. But the ball popped up off the turf, I caught it with the bone of my instep and it flew in. I joke in my after-dinner speech that I was aiming for the crowd, mishit it, and it went in. But, at that moment, the whistle blew and a million things happened at once. After the game I wasn't sure if it was in. No one seemed to know and it wasn't until I got changed and emerged back out onto the pitch to check the scoreboard that I realised I'd got a hat-trick.

The day after the final we had a dinner hosted by Eamonn Andrews. I don't remember being there, but we've got a clip recorded from the TV. Even today, our children find it highly amusing seeing footage of Judith's hairstyle.

The legacy of that day is that I became much more famous. Judith and I had often gone shopping at our local supermarket and were rarely recognised. But the first time we went there after the World Cup we were mobbed. The staff poured out from behind counters waving paper to be autographed, customers joined in, thrusting soap packets and, of all things, bundles of bacon for me to sign. I was backed up against the biscuit counter trying to shake a hundred hands at once. We got out of there pretty quickly. I used to have to phone local restaurants and say I was a friend of Bobby Moore. Now, suddenly, I could book a table in my own name with ease. It was amazing.

Over twenty years or so, the '66 team have played together almost every two years in some testimonial or friendly. We've played against the Germans in Germany and at Elland Road in aid of the Bradford fire fund in '86. That was the last real game we played together. The whole England team turned out and all the Germans started the game. Strangely enough, we beat them 6-3 and I scored a hat-trick. About 20,000 people turned up and we raised £50,000. My children were too young for '66 but they came to that game at Leeds and on the way home in the car my eldest daughter said she was beginning to understand the significance of the day and that they were all very proud of me.

I was in my car when I heard the news of Mooro's death. I knew he was ill. I went down to the gates of Upton Park after Bobby died because I'd seen it on the news. It was a shrine down there. I had to go with my wife, so we could see it for ourselves. It was amazing how people felt about Bobby.

Martin Peters

Made a total of 720 League appearances and won 67 England caps between 1962-80. Emerged into the limelight in 1966 after scoring in the World Cup final before transferring from West Ham United to Tottenham Hotspur for a record £200,000 in 1970.

I always called him 'Robert'. I'd say: 'Hello, Robert, how you doing?' I had tremendous respect for him. Everyone knows about his football prowess but people didn't know about the man. It's the man we miss.

He rang me in the January before he died. I didn't know he was so ill. I said: 'Hello Robert.' He said: 'How are things? How's the family? All right? How's Kathy? How's Leanne? How's Grant?' He had a standard patter but he even remembered their names. I don't suppose I would think to enquire about Roberta and Dean. Bobby rang to ask me to play in Malcolm Allison's testimonial but unfortunately I was already booked to play in the Michael Watson benefit match. Even though Bobby was terminally ill, he was still trying to earn money for his friend Malcolm.

In my early days at West Ham I didn't know Bobby to begin with. He wasn't outspoken, just one of the pro's I worked with. He worked tremendously hard to hone his game. Ability doesn't happen overnight. I noticed his dedication as the years went on because he would stay after our training at Grange Farm, Chigwell, to do extra work – I was the same: first to arrive and last to leave.

I broke into the first team in 1962. We were mid-table and Ron Greenwood put me and three other youngsters in. We beat Cardiff 4-1. After that I was in and out of the side and, a lot of people forget this, but I didn't play in the side that won the '64 FA Cup. My true position was midfield and although I was used in many positions, I got back in the side at left-back in the end.

During that time I wasn't close to Bobby. He was one stage ahead the whole time. He was only a couple of years older than me but he moved in different circles. The stars and entertainers wanted to be with Bobby Moore. A group of the players would meet around each other's houses to play cards while the wives chatted. But our captain wasn't part of that.

Both Geoff and I were late arrivals in the squad for '66. I played my first game against Yugoslavia in the May before the tournament started and knowing Geoff and Bobby was a big help because we played well together.

Mostly defenders didn't pass it short, they always booted it long, but Mooro would knock it to me, I'd draw an opponent, lay it back and he would come forward. When you see the old films, you realise how attacking he was. Bobby demanded the ball. It wasn't a case of giving it to him. He would even run in and take it from you if he saw an opportunity you had missed.

Although Alf Ramsey was direct with his comments he rarely criticised you in front of others – he would pull you to one side. On the rare occasions the boys sneaked out for a lager, he knew, but he didn't say anything as long as they were doing the business. No one went out during the World Cup though. The players gave so much to him because he gave so much to the players.

In the quarter-final, Argentina were just hooligans. They didn't want to play, just kick and bite and fight. After Antonio Rattin was sent off we got through on Geoff's header, but afterwards they urinated in the corridor outside the England dressing room and a chair came flying through the door – the Argentinians wanted a fight. That wasn't my scene but I think Jack Charlton and Nobby Stiles were up for it. The semi-final against Portugal was the opposite of the quarter-final – I committed the first foul and that was for a push just before half-time. Nobby won that match for us because he marked their star player, Eusebio, out of the match.

The beginning of the greatest occasion in English football history as Bobby and Uwe Seeler toss the coin.

The night before the final Alf secretly told those who were playing but asked us to keep it to ourselves. I was sharing with Geoff and we sat on our beds talking for about an hour before he finally said: 'Martin, I've got to tell someone. I'm in! I'm playing,' and I said: 'Great, so am I!'

On the day of the final I remember being very nervous. Two months before, I hadn't even played for England. It was real *Boy's Own* stuff. Travelling in the coach to Wembley was a fantastic sight. Everyone had flags. Just getting through the crowd up Wembley Way was a struggle. I'm fairly focused when I'm playing: dressing room, pitch, take in the atmosphere, check the surface – long stud or short stud? – get changed. But I take my time getting mentally prepared. I remember that day after I got changed I knocked a ball against the dressing room wall to warm up.

Bobby wasn't a demonstrative captain in the dressing room. From time to time, if he felt it was necessary, he would have a quiet word, gently gee people up. But he was very methodical. I remember watching him fold his handkerchief up. You don't fold your handkerchief up, do you? Or your underpants? But Bobby did.

Bobby had a superstition to be the last player to put his shorts on. He would wait 'till everyone had their shorts on and then put his on. But I used to take mine off again and then watch him take his off again. He never realised I used to do it to him. I didn't do it on the day of the World Cup final but I did it to him a few times at West Ham. Funnily enough, when I moved on to Tottenham, I continued the habit of putting my shorts on last.

What I remember most about the final was my goal. I got on the end of a deflection and volleyed it in. It was a tremendous feeling – When I was celebrating I was going back to the half-way line and my fingers were tingling. It was as though a bolt of lightning had gone through me.

I remember going up the steps to collect my medal. The wives were sitting just in front. I was pleased for Kathy because in the '64 Cup final with West Ham she was crying because I didn't play. After the final we had the official banquet and I remember some of the boys wanted to get away after the speeches and Bobby asked Alf, who said: 'Off you go lads.' Someone had tickets for Danny La Rue, and Bobby and some others went to the Playboy Club. I went to bed. I didn't want to go out and be loud and noisy. I just wanted to be quiet with Kathy, relax, take it easy on our own. I hadn't seen her properly for six weeks. She was 20 and Leanne was only 11 months-old and while I was away she had organised a house move to Barkingside for us on her own and that was traumatic for her. Sometimes it's good to be quiet. On the way back to our new home, though, someone crashed into the back of our car, but no one was hurt.

We got £60 appearance money and the FA gave us £22,000 as an after-thought for winning, to split pro-rata between those who actually played in the tournament. But everyone wanted it split evenly as a squad. It was a team decision. We got a grand each before tax.

Of '66, Bobby Charlton said: 'Time is enchantment.' I think that is true. The longer something goes on, the more wonderful it can seem. No English team has ever won it since, but people who watched the '66 final felt as proud as we did playing in it. It was against the Germans which was a big thing for the older folks. People have passed it down to their children, who have seen it on television and video. It was English football's greatest moment.

People say I left West Ham because I was in the shadow of Bobby and Geoff, which was rubbish. Why should I be number one in the side led by the captain of England and the man who scored three goals in a World Cup final? It's natural they are going to be more sought after than the person who got one goal. But if I hadn't scored, do you realise we would have lost 2-1 within normal time?

I wanted to be in a more successful team. I was 26 and if I didn't go then, it would've been too late. It was okay playing in such great games with West Ham, losing 4-3 and drawing 5-5, but I wanted more than that. As it turned out, I made the right decision moving to Tottenham. We won the UEFA Cup in 1972 and League Cups in 1971 and again in 1973 when I was captain. Lifting that cup was fantastic so I know how Bobby must have felt.

We all miss him at the World Cup reunions. In fact I thought we would never get together again after he died. I felt that strongly. He was number one. He was our leader. Even though he wasn't the oldest, he will always be our leader. In his absence Bobby Charlton has taken the mantle. I think about Mooro. I've got a busy schedule but sometimes when matches are on the television, I think: 'I miss old Robert'. He wasn't family, but he was close to family.

On the day he died, I couldn't believe I wouldn't see him again. Kathy and I miss the man. She used to go to Tottenham and Bobby would often come and talk to her when he was doing his Capital Radio work. Very shortly after his operation, I remember talking briefly with him at Wembley in 1991, when Tottenham played Nottingham Forest in the FA Cup final. He had on that old cap of his and I said: 'Hello Robert'. He said: 'How you doing, Martin? You all right?' He didn't look well, but he always insisted he was fine.

What can one say that hasn't already been said? He portrayed the proper image for our country. There were some who were half as good as him, but never as good as him. There isn't, and never will be, another Robert.

Gordon Banks

Arguably the world's greatest goalkeeper, Gordon's 24-year career was cut short by a car accident in 1972. Made over 500 League outings for Chesterfield, Leicester City and Stoke City and also won 73 England Caps.

Bobby was a very likeable man. He mixed with everybody, especially any new faces coming into the England squad. Bobby and Alf Ramsey often went talking together, asking each other's opinion about different things, exchanging views. On the field Bobby was such a great captain, always fighting and battling for every ball, geeing us up when things weren't going right. He never let his personal standards drop, no matter what the circumstances.

For me, it was great having him in the England defence because he read a game so well. I was good at positioning myself to anticipate dangers and threats, but Bob was even better. The two of us were right in the centre of the England formation and I could see from behind how good he was. He would often leave a bit of room for the opponent to receive the ball and as the guy put his head down to kick, Bobby would make a challenge – because he was momentarily looking at the ball, he couldn't see Bobby close in. Bobby did it so well, nipped attacks in the bud before they ever developed, which was superb. It was like seeing a master boxer at work – he studied what the other guy did and learned to keep his distance until the time was perfect to attack. He also gave a great deal of thought to where he distributed the ball once he'd won it, even under pressure.

In '66 we reached the final not really expecting to get there, although we were hopeful of doing so. The training sessions had got lighter as the match approached. Clowning around is something all teams do but we were worse than most. Our joking relieved the tension and we all knew each other well enough to know how far we could take the jesting and horseplay. It helped to relax us.

On the morning of the final we went through the usual individual routines. By the time we left Hendon Hall there was a big crowd and getting on the bus was an effort with people patting you, shaking hands and wishing you luck. As usual we had a police escort but obviously there was more tension on that particular journey. On route, we could see the fans making their way to the stadium and the two different sets of colours.

At Wembley Stadium, there was a big crowd outside the dressing room, too. They went crackers when we pulled up. There were cheers as each of us got off the coach. That was where we had to meet relatives and friends to give them tickets so we went in to encourage the crowd to disperse a bit and then came out again afterwards to try and find our families.

It built up from there: usual things, getting changed and that. I remember opening some of the telegrams – that was a monster task in itself, all them bloody letters and requests for autographs which were stacked high on the treatment table. The rest of the squad were in there giving us a hand with them – that was an important part of the team's success: the squad players who weren't in the team did everything they could to help. And, of course, amidst all the bodies and telegrams, Bob would be going round to everyone, offering words of encouragement: 'Everything all right? Have you got all you need?' that sort of thing.

Alf said beforehand: 'Gentlemen, you've worked hard for this, we've got this far, now let's get out there and get it won.' He shook everybody's hand, as did the trainers and the other lads in the squad, and next thing I knew we were walking up the tunnel, coming out on to the track and hearing that incredible roar. Wonderful. We'd savoured similar to that before, but knowing it was a World Cup final the noise was, that bit louder. Each team was trying not to look as nervous as the other, but we all knew how everybody felt. We'd never lost against West Germany and I virtually knew their national anthem by heart. Of course, being introduced to the Queen was another thrill.

If I remember rightly, it started to rain while we were out there and I knew I had to wear gloves because the ball always came off the turf quickly. Strangely enough, the warm-up is the most horrendous part – all the nerves are jangling, your legs feel like jelly, your hands feel weak, you certainly don't feel like your body will do what you want it to. But you want to get on with it. As soon as that whistle goes you know your concentration has got to be 100%.

Going one down didn't deter us. In my heart I thought: 'They've got the early goal but we've got time to get back.' We put them under pressure and the flow of the game see-sawed. When the final whistle went, we knew we'd won the World Cup and it was a wonderful feeling. I was nearly the last to collect my medal because I was going round congratulating all the team. Then all the squad players came over to me and Alf grabbed me and said: 'Well done! Great!' We hugged each other and I said: 'Well done yourself!' He was a lovely man and he didn't want the glory. The climb up the steps to receive the medal was a super moment.

We were remembered not solely because we won it. People were proud of the national football team and remember the '66 side because they've had little to cheer about since. When England win something, it will change again.

One last story about Bobby: After my save from Pele's header in the 1970 World Cup in Mexico I always tell people that while the ball was out for the corner, Bobby came over and said: 'Bloody hell, Gordon, can't you catch 'em!' The truth was Bobby came over and clapped me and tapped me on the head to say well done. It was his way of showing his appreciation from one professional to another. I can tell you, I was grateful to him on more than one occasion for rescuing us in tight spots.

Bobby Charlton

Made his Manchester United debut in 1956. Following a distinguished career which saw him make 642 League appearances and net 206 goals he retired in 1974. Bobby also won 106 England caps scoring a record 49 times. Knighted in 1994, he is a director at Old Trafford

Bobby Moore was very quiet and unobtrusive but, despite that, he had a lot of fun in him. He was captain of England for a good deal of the time I played for the national side and was an excellent skipper. He was genuine, a good

MOORE than a legend

leader and he linked everyone together. We won the World Cup in '66 because we were a group, we got on well together and Bobby was our captain.

The effect on the nation when he passed away was very moving. I believe everybody was so sad when he died because they can link themselves to '66 and remember just what they were doing that day with great affection. We all knew from the moment we won it our lives would be different. At the end of the final I said to our Jack: 'We can't do any better than world champions!' We were the best-liked team there has ever been in this country and there was a great affection for the lads. It was a tight-knit unit and when Bobby Moore died it signalled the beginning of the end of it. In fact, you could even say it was the end because it has not been the same since. We've had a few functions but it's not been the same because we weren't all there.

With Bobby being the first to go, I wasn't surprised by the reaction of the nation. He represented the '66 team which achieved the greatest footballing moment this country's ever had. Not just English people either: Welsh, Irish, Scots, Dutch, everyone had respect for his ability and they all liked him.

One memory I have of Bobby is when some of us went on an All-Star team goodwill tour to South Africa in 1979 and he got sent off for arguing against a multi-racial XI. On the tour, some of us flew on a little plane to a wildlife park. It was a nice trip and we were on the viewing platform overlooking a pond where animals came to drink. It was very peaceful, and I remember Bobby saying: 'There's hardly anywhere in the world where you can't actually hear any cars, buses, aeroplanes or anything, but a game park in Africa is one of the rare moments when you hear absolutely nothing.' And it was true.

When the plane took off to come back it was a rough runway and one of the stones fractured the hydraulic system and the wheels wouldn't come up, so we had to fly with the wheels down. We landed without difficulty but afterwards they said they had lost a lot of hydraulic oil so we were glad we were down safely.

The '66 team were all winners. And, just as importantly, most of them were good listeners. The players had a lot of character. Alf taught us to keep our feet on the ground. Bobby and the lads were all survivors. They all played for a long time, had long careers and possessed the right attitude for the game. It wasn't a bit of success and then forget it. They stayed in the game and that is only possible if the application is right. None of

65

them were more bothered about their own future and success than that of the team. Everybody was keen to do well and win but they were quite prepared to share it. We all believed in the team.

We persevered with the same system in the Mexico '70 World Cup with only a few different players and it worked reasonably well. We were a strong side, had some good new players who fitted well and with a little bit of luck could easily have won the World Cup again. When Gordon Banks dropped out against the Germans with a stomach bug we lost the greatest goalkeeper in the world and that had to weaken any team. Had that not happened, we might have won the World Cup twice. The defeat against West Germany was to be my last game.

I didn't see much of Bobby in the years after I stopped playing. We occasionally went to the same social functions but he was in London and I was in Manchester. I didn't see as much of him as I would have liked. Bobby was attentive, though, and whenever we met he would ask about the youngsters at United.

Bobby had presence. He stood out, because he was always noticeable in the crowd, with his bright blond hair, but it was also the way he played. He had confidence which people found attractive and reassuring. Bobby was an outstanding player in so many ways.

Ray Wilson

Made his Huddersfield Town debut in 1955 and as a 31-year-old Everton player was the oldest member of the 1966 World Cup final team. Plagued by knee and ankle injuries, Ray still played over 400 League games winning 63 England caps. Quit in 1972 to join the family funeral business.

I played with Bobby in the England team from when he started in 1962 until my last game in 1968. He was a better international than he was a club player. As left-back, we had a fair bit of contact on the field with him playing left side. He would be the first man I would look for if I won a tackle. He was always available to help out. Sometimes he would actually knock me off the ball to start a move. He was a better user of the ball than me and he wanted to be on it all the time. I was happy just to win the tackle and let Bobby Moore use it.

The defence never changed for years. The goalkeeper, Gordon and the back four – George, Big Jack, Bobby and me. We were settled defensively and therefore comfortable playing away matches. We used to get goals on the break because we had the solidity to win the ball, then we had people who could use it. We had a short tour before the finals and we didn't concede a single goal, so the defence was sorted. All Alf did was tinker the system further upfield.

The team was full of fighting lads with good hearts who never gave in. We could win games without firing on all cylinders, we were that good. Even today, as soon as I get in the company of the squad it was as though the final was last week. We get on so well. We all mixed, there were no little cliques that you sometimes get in teams. There were some powerful players there, but they were ordinary guys. There weren't any flash Johnnies. Alf picked the players he knew would fit. In retrospect, I can appreciate that.

Bobby was immense. No doubt about it, the player of the tournament. Some said he wasn't playing well at club level. If that was the case, I would suggest he was saving himself for the World Cup.

To relax, I would try and sleep. Bobby Charlton could be a bit edgy and would sooner be doing something and I was happy to go with him on a walk, but equally happy to stay in bed and doze. Everybody thinks being a footballer and travelling the world is wonderful, but you stay in hotels, you can only train for so long and the rest is spent killing time. We did very intense training, three times a day, before the tour. But once the tournament started we were playing every few days so the matches kept us fit and we only did light training, so that any niggles, sore feet or bruises had a chance to heal.

We had a great day out to Pinewood, though. We were watching a scene from that year's James Bond film, we'd been on the wine and champagne and I was leaning back on a chair when somebody knocked me right over while the filming was going on. There was a bloody clatter. It was on a bloody step as well and it dropped right down. They shouted: 'Cut!' and had to film the whole scene again.

I roomed with Bobby Charlton and on the day of the final we went into Hendon to do some shopping. We roamed about and wandered back about midday. Nobody really noticed us. You wouldn't be able to do that now.

I'd only been there a month before with Everton for the FA Cup final. It was ironic but I was 31 and I'd spent my time from age 17 without winning anything, so to get FA Cup and World Cup medals the same year was amazing. However, I'd rather have been Martin Peters or Alan Ball, just starting out on my international career, having won the World Cup because reputations mean a lot. When I used to play against some players they wouldn't take me on because they were in awe of me being a World Cup winner so I immediately had an edge.

When I think of it now, I am stunned by the enormity of what we did. When I watch the film footage I think: 'Christ! Did I do that?'

On the day, you try and enjoy it but it flies past. If it had stayed at 2-1 it would have gone down as a pretty ordinary final. The drama right at the end made it seem as though it had been a real thriller. At the end of normal time, Alf said: 'You've won it once, now you've got to go out and win it again.' When Geoff set off running for the last goal the defender actually ran away. All game Bobby was playing short chips up to him and Geoff was coming to collect the ball and lay it off. The guy never picked Geoff up all game and I bet when he thought about it afterwards he can't believe he had so much room.

We were a fairly communicative team during matches, which can only help. Always talking to each other, especially at the back, pulling each other into different positions. 'Watch your back!' 'He's on this side!' 'Push it square!' Bobby and I talked all game and nobody did more shouting than Big Jack.

Bobby was a responsible young man. I was six years older than him and I wouldn't have wanted the captain's job. Alf made him skipper at 23 and there was no objection, because when Alf made a decision it was usually pretty sound.

At the end of the final I remember being absolutely drained. I've seen some photographs after the game and I look about 90. I was knackered! It was purely and simply the occasion, playing extra time, and the tension. We were up till 4am the following morning. We had a big function that finished about midnight then we all split up and went to different clubs. I went to the Playboy club and finished up with Jimmy Armfield and his wife Pat before having breakfast somewhere. It had been a marvellous day and our captain had been a bit special.

Jack Charlton

Played a record 629 games for Leeds United between 1952-72 before managing Middlesbrough, Newcastle United and Sheffield Wednesday. Capped 35 times by England, Jack also became manager of the Republic of Ireland, resigning in 1995 to dedicate more time to his hobbies

Bob always called me 'Jacko' - nobody ever calls me that. When he saw me across a London hotel reception full of people, he'd wave his arms about and shout: 'Oi! Jacko!' Every time I visit places in London where I used to see Bob, I almost expect to hear him shout 'Jacko!' I know it won't happen, but I can't stop the feeling.

When you got to know Bob you realised he never made a fuss. I never saw him argue with anyone. In my playing days I seemed to spend my entire time trying to convince other players that Bobby Moore wasn't big-headed at all.

Bob wasn't a 'shouter'. The only time he might open his mouth in a game was if you did something stupid. If he didn't say a word, it meant you were doing your bit right. When we won a game, most of us would open a bottle of champagne or beer and be boisterous in the dressing room. Invariably, Bobby would take off his shirt and just sit and smile. He did things differently to us.

Bob was particularly good at taking the ball off the 'keeper and prompting an attack. One day I asked Alf why he picked me. 'I've watched you play,' he said. 'You're good in the air, a good tackler and I know you won't trust Bobby Moore.' I asked him what he meant and he added: 'If Gordon gives you the ball, you'll give it back to him and say: 'Kick the bloody thing!' But if Gordon rolls the ball to Bobby he'll pass it out. If he makes a mistake, I know you'll tuck in behind him and cover the vacated space.'

Bobby pushed up a lot - two goals in '66 came from his sorties up the field - whereas I was brought up in the north, where defenders took no chances. Bobby Moore was different. In the last seconds of the final, he was in possession on the edge of the box and there were shouts the game was virtually over. Instead of punting it, Bobby and had a look upfield. The time was up, it was 3-2, and he was saying to the Germans: 'Come and get it.' They went to close him down, but Bob played a casual one-two with little Ballie in the box. I was screaming at him to hoof it, but Bobby started to dribble out of the box. Two German players anticipated that move and - if you look at the footage, you'll see it - Bobby ran between them. If he'd lost the ball, we were finished. He moved into the midfield with the ball and I'm still screaming at him to whack it out. It was agonising for me, but he checked, looked up, took all day about it, then delivered a curler of a ball to Geoff, who was running, and goal number four was made. In one go Bobby did about six basic things I'd always been taught not to even contemplate! Right or wrong, if you're as good a player as Bobby you could get away with it. So I stood there, watched him and thought: 'I'll never be able to play this bloody game!'

The '66 tournament captured the imagination especially because of the final itself more than the earlier games. It was the drama, the timing of the goals, going 1-0 down, then 2-1 up, 2-2, extra time, the controversial third goal, the triumph of that last goal. You don't forget a match like that, do you?

During our time with the England squad, we found that Alf rarely agreed with our ideas, so when we had one, we told Bob and asked him to mention it to Alf. Bobby would do so and Alf would usually go along with it. Some of us didn't always obey the rules although we never broke them to any great degree. It was mischief more than anything. We'd go for a jar now and again when we weren't supposed to, but we liked Bob to be with us because Alf wouldn't send him home if we got caught. Bob was our protection.

At the Mexico '70 World Cup, me and Bob used to sneak to an old church and sit on the steps in the sun for 10 minutes, which was totally against Alf's sunbathing ban. We never did it for long because we were both susceptible to the sun – we only had to be in it for a few minutes before we went pink.

Along with Stephanie, Bob came over to Dublin as a guest of the Irish FA at a Player-of-the-Year dinner. We went out afterwards for a drink and a chat and he looked well. About a month or so later – it wasn't long afterwards – I saw him on TV at the Wembley match. When the camera focused on him my heart fell to my stomach. I looked at Bob and thought: 'He's serious.' A week later, he was gone. Once I'd seen him at Wembley, his death wasn't a shock. There was no big funeral and, in a way, I'm glad there wasn't. I felt that you needed a bit of time for Bob's death to sink in. We were all invited to the memorial service but, strangely enough, that wasn't a sad occasion. There were some light-hearted moments and people said things about Bob in a fond way. Knowing Bob, he wouldn't have wanted tears. It was a good wake. We didn't talk about him at length on the day, there was nothing to say really. We felt for him.

Bob had a great deal of style. One day I met him in London and we went to a favourite club of his behind the Grosvenor House Hotel. When we pulled up outside in Bob's car he got out and the guy on the door said: 'Hello, Mr Moore!' Bobby handed him the keys and the guy jumped in the car and went off to park it. I'd never seen anybody do that before and ever since I've always wanted to have a big car and be well-known enough to give the keys over and have someone park it for me.

I was a late starter to the international set-up and Bob looked after me from the moment I joined the England squad. Even now, when we get together for '66 reunions we don't say a great deal about him. It's not necessary. We all know. I've got a picture at home with Bobby Moore's autograph on it. To me, it's priceless.

Alan Ball

Made over 750 League appearances for six clubs including Everton, Arsenal and Southampton between 1962-82. Alan was also awarded 72 England caps and subsequently went on to manage several teams including Blackpool, Portsmouth, Stoke City, Southampton and Manchester City.

I first met Bobby Moore when I joined up with England in '65. I'd played against him before that but hadn't really been in his company until we got together with the England squads.

My first impression of him was that he appeared aloof but he was, in fact, very approachable. Bobby had an air about him which frightened people off. Underneath, he was a very lovely man and I'm sure people were in awe of him because he was a great footballer. He had a wonderful sense of humour – very dry, impish, cheeky. And he was very loyal to his friends. Very loyal.

I became very good friends with him. What can I say? He treated me marvellously and always had time for me, making me feel at home in the England set-up. He was a calming influence on me, too, and helped in the way that senior pro's do – before and after games – and all the time we used to speak football. I roomed with Bobby all over the world for three years, every time the England team went away. His calmness was reassuring and I spoke to him about his knowledge of the game. I picked things up from him that were important, especially the use of space and reading the danger.

My own memories of '66 are pretty clouded really. It happened while I was very young. I wish it could have happened later in my life when I could have appreciated it more. I was certainly aware of the pressure of the big game before the final, but was too young to be really nervous. The day flashed by. I roomed with Nobby in the attic room at Hendon Hall – I think they put us up there because we were the only ones fit enough to get up the stairs. On the day of the final I went shopping and bought a watch…just for something to do really.

Before the game, there was a telegram from my father waiting for me in the dressing room. It said: 'You're there. Don't miss a minute of it. Be magic, little man.' In fact, it was the most instinctive game I played in my life. Luckily I had young legs that kept me running and I gave everything I had. I recall it being a very enthralling game for all watching. A lot of people played well on the day, especially Bobby Moore.

When Nobby played the ball down the wing for me to chase - the move which led to Geoff's second goal - it was ten minutes into extra time and I

> **"The telegram said: 'You're there. Don't miss a minute of it. Be magic, little man.'"**

thought 'I'll never get that', but I managed to outpace Schnellinger and reach it. I knew Geoff liked it delivered early so I whipped it into the near-post space and he cracked that shot against the bar. I couldn't tell you whether it was in or not.

When Bobby played that great ball to Geoff for the last goal I was running through the middle, square with Geoff, shouting at him to knock it to me. We were two against one and, if he'd passed to me, I could've walked it in. I was about to curse him for being greedy when he hit it but the words stuck in my throat - then I was cartwheeling and yelling with everyone else.

As we walked off Alf said to me: 'Well done, you'll never play a better game in your life.' I swopped shirts with Nobby, as we had agreed, and gave my medal to my mum. We got a £1,000 bonus, which was taxed. It wasn't a lot, but it didn't matter. It was one of those things in your life that you would have done for nothing. It was my job. And just to be able to win the medal and take it home to my father was the be-all and end-all for me.

I've got lots of happy memories of Bobby. As I said, he was a lovely, lovely man. And a very good friend. My father has passed on and I think of him every day. And I think of Bobby every day, too.

Roger Hunt

Made his League debut for Liverpool in 1959. Roger scored 18 times for England in 34 games before joining Bolton Wanderers. Ended his career in 1971 and now runs his own haulage business on Merseyside.

Bobby was very ambitious with a strong determination to succeed. He was a last-minute call-up for the World Cup squad for Chile in 1962. But on the plane over he grilled me about the England set-up and was very inquisitive about how things worked at Liverpool. He wanted to know it all.

We won the warm-up match 4-0 against Peru in which Bobby got his first cap. We got through the group matches but were beaten by Brazil in the quarter-finals. As soon as he got into the squad Bobby became an automatic choice and Alf made him captain when he was only about 22.

I was classed as an inside-right, but Alf Ramsey changed the formation from wingers to 4-3-3 and 4-4-2, reducing the front men to two, so I became an out and out striker. Virtually all my career at Liverpool was spent playing with wingers, so I would play for England using one system then return to Liverpool and play in an entirely different one. Sir Alf did toy with wingers for a while, but once he tested the 4-3-3 he always knew that was our strongest shape. Basically it bolstered the midfield, you lost an attacker but gained an extra man in midfield and the emphasis was then on the midfield players to get forward. Another reason why it worked was because he had such good distributors of the ball, like Bobby, who could pick out Geoff or me at any given moment. Usually play-makers who can pass like that are in midfield and rarely in the centre of defence. Bobby had been an attacking wing-half with West Ham before he moved into the centre of defence so his pass-

71

ing was as good as anyone's.

The final in '66 was a dream. Playing in a game like that was something you couldn't envisage. When I was young, the height of my own ambition was playing in an FA Cup final. It was such a fantastic day and such an unusual game. I vividly recall standing there while the national anthem played, but a lot of it is a blur.

I played in the England set-up with Bobby for some six years and he was a great captain, a great leader. He had the respect of the players because of the quiet and efficient way he went about his work. Unflappable and immaculate, he didn't have an outrageous personality. He was 'The Golden Boy' but he was still an ordinary bloke, if that makes any sense. Bobby was an impressive man.

George Cohen

Retired prematurely in 1968, having played 409 matches for Fulham over a 13-year period. George who earned 37 England caps, recently overcame his own five-year battle against cancer and is now a property developer.

Bob took the seriousness about his personal appearance on to the pitch. He hardly fell over and always seemed to come off as clean as he went on. If one of us made a tackle, he was very quick to sweep up any loose ball. He was also very adept at choosing the right moment to close in on an opponent who had taken a poor touch. Winning balls is one thing, but Bob was particularly good at getting his body shape, balance and positioning right after making a tackle, to get himself out of any trouble. Although he might not have been a jumper like Big Jack Charlton, he would always make it difficult for an opponent to get a clean head on the ball.

If we were under attack, we would funnel the ball out wide, so the danger wasn't in front of our goal. We would attempt to channel wingers down the outside so we could pin them between the line and reduce their options. If they moved infield, they had more room to play and could do more damage. We did that with Eusebio in the semi-final kept him on his wrong foot and out of range. Gordon was a great shotstopper so Eusebio would have to hit a terrific shot to beat him from way out. Our system made him dribble or pass sideways.

Many of the continental sides we played against were particularly good at wall passing, where the man on the ball played a one-two with a colleague on the edge of our box and went for the return, prising your wall of defence open in the space Alf called the 'area of interception'. Bob was great at anticipating what the man receiving the ball would do, whether he would make the return pass or take it himself. If you got it wrong, you could be caught in no man's land with the attacker behind you, but Bob would time his tackle perfectly and kill the danger.

The key to our success was that we understood what each other's game was supposed to be and that came with experience of playing together over such a long period. The players in the team compensated for each other's strengths and weaknesses. My asset was speed and recovery, whereas others, like Bobby Moore, distributed well. There was great team spirit and it was well-balanced. It didn't matter what you did, whether you played cards or went for a walk, everyone joined in. You did things with whoever happened to be there at that moment. Jack Charlton always said the spirit was greater than that of any club. Neither was there any personal rivalry in the squad at all, even when people were competing for the same places. Alf's changes were gradual and the camaraderie built up over time.

After the Uruguay game, Alf arranged for us to go to Pinewood Studios for the day. We saw the making of *You Only Live Twice* and chatted with Sean Connery. Norman Wisdom did an impression of a one-man football team and Yul Brynner, who was filming *The Double Man*, a spy thriller, talked about training horses on the Russian steppes. We also met Britt Ekland, Cliff Richard and George Segal. Alf made a speech, thanking Sean Connery for his hospitality, but he called him 'Seen' Connery. We were all laughing and Jimmy Greaves joked with Bobby Moore that it was the funniest thing he had 'Sean' or heard. The trip did us good.

Bob pointed out that I always walked out in the line-up after him. I wasn't convinced, but every time I see myself on television or in photographs, there I am, right behind Bobby in second place. He was absolutely right.

At the final, you could almost feel the England fans willing us to win. The Germans were favourites and I believe you could still get decent odds on us to win. The ball comes off the Wembley turf two or three yards faster than a normal pitch because of its spongy nature. It's very wearing and the longer the game went on the more tired the Germans became. The sense of occasion was overpowering and that spurred us on. At the break before extra time Alf said: 'Look at those Germans, they're laying about, their socks are down, they're finished. You've won it once, now go out there and win it again!'

At the final whistle, Nobby jumped on me and tried to kiss me right in front of the Royal Box. Heaven knows what the Queen thought. He was very excited and I was too tired to fight him off. I remember those bloody steps, it was like climbing a mountain. I didn't notice how tired I was until the game finished but it was some feeling watching Bobby lift that trophy.

Nobby Stiles

Spent 10 years with Manchester United making 312 appearances. Nobby also played for Middlesbrough and Preston North End but after a spell in management he returned to Old Trafford as youth team coach before leaving in 1995. Represented England at every level, winning 28 full caps.

I t's hard to put your finger on what made Bobby so special. But when all the '66 lads get together there's something missing. It isn't right without him. Mooro was our leader and we looked up to him. When he went, something went from us, too. He epitomised what '66 was all about.

I was 24 years old in '66 and Bobby was only a year older than me, but he gave the impression he was much older, like late 20s, early 30s. It was this unique manner he had. You just felt at ease with him and yet, in some ways, you didn't know him. He had an aura, someone you could look up to.

I will always remember one magic moment in the '66 final. It was at 1-1 and our defence had been pulled over. Emmerich had made a straight run down the middle and I said to myself: 'He's through!' But Bobby read it so quickly and did that tackle of his – he was last man and if he hadn't made it, we would have been in trouble. But it was even better than the tackles in Mexico four years later because Bobby came from nowhere and from the way he was facing, wouldn't have been able to see the situation develop in the first place – his instincts would have expected someone to make that run so he'd started to come across in anticipation. As I watched it happen I thought: 'That's the tackle that's won us the game'. It must've demoralised the Germans as much as it inspired us. He didn't just win the ball, he slid it out wide to George Cohen and it started an attack for us. To me that was the key point in the final.

We didn't start well in that final and went 1-0 down. We regularly started playing after we'd given a goal away, but it was Mooro who got us back in the game. He'd gone forward, and as quick as anything, sent in that floating cross for Geoff to head in. He was so far ahead of everyone else in his thinking and at times he made it look like he was walking it.

For England I played just in front of Mooro and Jack Charlton, the centre-halves. Because neither of them were that quick, my job was to hustle and intercept, but also to enable any of the back four to go forward. If Ray Wilson or George Cohen went forward, I would tuck across on the right or the left; if Mooro went forward, I would slip into his position, and if Big Jack went up for free-kicks and corners, I tucked into his spot. At Manchester United I played centre-back which meant I could comfortably rotate positions with Mooro and Big Jack at any moment during a game. We had a good understanding.

People said Alf's formation was 4-4-2 or 4-3-3. It wasn't. No way did Martin Peters or Alan Ball play a rigid 4-3-3. In fact, it was more like the system they now call the diamond. The system

Bobby and Nobby Stiles covering the danger.

we played in the World Cup was a back four, then myself in front, with Bobby Charlton ahead of me at the foot of the diamond so that he could make those surging runs, Ballie on the right, Martin Peters on the left, and you had your two front men, Geoff and Roger Hunt, interchanging all the time, often playing with their backs to goal and seeking space in the corners. Geoff was the main target man with Roger working off him. It was a very fluid and changable system and we all swapped roles whenever necessary – Ballie and Martin Peters kept appearing on both wings and at one point in the final Big Jack went bombing down the left-wing and got a cross in and if we were attacking Ballie might make a run across field and George Cohen would overlap on the right. If you had to pin the system down it evolved into a 4-1-1-2-2.

My strength was hustling opponents in front of Big Jack and Mooro, making them hurry into attempting rash passes, or, if I won the tackle, giving it early to Mooro or Bobby Charlton or Ballie for them to use the ball. That's what made us such a great side: We learnt to play to our strengths.

I had been slipping out to mass every morning during the tournament at about seven o'clock. Ballie was my room-mate and I hadn't told him, but he knew I'd been sneaking out and didn't let on. He was pretending to be asleep and as I was creeping around the room he said:'You're not going today, are you?' But I did.

I don't remember much about the final, only fragments, like the Mooro tackle. I remember diving on George when Geoff had scored the fourth goal and I'd pushed him on the ground. He was saying:'What the hell are you doing?' and I shouted: 'What do you mean, what the f*** am I doing? We've won the f***** World Cup!'

The memories fade. I don't recall much about going up the steps to get my medal. People say I did this little dance during the lap of honour, but I didn't know what the hell I was doing, I was just so delirious. How I did a jig I don't know because in extra time as I went to send a cross over, I felt my energy drain away and the ball rolled off my foot for a goal kick. I thought:'I can't move. I've gone'. It was like what happens to marathon runners. I was looking around and little Ballie ran past and shouted:'Move, you bastard! Move!' That got me going.

After the final and the banquet, me, Ballie and John Connelly went out with our wives, Kay, Lesley and Sandra. Mooro said we were welcome at the Playboy club, so we went there but we were the first to arrive and they asked us to stand behind a rope and wait for the other lads, but we said it was getting late and we hadn't seen our wives for some time. We were ready to start celebrating and didn't want to wait. Luckily enough, Geoff had invited us to Danny La Rue's club so we got in a cab and went there. Danny was in cabaret with Ronnie Corbett and he had laid on a big cake for us with a World Cup on it. We had a fabulous night. Little Ballie finished up on the stage at four o'clock in the morning singing *Catch a Falling Star* and when we came to pay the bill they said:'It's all on Danny. He's so proud of you all'.

After '66, the squad had a very close relationship. Whenever you played them, the recognition was instantly there from all of the lads. It was a bond that would never be broken. If you ask all the 22 lads in the squad about it, it was a special time. But we were lucky. We had the best captain in the world. Bobby Moore was a most outstanding centre-back and a most outstanding person.

MOORE **than a legend**

Moore tributes

The day Bobby passed away was one of the saddest of my life. He was my captain and my right-hand man. Bobby was the heartbeat of the England team, the king of the castle, my representative on the field. He made things work on the pitch. I had the deepest trust in him as a man, as a captain, as a confidant. He was already in the England team when I took over as manager and he was the first player I turned to for a breakdown of his England colleagues. We met in secret, talked our way through 20 players, and at the end of meeting I had decided that this was the man I would entrust with leading England to the glory I felt sure I could bring the country. And Bobby went on to become one of the greatest defenders world football has ever seen, one of the best captains.

I could easily overlook his indiscretions, his thirst for the good life, because he was the supreme professional, the best I ever worked with. We would not have won the World Cup if Bobby Moore had not been our captain.
Sir Alf Ramsey

Super player was Bobby. Even from the word go, when Ron Greenwood stopped him from packing his kit for a club trip to southern Rhodesia and told him that Walter Winterbottom had increased his party to twenty and had picked him to go to Chile, you could see Bobby Moore was going to be a great player for England.

But Bobby nearly missed the World Cup final. On the 27th July 1966 he went down with tonsilitis, the day after the semi-final win over Portugal. We were worried it might develop into something worse, but the emergency proved the wisdom of having our own physician on the spot, Dr Alan Bass. The vital recovery hours are the first two or three after the player has gone down. It is imperative to get an instant diagnosis, especially in this case, when we had only two full days to get Bobby fit. Dr Bass got cracking right away but if we had left matters for a day, the tonsilitis would have got such a hold on Bobby it would have taken five days to clear up. That is how close Bobby was to missing the final.
Harold Shepherdson, England team trainer

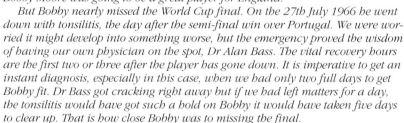

Chapter 4
Boleyn boys
(part 2: 1966-73)

Harry Redknapp

Played on the Hammers' right wing between 1965-72 before moving to Bournemouth, who he managed until he became assistant manager at West Ham in 1992. Succeeded Billy Bonds as manager in 1994.

He was The Guv'nor. The most lovely fellow you could wish to meet. Bobby had something about him that stood him apart from everybody. Never mind how the fans felt, he was even a hero to those who played with him. It was every boy's dream to be Bobby Moore. I loved him.

There was nothing flash about Bobby. Sure, he looked the part, good-looking, smart, but he wasn't arrogant. One night me, Frank Lampard and Bobby had played at Wolves and we got the train back and went for a swift beer in the Blind Beggar – you know, the one at Whitechapel where Ronnie Kray shot George Cornell? It was a good pub owned by Patsy and Jimmy Quill. They were Arsenal fans and Bobby and I were big mates with them. We were standing at the main bar, it was fairly empty, nice music and it was early, about seven-thirty.

I went through the little back bar to the toilet and there was a big fellow standing in my way, like someone out of a gangster film: black overcoat, white pocket handkerchief, black hair and he had this big scar on his face and if ever you've seen anyone look like a hoodlum, it was this geezer. He said: 'Oi, tell your mate, Bobby Moore, I'm going to cut him from here to here,' and he drew his finger across his throat.

I said: 'Why? What for?' The guy said: 'Cos he thinks he's a f***** film star, that's why.' I said: 'Do you know him then?' 'Nah,' he said. 'But I'm gonna get him.'

I went back in the main bar, but before I had a chance to tell Bobby about the geezer in the other bar, Bobby had drunk his half and said: 'That'll do lads, see you in the morning', and left the pub to meet Tina for a meal, so me and Frank followed him out. On the Sunday morning he came in to train and I said: 'Bob, it was lucky you left the pub when you did,' and I told him about the geezer who wanted to cut him up. Bobby hadn't even seen the guy.

Bobby rang up Patsy and Jimmy and said: 'I won't be coming in the pub anymore, there's a fellow in the back bar wants to cut me up.' They said: 'What does he look like?' and Bobby replied: 'Harry said he was dark with a big scar on his face.' They said: 'Don't worry about him. We'll sort him out.' Anyway, that night, the fellow went in the pub and Patsy and Jimmy took him to one side and had a chat with him, and, funnily enough, the outcome was the geezer never showed his face in the pub again. But Bobby didn't even bloody know him. When you're in the public eye there is always someone who thinks you're a big-head without knowing you. But everybody who met Bobby, loved him. He was a guy you couldn't dislike.

Bobby once told me that he wouldn't have been a player if it hadn't been for Malcolm Allison because he always got something extra out of Bobby. When he first went to West Ham all the other youngsters had played for England or London Boys and he felt he wouldn't catch up. When he told Malcolm he said: 'Don't be silly. You'll be better than all of them.' Because Malcolm believed in him so much Bobby was forced to believe in himself.

Once, Bobby told me, Malcolm was driving past in his car and asked: 'Want a lift home?' and Bobby said: 'If you could drop me off in Barking, that would be fine.' But Malcolm snapped: 'Tell the truth, you want a lift home but you're too frightened to ask?' Bobby got a lift home and after that, Malcolm would bring him to training and drive him home.

When West Ham were going to sign the apprentices, they had one position left and Bobby was a borderline case, but one particular youth match, Bobby said, changed his career. West Ham played Chelsea and he was marking Barry Bridges, who was the best youth player in the country and had already made Chelsea's first team. Bobby told me: 'I marked Bridges and followed him all over the field, wherever he went. We drew 0-0 and I was really pleased with myself and I thought Malcolm would

give me a pat on the back but he came in the dressing room at the end of the game and shouted: 'If I ever see you play like that again, I'll never talk to you again. You just followed Bridges all over the field. When your goalkeeper got the ball, you never dropped back and made the 'keeper roll it out so you could start attacks from the back, did you? When your left-back got it, you didn't drop inside so he could pass it square, so you could chip the ball up to the centre-forward, did you? I want to see you do those things and if you can't, don't talk to me. I'm not giving you any more lifts home.'

Bobby swore that was the making of him and if you look at Bobby's game, he would come and get it off the goalie and play it out, starting attacks, and he would drop off, get the ball from the left-back and chip it into Hurstie's chest. That was an essential part of his game.

Did we have some nights out or what? There's a few that I couldn't repeat. Dear, oh, dear. One Wednesday night we played so bad up at Stoke Ron Greenwood said: 'No one goes out tonight, you're all confined to the hotel.' We used to like going out in Stoke because there were a couple of good clubs, so some of us sneaked out the window at the back of the hotel, ran across the motorway and found some cabs. We had a good time and came back about four in the morning. Climbing over a fence to sneak back in, Bobby slipped and a spike went into his leg. We'd all been drinking and we couldn't get him off this spike and we were all giggling. Eventually we got him off and carried him back to the hotel. The physio, Rob Jenkins, secretly patched Bobby up but he had to limp about on the train home the next morning, and we kept him out of Ron's way, so he couldn't see. When we got home we had to report back in the afternoon and Bobby turned up saying he had tripped in the garden and landed on a fence. But Bobby was out for three weeks because he landed on a spike while out on the booze in Stoke.

One Christmas Eve all the West Ham lads were having a drink, dancing about and having a good time at The Globe in Stepney. About half-past three in the afternoon, the phone rang and it was Tina – she had been phoning round all the usual pubs to track him down because they were supposed to be going out and she was at home wearing her evening dress. 'Come on home, Bobby', she was saying. 'We've got that function to go to in the West End,' and Bobby said: 'Okay, I'll be home in twenty minutes.'

An hour later, Mooro was still there. The phone went again and Tina said: 'Are you still there? It's getting late. We'll miss the ball.' Bobby told her he would finish his drink and be on his way home, but then he carried on dancing. We were all very merry. About half an hour later the phone rang again and it was Tina: 'If you don't come home right now, I'll tell your mother!'

An hour later Mooro was still dancing, very legless, when in walked his mum, a lovely little old lady of 68 who started to drag Bobby out of the pub, saying: 'Come on, son, you've got to go home. Tina's waiting.' Bobby shrugged his shoulders like a naughty schoolboy and let her lead him out, complaining: 'Mum, it's okay, I'm 31 and I'm the captain of England.' As she was dragging him out she kept saying to us: 'He doesn't normally drink, you know, someone's mixed his drink.'

I watched him play for Team America against Brazil in a bicentennial tournament one year. Bobby was brilliant, playing in his usual role and when the game finished Keith Eddy of the New York Cosmos ran up to swop shirts with Rivelino, but he wouldn't swop shirts with Keith. I can see Rivelino now, he shook Keith's hand and ran 80 yards up the field chasing Bobby, who was almost walking up the tunnel, tapped him on the shoulder and pleaded with Bobby to give him his shirt, which Bobby did. Rivelino was a great Brazilian superstar yet he wanted Bobby's shirt.

Everyone will tell you how infuriatingly tidy Bobby was and I'm the most untidy person in the world. Bobby even used those bloody shoe things that keep the shape when you're not wearing them. He put his ties on a rack and when he'd finished the away trip, his gear went back in the case the same, and he folded his ties in with his shirts. I used to stuff it all in my case, sit on it and jump up and down to shut the thing.

Bobby was always there for you when you needed him. In New York one year we played Santos of Brazil and the night after Bobby had arranged tickets for all the lads to see Diana Ross at the Waldorf Astoria. It was her first ever solo concert after she left The Supremes. We started off in the New York hotel bar and Bobby said to the barman: 'Put it all on a tab.'

After about three hours, everyone was having a good booze and before we knew it the world and his dog were putting their drinks on our tab – bleedin' people we'd never seen before. A load of air hostesses arrived, a big crowd, bodies everywhere, I was talking to someone and I heard Bobby say to me: 'Harry, we're going soon, the concert starts in so and so minutes', something like that. Anyway, I was chatting away when suddenly these two big bouncer geezers wearing bow ties came up and handed me a bill. I said: 'Lovely, all right mate, sure, no problem, we'll pay it now, mate,' but I looked and it was about a thousand dollars – about six hundred bleedin' smackers. I only had about thirty quid on me. 'I'll just get the lads,' I said, but when I looked around they'd all gone. Straight up, I was the only one left. So I said to the bouncer: 'Sorry, mate, they've all gone.' He snapped: 'Your buddies have gone, but you've got the bill, so what you gonna do about it?'

Someone suggested we go in the office to sort it out, which we did, and they gave me an ultimatum: 'Pay the bill or we call the police.' I knew the lads had gone to the concert, so I phoned the Waldorf Astoria and they got Bobby on the line. 'What's going on?' he says, 'Where are you?'

'I'm at the New York hotel,' I replied.

'What are you doing there?' asked Bobby.

'I'll tell you what I'm doing here – I'm stuck here with this f****** bill, aren't I?'. He said: 'Well, all those other blokes were drinking more than us so I left the bill to them.'

'Well, that's nice,' I said. 'But they've all gone, I'm here on my own and there are a couple of big gorillas here not very happy with me.' 'All right,' he said, 'five minutes and I'll be back.'

I was stuck sitting with these big monsters glaring at me and eventually Bobby

> **"This geezer looked like a gangster. He said: 'Tell your mate Bobby Moore I'm going to cut his throat!'"**

walked in. 'How much is it?' he asked. I told him and he paid it, just like that, not a quibble. 'Okay,' he said, 'let's go'. He bailed me out before these two big monkees could strangle me and we went to see Diana Ross.

It was a crime he was lost to football. I've heard people say Bobby wasn't a good manager, but what do people know about that? When he went to Southend, they had few facilities, no resources, no players and no money. He found it difficult, but no less difficult than Kenny Dalglish or Kevin Keegan or Alex Ferguson would've found if they had gone there.

Bobby always said: 'If ever I get a job, Harry, I'd like us to work together.' When I came back from working in America he had been approached for the manager's job by Oxford City – they had big plans. Bobby said: 'H, let's have a year here, see how we go.' It wasn't easy. It was part-time but, as usual, Bobby put everything into it. I would sit with him at some bleak places in the middle of winter with about 80 people watching. It'd be pouring with rain, freezing bloody cold, and I'd look at Bobby and think, 'It's bad enough me being here but what is the captain of England doing

MOORE **than a legend**

here?' He deserved better.

The season West Ham were promoted, we had to play at Grimsby in early November '92. Miserable night, freezing cold and when I walked out on the pitch before the game I heard:'Harry-baby! 'Aitchy-boy!', so I looked around and there was Mooro with that peaked cap on, bloody great coat, eating fish and chips, doing his commentary for the radio. He had more to offer than travelling all the way to Grimsby on a poxy cold night, chipping in a few comments for a couple of quid. He should've got the opportunity to be involved in something worthwhile in football.

Terry Venables loved Mooro. He knew what qualities he had. I'm sure when Terry was made England manager, he would've involved Bobby somehow in the England coaching set-up. Looking back, it was a great waste Mooro wasn't utilised at West Ham after he stopped playing. I think there might have been some friction with Ron Greenwood before Mooro left for Fulham, which was sad. He should've been allowed to write his own job description at the club. Think of the knowledge he could've given the kids? It would have been fantastic just having him around the place. I tell you this, if he was alive now, he'd be working at West Ham. There are no two ways about that. And if the only job he'd take was mine, he could f****** have that and I'd be his assistant!

Bobby showed what he was made of when he was ill. About two years before he died, he came and spent a couple of days with me in Bournemouth. We had three lovely days: a wander round, a few walks, a few nice lunches, nice weather, terrific. It takes some bollocks to get on with a burden like that without letting on or cracking up, doesn't it? Never once did he say:'Oh Harry, I can't go on.' I knew he was ill but he never complained, never said a word. Just got on with it.

He was The Guv'nor and I miss him, you know?

Frank Lampard

Established himself in the West Ham first team in the 1967-8 season. His two international caps were almost eight years apart. After his free transfer in 1985 he spent a season at Southend United with Moore as player-coach. Now assistant manager to Harry Redknapp at West Ham.

I cried when Bob died. I cried at his funeral as well and I still get a lump in my throat when I think about him. What a waste. Look at those tributes from all over the world at the gates of Upton Park when he died. Remember he came from our manor.

In many ways, Bob was a father-figure to me. My dad died when I was two so I was brought up by my mum and nan and grandad in Canning Town. It made me more determined to be a footballer because, being the man of the household, I wanted certain things. My mates either went off to work in the docks or were probably robbing banks or something!

As a kid I would walk up to the West Ham ground and watch reserve games, and on the odd occasion, a first team game. I remember seeing John Bond and Noel Cantwell, the full-backs, playing, Three years went by and Bobby Moore came to the fore. Wally St Pier, the chief scout, invited me down to train for two nights a week. I went along and they offered me an apprenticeship at fifteen.

Suddenly I was running alongside Bobby in pre-season training and mixing with all these great players, my heroes. You could see how some trained better than others, some were good runners, some were bad, but every time you looked over at the first team training, Bobby was the one really training hard.

Once I watched Ernie Gregory making the first team do 100-yard sprints and I was waiting to pick the cones up when they had finished. There were five of them sprinting in a race and Mooro was running and Ernie was bellowing at them: 'Come on! Grit your teeth!' and Mooro snapped back: 'It ain't me teeth that's hurting, it's me bleedin' legs!'

When I broke into the first team Bobby took me under his wing. I can remember vividly what happened coming back on the train from my first away game. Going away on trains and such like was a bit strange to me and we were sitting on the train and I was four tables away from Bobby and he had an empty seat next to him. He beckoned me over, which was a big thing because although you worked with the senior pros, there was a distance there. I sat next to him and Bob asked: 'Where do you come from?' and other questions like that. Basically, just small talk. In fact, he handed me a can of lager, but it meant a lot. That incident really put me at ease. I'll never forget it.

I copied a lot of his habits. Like him, I became ruthlessly tidy. I finished up being his room-mate for away games for eight years and, from watching him, I learned how to handle myself and how to deal with people. He never got flustered at anyone who pestered him.

Mooro never yelled at anyone. Me and Billy Bonds would give people stick if they weren't doing it on the pitch, but all Bob did was look at you. If you gave the ball away, he'd give you that look of his. All upright, with his chin tilted up, like he was Nelson's column looking down at you. The look said: 'What did you do that for? We don't do that, we don't give the ball away here, we have a code between us.' That look. It was all you needed to make you squirm and feel very sheepish.

Coming back on the train from away games, we would be fifteen minutes away from King's Cross and Bob would take his suit carrier from behind the seat and go into the toilet. He'd come out of that tiny toilet a few minutes from the station wearing a clean shirt, tie, suit, everything, like he'd stepped out of Harrods window. I can see him now, all his made-to-measure suits with double cuffs, his hair all groomed lovely. Invariably he would be meeting Tina, his wife, and going to some fancy restaurant in the West End. Bob had class, whereas the rest of us would put the kit in the back of an old transit, all pile in and maybe go down the Baker's

Arms for a quick pint before going home.

Bob would train on Sunday mornings. We had a treatment room at Upton Park then and Bob would turn up early, put a tracksuit on, tuck a towel in around his neck and jog around the pitch. He would probably have been out socialising the night before and he'd do some laps, have a shower, clean set of clothes and he'd probably be off up the Bald Hind or The Retreat at Chigwell for a couple of lunchtime beers. Bob had it right. What I learned from him enabled me to last nearly twenty years in the professional game.

One trick I learned was playing balls with the outside of the foot. I was a right-footed left-back, but I liked tackling on my left side. When I got into the first team Ron Greenwood took me to one side and said: 'If you don't like playing the ball with your left foot, let the ball run across your body and play it with the outside of your right foot. Watch Bobby or Martin or Johnny Byrne, they can do it because they've worked on it.' I watched to see what he meant and they were doing it all the time in training. Even for short five-yard passes, Ron said if you played the ball with the outside of the foot you were already moving forward. So I tried it and cultivated it. It got me out of a lot of trouble. Bob was the master at it though.

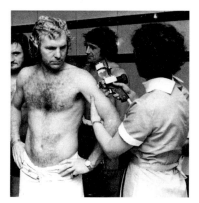

I played for England only once at Wembley, against Yugoslavia. Alf Ramsey was manager and I came into the squad because someone pulled out. I didn't know I was going to play and the day before the game we were on the coach on the way back from training and Alf bent over the seat – Bob was sitting opposite me – and said: 'You're playing tomorrow'. It was a shock. Bob looked at me and he said: 'Well done. They can never take that cap away from you.' He had played a hundred odd games by then, but his words have always stuck in my mind.

Receiving his flu jab while a pensive Frank Lampard and Bobby Ferguson await their turn.

I played left-back in the match and Bob played left-half. During the game, one of the Yugoslavian forwards dribbled towards us and we jockeyed him a bit – sometimes we used to jockey too much – but we backed up as the fellow ran at us and he passed the ball out wide to the wing. Bob and I expected a winger to be over-lapping, but when we looked there was no one there and the Yugoslavian forward ran and kept the ball in play. After a couple of passes the ball eventually went off for a goal-kick and as we were jogging back up the pitch Mooro said to me: 'Bloody hell, Frank, the geezer passed to himself!' We were supposed to be concentrating and being serious but I was in stitches.

Sometimes, if the squad went away pre-season we would pop out for a few lagers and get back to the hotel about eleven o'clock. Ron would often be sitting there in reception and we'd all sit down with a coffee before we went to bed.

Ron would start talking football and where Bob normally held back, he would join in and come out with enlightening technical examples and stories. The times when he did speak, people listened. Maybe he could've spoken up a bit more.

When you are held in such high esteem by everyone, people are a bit frightened of you. Bob preferred the company of people who weren't awe-struck. He liked people who didn't look at him as captain of England, and didn't know what to say to him. A couple of my mates got on with Bob easily because they treated him as plain old Mooro and he could relax. Sometimes, when he knew I was out with them on a Sunday lunchtime, he would turn up for a lager with us. In fact, Bob liked lively characters around him like Harry Redknapp and Johnnie Charles. The outgoing guys brought Bob out a bit. If there was a function to go to, I used to hear him shout: 'Charlo, you fancy that?'

We would socialise, go drinking, but he was always so perfect. Where most people have a drink and go wobbly and talk nonsense, you never saw Bob do that. I used to think: 'Blimey, we're all over here swaying,' and he'd be in his corner, leaning up at the bar, looking perfectly sober and sensible. Maybe the corner held him up!

"Mooro said: 'Bloody hell, Frank, the geezer passed to himself.' We were supposed to be concentrating and being serious but I was in stitches"

Sometimes I felt he was too tolerant of people. He was always so charming. When he lived in Chigwell he was surrounded by a lot of money people who wanted to be in his company and the celebrity circle started coming to our games, basically because of Bob. They had met him in the West End and sometimes he suffered some of them more than he should. He was too nice, I guess.

He never got flustered on the pitch. The more people panicked around him, the calmer he was. Amidst mayhem, he'd trap the ball and flick it out with four attackers flying after him. It inspired the rest of us to be so cool when you saw him pass it out and go jogging up the field...you know how he used to run, like with a little waddle?

One trick he used to great effect was to drop off his attacker and take the ball on his chest. When the cross came over he would run with the attacker to head it, but he would back off a few yards, the guy would head it on and Bob would allow it to land on his chest, let it drop and he'd be starting an attack. The other guy wouldn't even have realised Bob had dropped off him. We try telling the kids here at West Ham: 'Learn from Bobby Moore – know when you aren't going to reach the ball, so don't try and reach it and get beaten, drop off.'

Once we were playing away somewhere and I was sharing a room with Mooro. At eight o'clock on the Saturday morning there was a bang on the door – it was the time when Brian Clough of Derby had supposedly come in for Mooro and me. It was only paper talk. Bob was still in bed, asleep I thought, and I was in the bed nearer the door, so I got up to answer it and Bob opened an eye and said: 'Don't open it, it's a reporter!' So I jumped back into bed. There were a couple more bangs

85

on the door and then the guy went away. Bob instinctively knew it was a reporter. He was uncanny about stuff like that. We found out it was a reporter because he had left a message at reception.

Years ago you got stick from the rowdy crowd in the Chicken Run at Upton Park. They always had a go at a winger or a full-back, whoever was on the outside. Bob rarely played near the Chicken Run, but there was never a murmur of abuse at him anyway. He made less mistakes than anyone so perhaps they should have played him near The Run and given the rest of us a break!

After Bob had left the club for Fulham, I remember doing some day-to-day task and thinking: 'Mooro would've done it like that'. I've found myself treating some of our youth kids in a different way because it was how Bob would've done it. The spirit of Mooro lives on because what I learned from him will never die. I've been in nice restaurants with my wife, Pat, and said to her: 'Mooro would love this place, wouldn't he?' He wasn't a snob, but he loved places that were the business, the proper thing.

I was at Southend with Bob for nearly a year. I was player-coach and he was manager. I'd always find him in the medical room before training, talking to the players. I'd hear him say: 'How are you?', 'All right?', 'Go out last night?', 'How's the leg?', 'Are you sure you want to train?' 'Don't worry if you can't.' He always had time for the players and treated everyone the same.

Striking the right balance in management is very hard. You have to be careful or some people think you're soft. Not all the players at Southend liked Bob, but it's impossible for everyone to like you. But if anyone didn't like Bob, it was their fault because Bob was a person to like. The combination of people being frightened of him, plus Bob's natural shyness, would mean some people might make a conclusion that he was being funny with them, but that wasn't the case.

When Bob was ill and he lost weight, he stayed as tidy as ever. He was brave and faced the illness head-on. But that's how he was, see? He wouldn't panic. He'd take it. Actually, there was a time, before he was ill, when I used to say to him: 'Speak up more! Say something about something, will you!' But he wouldn't. Always so calm and collected. Maybe he held it in too much. He never made a fuss about anything, even when he was ill. Maybe, sometimes, he should've made a fuss, but I guess that wasn't his nature.

I miss him. Oh yes. It does me up like a kipper every time I walk out at the Chadwell Heath training ground. I look out there and I can see all of them – not just Bobby, but Budgie Byrne, Bondie, all jogging round, you know? Bob was a bit on the tubby side as a lad, lacked a few things, but he worked at his game and made himself into England captain and, I'd say, the best defender in the world.

Billy Bonds

Joined West Ham in May 1967 from Charlton Athletic and played a club record 793 games. Billy was appointed manager at Upton Park in February 1990 but resigned in August 1994. Now manager at Millwall.

I was in awe of Bobby. He's the only player I ever looked up to, much more than just the usual respect you have for fellow pros. There was something special about the man. Everything he did was absolutely spot on, both on and off the field.

When I was 13 I played for a boys' club at Eltham and we used to train at my junior school, Middle Park, every night. That year we won the league, the cup, everything, and Mr Flowers, the fellow who ran it, got Bobby Moore to come over and present the medals. We trained in the school hall and Mooro and Tina sat up on the stage with Mr Flowers and we showed them dribbling exercises and then Bob presented the medals to us. He was all suited up with his blond hair and he looked a million dollars to us kids. We were sitting there with our legs crossed on the floor staring up at him. He was a superstar.

I started at Charlton, played there 'till 1967 and ended up at West Ham. Who would have thought, that night when I was a kid getting medals from Bobby, that I'd be playing alongside him as right-back and he'd be the centre-half. In the end, I took over the skipper's job from him which was a big honour for me.

I never really got to know Bob well, although he was very friendly towards me. I suppose it was because I was so in awe of him. He used to call me 'Daffo'. He'd say: 'Come over here, Daffo!' Whenever I sat with him on the train he'd ask a hundred questions and directly I asked him one, I wouldn't get anything out of him. So I just shut up and let him ask the questions. I very seldom socialised with him and was renowned for getting out of the bath and going straight home.

On the field, he was very cool when we were under the cosh. He even looked cool. That calmness rubbed off on us. He was good to learn from. If you couldn't learn from him, you couldn't learn from anybody.

I once got the hump with Bob during a game at Sunderland because he wagged his finger and was shouting something at me, or so I thought, but I should've known better because he never really had a pop at anybody. I was about to lose my bonce and have a go back at him, but he was shouting at the linesman who had missed an offside. When I turned around and realised he was talking to the linesman, I felt bloody rotten for my reaction.

Everybody remembers the '66 World Cup Final. I was sitting in the living room with all the family crowded around a TV with a couple of greyhounds on the floor.

I didn't have much contact with him after he left the club. I talked to Mooro a few times when he was doing his radio work. The last time I saw him was on a freezing cold night at Grimsby, the season West Ham were promoted. The stadium was empty, everyone had gone home and I was doing an interview. He came down from his loft where he did the commentating and had a chat with me.

I'd heard he wasn't well but it was still a complete bombshell when I heard he was seriously ill and struggling badly. I liked him a lot and respected him so much.

Brian Dear

Played his first game for the Hammers in August 1962 and his last match for them in 1969, making 63 appearances. He is now restaurant manager at Southend United.

Mooro told me this great story about how the penalty came about in *Escape to Victory*. You know they always have a token American in these things to sell the film in the States? Well, Sylvester Stallone was worried that his role wasn't heroic enough and he wanted to save a shot then dribble the ball all the way up the field and score the winning goal. Mooro and Pele said to him that it just wasn't done, that goalkeepers didn't beat 11 players and score and that, if he did it, he would make a prat of himself. So that's where the idea of Stallone saving the penalty came from.

'Can you guys hit a soccer ball in a certain spot?' says Stallone during filming one day. 'Of course we can,' replies Pele. 'We're professional players.' So Stallone says: 'Right, be out here tomorrow morning early at 6am and we'll try something.' So the next day all the players get up early and go out onto the pitch where all the film crew are set up. Stallone is in goal and he asks Pele to put the ball right in the top corner. So Pele steps up, kicks the ball where Stallone wants it, and he goes to dive at the ball. All of a sudden he leaps off the ground, flies right up in the air above the crossbar and catches the ball. The players can't believe it because he's gone and installed a trampoline in the goalmouth and it looks ridiculous. 'Fabulous! Great! Outstanding!' shout all the film crew, clapping Stallone, and Mooro and all the players are hiding their faces and sniggering. But that's how it happened and you can see it on the film.

When they filmed the bit with Pele's goal, the overhead kick, where Bobby crossed for him, Mooro said to me: 'Stag, one take only. We did it first time. And that's the one they used in the film.' As if those two would take more than one go to do that? But he was like that at West Ham. Others would do exercises until they perfected it, but he would do it first time. If it was volleying with Martin Peters they would go bang, bang, and it was done. Unbelievable.

Bobby knew his way around the West End like a sewer rat. Every one-way street, every nook and cranny, and he would find little bars and places you wouldn't know existed. We used to go to The Wig and Pen by the Law Courts, Vagabonds and the 21 Club in Great Chesterfield Street – you would get a big bowl of Mediterranean prawns and a violinist would come to the table and play. When Bobby used to walk into Churchills for a drink the old boy on the piano would play 'I'm Forever Blowing Bubbles'.

Bobby would always be in town doing something. You never knew where he was going, but he was going somewhere. Everyone knew him. Bobby Moore could go anywhere in London because he behaved himself. We often went to this fish shop in Marylebone for fish and chips or we would go to Langans restaurant. Bobby liked it there. It was usually packed with people and he'd walk in and there would be a table lifted from somewhere and they'd lead him to a nice position and plonk it down. Whether it was a little pub or Annabelles, Bobby was always welcome, but he never expected any special treatment. Everyone got something out of Bobby. To be with him, you would be in nice company, the right people, the top people.

We used to go to Water Rats balls. Mike and Bernie Winters were on our table once and Mooro said: 'Bernie, what do you want to drink?' and he said: 'I'll have a bottle of rum please, Bob.' In those days, all those stars were on their way up and footballers and showbiz people had an affinity. They would all go along to Bobby's pub at Stratford or The Black Lion at Plaistow: Jimmy Tarbuck, Kenny Lynch, Max Bygraves, Eric Sykes. They even used to go outside and play football with the kids in the street. The publicans loved it.

Tarby and Lynchy phoned up and said they'd challenged the Mayor of Margate to a football match and would we play? So Bobby, myself, Harry Redknapp, Frank Lampard and John Charles went down there. Lynchy and Tarby played, so did Tommy Steele, Mick McManus and Ronnie Hilton, who sang *'The Mouse in Old Amsterdam.'* We thought it was going to be a joke game but 6,000 people turned up. We got a penalty and Tommy Steele was about to take it when Tarby ran up, shot and scored. There were bloody murders in the dressing room at half-time. I said to the referee: 'You better give us another penalty because Tommy Steele's got the hump.' I don't think him and Tarby talk to this day over it. It was so funny.

Two big friends of ours, Lou Wade and Del Simmons, came with us that day and we all went to the show in the evening. Bobby had a previous engagement in town and had to leave but Tarby stood up and said: 'Bobby Moore has had to go but we've got Deltoni Simmeroni from the Italian soccer league.' We all finished up on the stage.

Two friends of mine, Colin Spencer and Vic King, had an office cleaning business. We all went to a huge charity dinner at the Anglo-American Sporting Club and they invited Bobby along as their guest. During dinner Jarvis Astaire came over and he asked Bobby if he could do a radio interview. 'Excuse me, Jarvis,' I said, 'Bobby is a guest of Mr King so he can't just go off. Mr King has paid for the tables, so you'd better ask his permission.' Jarvis asked and Vic King said: 'Yes, but it'll cost you £100 for the charity.' Jarvis agreed and Bobby went off and did the interview, but when Jarvis asked him, Bobby looked at me as if to ask if he should go. He wouldn't have said anything. I had to say it for him.

Brian Dear doesn't seem to see the funny side as his team-mates inspect the plaster covering his broken leg in '65.

Bobby and I went round Colin's house for a drink once.

MOORE **than a legend**

Colin is really sports mad and his son is called Stanley Matthews Spencer but, ironically, he was never really a sports-minded kid. Colin, all proud to introduce his son, said: 'Stanley, come here! This is Bobby Moore, captain of England.' And Stanley looked up and said: 'Never heard of him, dad.' He was only a little lad and Mooro didn't take any notice. He said: 'He's a good lad' and tapped him on the head. 'How about a drink then, Stanley?' said Mooro, 'Gin and tonic? A gin and tonico for Stanley here.' That's what Bobby used to call it: Gin and tonico.

One of my friends, Bobby Hill, was having his 21st party at his house and his dad asked me if Mooro would come. I said: 'Can you pop round my mate's house, it's his birthday?' and he said: 'Yeah, of course.' Bobby never minded doing favours like that. Nothing was too much trouble.

In the early days at West Ham, Bob and I would go down to Smithfield market on Fridays to see two lads we knew who had a butchers there. We took them match tickets and Bobby would put on an apron and a boater and serve people meat. One of them would give us a tenner and say: 'How's the kids?' We didn't have kids then but we used to tell him we did and we used to walk out of there with a tenner and bags full of steaks.

Bobby's mum and dad were nice people. His dad went blind and he had a bad illness before he died. His mum was a typical mum. 'My Bobby this' and 'My Bobby that' and if she had seen Bobby run someone over in a car in front of 10,000 people, she would swear on 50 bibles it wasn't him. She was a secretary at William Warnes and, when they were groundstaff, Harry Cripps, Andy Smillie and Mooro worked there in the summer, doing anything to get a few extra quid. But it was purely sunbathing, very little work.

At the christening party for Bobby's son, Dean, a policeman arrived in a Morris Minor, knocked at the door and told us someone had complained about the noise. Within minutes, Bobby had him inside, his hat was off and he was up dancing around the lounge with Rob Jenkins' wife, Anya. The policeman stayed for about two hours.

When West Ham went to America we stayed in a big apartment building on 86th Street and we arrived there very late one night. We were given our rooms and Bobby was sharing with Peter Brabrook and John Bond, but because they got to the room first and nicked the two decent beds, Bobby was left with a silly little camp bed. Mooro said to Ron: 'Bloody hell, Ron, what's going on? I've got a bleeding camp bed!' It was so funny. It could only happen to Mooro. He got some money and disappeared to a hotel for 24 hours. Only he could do that, no one else would have got away with it.

After the '66 tournament, the squad were given World Cup cars and Bobby was going on holiday. He said: 'You may as well have it while I'm away, there's no point in it being parked outside my house.' I was driving around in that car with Bobby Moore's name on the side for a month. I loved it.

We were in a club with Jim Baxter in Nottingham one night and he said: 'I bet I can drink more Bacardi than you, Mooro'. At the end of the evening, Jim was on his knees and Mooro was looking down at him. Baxter's claim to fame was scoring when Scotland beat England 3-2 at Wembley after '66 and he kept mumbling over and over again: 'We beat the f****** World Cup winners!' But Bobby never batted an eyelid. He thought it was hilarious.

Practice matches were fun. If you were in the reserve lot playing the first team you'd want to kick lumps out of them. Ernie Gregory would say: 'Come on, lads, we'll do this first team mob,' and he would get us wound up. One game at Chadwell Heath, I was going round kicking everyone and went into a tackle with our centre-half, Alan Stephenson, and I cut his ankle. Mooro said: 'Sod it, Ron, I'm off. He's a bloody nutter!' and he walked off. He was good lad, Mooro.

When you roomed with

One of Bobby's 24 League goals for the Hammers – in a 5-1 victory at Sunderland in September '67. The other Hammers pictured are Martin Peters, Peter Brabrook and Trevor Brooking.

him, he always took a bath in the mornings. I'd say: 'Leave the bath, Mooro, I'll use it.' He'd reply: 'Stag, the water is dirty. You can't use that!' and I'd say: 'We all get in the same big bath after a game, so what's the difference?' In the changing room, he would never put his trousers on standing on the dressing room floor, he would always stand up on the bench and put them on. He never looked scruffy.

Bobby and Martin Peters came to a Tottenham game to help entertain some business associates of my friend Colin. Bobby had a glass of wine and spoke to these people and they were very impressed. Colin wanted to treat the boys so he gave me some money. Bobby said: 'Stag, I've got to do a radio thing in London,' and he left. I followed him outside, handed him the money and said: 'Colin wants you to have this.' But Mooro put it in my pocket and said: 'Take Jan and the kids out for a bit of grub' and he walked off. I never saw him again. A few weeks later he was dead.

Just before Bobby died, we were supposed to meet for lunch, but he phoned to cancel and said: 'I'm not feeling well, Stag. I've got flu.' Apart from his family, no one knew what was wrong. It was kept a secret until he issued that statement, which took a lot of guts.

I was at a lunch not long ago and someone asked Malcolm Allison what made Bobby a great player? Malcolm said he'd sat at Wembley with Raymond Kopa, the French centre-forward, watching Bobby play and when Bobby gave a bad pass Kopa said: 'If he hadn't done that, I wouldn't have known he was playing.' Malcolm also said if he had to put his life on the line with somebody, Bobby would be the man he'd choose.

When I visit Upton Park I always give the old bronze statue of Mooro a rub and little kiss. In fact, we're doing a Bobby Moore Lounge at Southend. We've had a plaque made, got some pictures, one of his old England shirts and a track suit. It will be a nice tribute to him.

Bobby was the main man. He played the game easy. He always wanted the ball. He was never afraid to receive it in any situation. In fact, he never seemed to be afraid of anything, did he?

John Charles

Played for West Ham from 1962 to 1970, making 141 appearances.

Bobby stood out, even on the training field, because he was such a big guy. I don't mean tall, but he appeared bigger. He had legs like treetrunks. Even when he was 17 or 18, he was big and when he won a tackle, sometimes dropping to one knee, he looked so cool.

For a long time, he was in the first team and I was in what was known as the 'A' team. I made my debut in 1963 against Blackburn with John Sissons and Martin Britt. Ron Greenwood thought we deserved a try out. When I was switched to full-back, that's where I played most of my games alongside Bobby. He just stroked the ball about and was always there to tell you what to do. He had a lot of style in the way he moved. Do you remember how he used to jog when the ball was played up the other end? He did this thing where he bent his arms and held his fists tucked in, stuck his chest out and just gently jogged across the back, always watching, checking our move was unfolding the way it was supposed to, sweeping back and forth in case the play changed direction and he was ready. It was like watching a strutting bulldog. He was really cool. But his example made the game easier for you.

Bobby and I used to drink a lot with Johnny 'Budgie' Byrne at The Retreat pub in Chigwell. We would go in there after training for a swift half. Sometimes, at about 7.30 in the evening, I'd take a wander up there and find Mooro or Budgie in there.

Bobby dives to save Mike Bernard's penalty . . . but couldn't keep out the rebound.

Budgie was a good bloke, game for anything. I went into a local pub one day and the landlord said: 'I met a mate of yours in South Africa – Budgie. He's given me a present for you.' I wondered what he meant but he went upstairs and came back with this scroll. It read: 'Dear Charlo, now they've released Nelson Mandela, you can come out here and visit me!'

Most of my photographs were destroyed in a fire, but I've got one in my kitchen of me and Bobby playing for West Ham. It helps remind me of him. I was working on my greengrocer's stall when I heard the news of his death. I took my grand-daughter down to West Ham to see the flowers. I was gutted for him, to go like that. It upset me.

Trevor Brooking

Started as an apprentice at West Ham in 1965 and played 635 games before his retirement in May 1984. Trevor won 47 full England caps. Today he is a TV and radio broadcaster.

I have never seen a reaction across the country to a sportsman's death like we did after Bobby's passing. There was a genuine sadness. You could have heard a pin drop during the minute's silence in the snow up at Sunderland v West Ham and wherever I went, supporters came up to me and said: 'I'm very sorry about Bobby.'

I joined West Ham United two months after they had won the European Cup Winners' Cup in '65. I had watched the team from the terraces, so being some-what awestruck to start with, I passed the ball on very quickly, rather than do some-thing with it myself.

West Ham's playing style under Ron Greenwood was quite European and very unlike other English teams. He put the emphasis on passing and expression of flair. With a player like Bobby Moore, we could initiate play from the back. Bobby was an unusually accurate passer for a defender and very few players have matched his distribution from deep positions since.

"Bob said: 'Anyone else fancy it?' No one volunteered so he said: 'Okay, I'll go in'. He did very well. He nearly saved a penalty"

I went to see the semi-final against Portugal in '66 but I watched the final on television at home. My mum had gone to the hairdressers and my dad was waiting for the final whistle before going to pick her up, but the West Germans equalised so he promptly sat down and mum was kept waiting. It was an understandable delay!

Bobby always took responsibility. In 1972 we had a League Cup run which ended in the semi-final after four ties against Stoke City. After the home and away legs we were level, so we went into extra time at our place and Gordon Banks even saved a penalty from Geoff Hurst.

After a 0-0 at Hillsborough we played the fourth match at Old Trafford. Bobby Ferguson, our goalkeeper, got concussion during the match and went off. Clyde Best was our stand-in keeper but he said:'No way, man. I can't go in goal in a game like this.' Bob said:'Anyone else fancy it then?' No one volunteered so Bob said: 'Okay, I'll go in.' He did very well. He nearly saved a penalty, stopping the initial shot but couldn't prevent the follow-up from going in. Mid-way through the second half Ferguson came back on. It was a dramatic match but we lost 3-2.

People talk about the time Bobby headed the ball and knocked a referee out and blew the whistle, but on another occasion, I knocked a referee unconcious by accident and Bobby took charge of the situation again. I was wandering away from a throw-in, as if I wasn't interested, hopefully trying to fool my marker, then I turned quickly to go back towards the space that had been created. But, unknown to me, the referee had wandered behind me and as I turned I caught him on the temple with my elbow and knocked him spark out. Everyone stopped, not knowing what to do, but Bobby sprinted over about 20 yards, picked up the whistle and blew it. The referee had to be taken off, the linesman took over and somebody else ran the line. Thankfully, the referee was fine and I saw his wife after the game and she joked:'Thanks, I've been wanting to knock him out for ages!'

For me, Bobby's strength of character was one of his best attributes. Many people might have crumbled when faced with some of the difficult problems he had to surmount, but even with the bracelet affair, and the Blackpool thing, he seemed very relaxed and appeared, certainly outwardly, able to cope.

Clyde Best

Played up front for West Ham between 1969 and 1975. He now coaches the Bermudian national team

For a man of his magnitude to be an ordinary person, is really something. Bobby Moore was the best player in the world. I've seen Beckenbauer play, but Bobby was better. Soccer is played from the brain, and Bobby did that better than anyone. In a match, while others thought about doing something, he had already done it. After he finished playing, he should have got the accolades people are giving him now. He played the same way whenever he put on his boots – whether it was playing on Saturday for West Ham or in training or practice matches, he kicked every ball like the World Cup depended on it.

I was just glad I had an opportunity to play with people like him in England. Because of him, I have been able to achieve what I have.

upstairs and downstairs

Rob Jenkins

Physiotherapist at West Ham United from 1966 until 1990.

I'll tell you about that time in Blackpool. There was me, Jimmy Greaves, Bobby, Clyde Best and Brian Dear. It was New Year's party season and we'd seen some friends off and a second cab was sitting there, so the five of us jumped in it. We had a walk and met Brian London, who invited us to his club.

We popped into his place, The 007, and there were people disco dancing. Me, Mooro, Greavesie and Stag had a couple of lagers and Clyde had an orange squash. And that was it. We had a chat with Brian London, went back to our hotel and ordered a plate of sandwiches. It was the hotel porter who rang up the paper.

The pitch was an ice rink. Treacherous. It should have been called off. Blackpool adapted to the conditions and annihilated us. One of their players, Tony Green, had a magic game. Ron Greenwood was very upset we were beaten. He didn't take too kindly to drink.

It was the combination of the circumstances: Blackpool, New Year, losing 4-0 and going out of the FA Cup. I've seen some players really worse for wear the night before a game and they've played blinders. These sort of incidents happen at all clubs.

However, the quality of the lower teams was greater then. You could play a Third Division side and be in bloody trouble. That happens very rarely now. The cream has risen to the top and there's nothing underneath. West Ham were the last side outside the top flight to win the FA Cup, back in 1980.

If I had to pick a time in my life which was the most exciting, it was the 60s and 70s. It was fabulous. I was at West Ham for 25 years and to me it wasn't like going to work. I loved it. Football burst into life with everything else.

My dad, Bill, was physio at West Ham until he died in August 1966. He'd had some heart trouble, so I gave away our tickets for the final because I was worried he might get over-excited, but in the end, I nearly died it was such an enthralling game!

We had a gang of people round afterwards for a few drinks but my dad started biting people. He was terrible after a few drinks, like an animal. He bit my friend's foot through his leather shoe once. So I went out celebrating with some friends and we all got back drunk. I put a great big saucepan of baked beans on the gas and we went back into the front room and put on some music. My first wife was woken by the noise and she came down and poured the saucepan down the sink. I quickly put the plug in and we all got spoons and ate the beans straight out of the sink! That was the night of '66 final.

When dad died a few weeks later, I was already his assistant and they gave me the senior physio's job. My first game was at home against Chelsea when their team lined up to applaud our World Cup heroes: Bobby, Martin and Geoff.

Bobby was a notoriously bad sleeper. He would often sit in my room on away trips. He'd chat, maybe have a small beer to help him relax and watch the television. He could only sleep if he felt relaxed. He used to turn in about midnight but was a notoriously early riser as well and he used to like a walk on a Saturday morning before a game.

If you went for a walk with Bobby in a foreign town, which I often did, and you had to get back to the hotel, I wouldn't know where the bloody hell I was. Not Bobby. He was like a homing pigeon. Just like on the pitch, he always knew where everything was. Wherever we'd managed to walk to, he knew how to get back. It was uncanny. You'd just follow him and you'd be back at the hotel.

John Radford was in an England squad with Mooro and he told me they had a team meeting with Alf Ramsey one afternoon after training and Bobby was sitting at the front. Alf was

Moment to savour for physio Bill Jenkins, Rob's dad, holding aloft the FA Cup at Wembley in '64.

droning on and pointing at his blackboard when suddenly they heard snoring and Mooro had fallen asleep. Alf just carried on.

Bobby had a couple of superstitions. He would touch the top of the door jam on the way out of the dressing room and he'd never shave before matches. He'd always shave after games - in the bath with a razor and proper soap, because he felt it gave him a closer shave.

Mooro was a bit mischievous when it came to pretending. We had a club trip to Bermuda and this American woman kept staring at Bobby and saying: 'Gee, whizz, don't I know you from somewhere?' Mooro wouldn't tell her. Suddenly she said: 'I've got it! You're the drummer from the hotel band!' Mooro played along and said: 'Oh, you've found me out,' and he kept pretending to play the drums by rapping his fingers on the table. He did it every time this woman came past. We were all laughing but he was very good at keeping a straight face.

Ron Greenwood took us to Egypt and we stayed at the Nile Hilton. Everyone, including Bobby, went down with food poisoning from the hotel food and we had to play this side from Cairo with most of our team suffering from stomach bugs. A few of them had to keep coming off the pitch for the toilet during the game and we got thrashed 4-1. Ron wasn't pleased. He often took us away on trips. We went to play TSV Munich 1860, were two goals up but lost in the last five minutes. Ron flipped his lid. I don't think we went on any more trips after that.

In training once, Ron fitted the players up with hearing aids so he could give them instructions during the game. Greavesie said he had a bad game because the thing fell out and he couldn't hear what Ron was saying!

Bobby barely had a handful of injuries in his career, but he loathed getting cuts. If there was anyone cut, they called in Doctor Bell. He was an old guy and he was bit shaky when he stitched anyone up and Mooro preferred me to do it. I'd put small stitches in him and he'd say: 'Don't tell Doc Bell!'

If there were any boxing dinners on offer he would ask me to go. We attended all those screenings of the big fights between Ali, Frazier and Foreman. At one dinner with live boxing, we'd had a few drinks and were watching a very boring light-heavyweight contest. When no one was looking, one of Mooro's mate's took out of his bag a big rubber willy with 'BOLLOCKS' written on it and flung it into the ring. The two blokes were fighting and this rubber willy was bouncing about in the ring and everyone was laughing. The referee kicked it out of the ring but didn't stop the fight. Jarvis Astaire, the promoter, came over and said: 'It was someone on this bloody table! Was it you Mooro?' and Bobby said he wouldn't do a thing like that. They never found out.

After the fights, we'd always finish up at a nightclub and Mooro would be at the bar. Bobby would drink as much as any of us and wouldn't need to go to the toilet. Yet we'd all be in and out of the loo all night. Mind you, it was usually after a training session, so he'd probably had a run to dehydrate himself.

Bobby found crudity distasteful, which is unusual among footballers. He didn't mind dirty jokes but he kept farting and bodily functions in their place. I don't think he spat either. He considered it rude and unnecessary. All footballers spit. They even spit at each other nowadays.

Bobby's attitude to football was very serious. He liked to live, sure, but at the same time he did his job. He was a tremendous professional. His clothes were so spotless I used to scrounge his old suits. I'd say: 'How much do you want for that suit when you've finished with it, Bob?' I had some lovely gear off him.

My auntie used to go in the players' lounge after the games and she said when Bobby walked in, it made her shiver. She reckons he had the bearing of a prince. I know exactly what she meant.

Eddie Chapman

As a player Eddie joined West Ham in 1937. He became secretary in 1956 and retired in 1986.

I used to see Bobby in my office quite a lot. The longest talk I had with him was after that bracelet business in Bogota. An awful experience but he always seemed to be thinking of others before himself most of the time. He was a bit of a lad in his way, but more so outside the West Ham club than he was within it.

I can't think of anyone who didn't like him and he had an ability to adapt himself to any company. He was an only child but he wasn't flamboyant. He wasn't exactly shy, but he was within himself a bit. When he left the club, we didn't see that much of him but Bobby's son, Dean, was a big West Ham fan and Bobby often phoned up for a ticket for him.

I do think it is a great shame with all the things that happened after he died, all the tributes, he didn't know just how much he was thought of by everyone. I believe the reason he was thought of so highly was because of the example he set. Even by people who never saw him play.

Ernie Gregory

West Ham United goalkeeper from 1946-60, Ernie made 406 first team appearances before coaching at Upton Park until he retired in 1987.

Bobby was one of a batch of amateur groundstaff that Ted Fenton signed in the 50s. They used to do the sweeping, painting and odd jobs. When the lads were playing in the youth team, all about 16 years-old, I remember Reg Pratt, the chairman, talking about what promising kids they were and what a great future the club had.

Bobby's teacher brought him to West Ham. Even as a kid he showed the signs of a great player and had started making passes in between opponents, taking them out of the play. He was a polite boy. Always called me 'Mr Gregory'. I played with him in the first team in my last season, which was Bob's first season.

I'm not sure Bobby would have made a straight centre-half in the old-fashioned 'W' formation. I remember Walter Winterbottom returned from Scotland excited about Bobby's role for the under-23s because, for the first time, Bobby had played loose, around the centre-half, picking up the pieces.

Bobby's extra training was legendary. We were staying in a hotel in the States when there was a knock at my door. It was Bobby and he said: 'Ern, do us a favour? Take me down the track, give me a work-out?' Bobby knew that if you didn't have discipline off the field, you couldn't be disciplined on it.

In about '68-'69 we were touring Germany and went to watch the Cologne v. Liverpool match. Before the start, we had to walk around the pitch to get to our seats and the crowd at that end – all Germans – stood up and cheered him. 'Bobby Moore! Bobby Moore!' they cried. When we got off the plane in Egypt, there were thousands of locals screaming for Bobby. He could've had the treatment of a film star everywhere he went, but he never took advantage of it and he never threw his weight about.

We have two tickets for the box at West Ham and if he was there doing his radio work he would always come over, kiss the wife, and say: 'Hello, Ern, hello Yvonne, how are you keeping?' It used to make my wife's day.

Happy memories. I'm sorry I can't remember more.

Edna Sheridan

At Upton Park for 20 years, Edna worked on the telephone switchboard.

After he died, what a turnout at the gates! The tributes all those people left, it just goes to show how much people thought of him. Of course, being on the switchboard, I had everyone ringing up to find out what tribute the club was going to arrange. It was a traumatic time. I would get grown men crying down the phone and, in the end, I'd be crying with them, you know? People would phone up just to talk, especially from abroad and those who couldn't get down to the ground to pay their respects. But all the flowers and things: the response was marvellous. I got choked up a lot. I just couldn't help it.

Eddie Baily

Long-serving assistant to Bill Nicholson at Tottenham Hotspur, Eddie joined West Ham United in 1976, and worked for 17 years under Ron Greenwood and then John Lyall

We respected him hugely as an opponent. Bill Nicholson and I would look at their formation and say we've got to put Moore under a bit of pressure. No one likes being made to do things quickly, so we tried to work out how they were going to stick their passes in and who was going to do it. Everything comes from source and Bobby used to deliver a lot of it. It says a lot about Bobby that we were more worried about him than their forwards.

 ## Moore tributes

I know I shall not offend any of our players, past or present, by saying that there is nobody who has matched the stature of Bobby Moore. He had footballing skills in abundance, but it was his personal qualities that made Bobby stand out from the crowd. At West Ham we were privileged to have had Bobby as a player for the greater part of his career. It would have been so easy for Bobby to have sought fame and fortune at a glamour club. West Ham can indeed be forever mindful of Bobby's loyalty to the club. I take comfort in the fact that even in death he has enhanced the game of football. All of the publicity has reminded the world of how the game was played and the standards of behaviour that were displayed in the golden years when Bobby Moore was captain of West Ham United. I hope that the nation remembers and learns.
Len Cearns, former chairman of West Ham United who died in October 1993

Bobby was a man who lifted everyone's hearts. As someone who grew up in Barking at the same time as Bobby, I know only too well the dreams and hopes he inspired during the journey from obscurity to greatness. Those fortunate enough to have seen him play at his peak will remember Bobby for the rest of our lives and I am sure his story will be passed down from father to son, grandfather to grandson.
Terence Brown, chairman of West Ham United

Chapter 6

Grand masters

Pele

Considered by most to be the greatest player that ever lived, Edson Arantes do Nascimento made his League debut for Santos in 1956, eventually scoring more than a thousand goals in his career. He retired from the NASL in 1977. Pele won three World Cup winners' medals – in 1958, 1962 and 1970. He is currently Brazil's Minister for Sport.

I first met Bobby Moore in England at the 1966 World Cup. His strength as a player was that he marked other players very well. It was very difficult to dribble past him and when he had the ball, he distributed it very well. He was a strong player, but a clean player.

Hhe was very serious about his football. He was a great example to youth. People often ask me about the swapping of shirts with Bobby in Mexico in 1970. I had seen other games on TV where players swapped shirts. I chose Bobby because, for me, he was one of the best defenders at the World Cup and because I admired him greatly. I do not keep many momentoe s, but I have kept Bobby's England shirt. It is my prized posssesion in my trophy room.

When we played together in the North American Soccer League in the 70s, he was with San Antonio Thunder and I was with the New York Cosmos. I played against him a few times but Cosmos were the better team.

When we played for Team America against England, playing alongside him was a pleasure – much better than playing against him. It felt very comfortable because I never had him on my back, tackling me. It was a fantastic opportunity to spend more time with him. I got to know him better and to admire him as a friend.

When we made *Escape to Victory* in Hungary it was great fun. I remember very clearly that Bobby made fun of Sylvester Stallone. He kept saying to Stallone that if

Bobby in America.

he had to play soccer for a living, he would die of starvation!

The last time I saw Bobby was at the World Cup in Italy in 1990. I was very sad when I heard he had died, especially in such unfortunate circumstances. We were such good friends off the field and words could not sum up the grief I felt for his passing. It's very hard when you have lost a nice person like Bobby Moore. Everybody who knew him will have wonderful memories of him.

The only thing that I want to say is that his death was a big loss for the human race. He was a great sportsman and an honourable gentleman. The world misses him as a player and a man. He proved himself to be one of the most important figures who ever played the game. Children should remember him as an example of the good in this world.

Franz Beckenbauer

Captained Bayern Munich to three successive European Cups from '74 to '76 and West Germany to the '74 World Cup. Franz also went to America and played in the NASL for New York Cosmos. After a short spell at Hamburg, he retired before taking over the German national side. When Germany won the 1990 World Cup he became the only man to win the World Cup both as a player and manager.

Bobby Moore was always a football idol for me as a young player. I looked up to him. The news of his death stunned me. He was too young. A lot of players in the world have lots of the same abilities, but what makes them different and determines their greatness? It is the personality. Their character. That is the difference. I think Bobby was like Pele. I played against Pele many times, and with him for one year, and he was probably the best player in the history of the game. But, for me, Bobby Moore was the best defender in the history of the game. The character of both, the ability on the field, and their lifestyle and attitude off the field. They are almost the same. Pele and Bobby Moore, they were, shall we say, almost perfect people.

The first time I saw him play on television was in the European Cup Winners' Cup final between West Ham United and 1860 – they were the local rivals of Bayern, where I played. At this time he was very young, but he was the captain of the English team, and it is very unusual to have a captain so young. Normally the captain of the team is maybe more older and more experienced, so that speaks for Bobby and his personality. The first time I met him on the field was in January 1966 – when the German national team played for the first time at Wembley. It was a few months before the World Cup, we were beaten 1-0 and Nobby Stiles, who was not a renowned goalscorer, scored their goal.

Quite often Bobby and I had private meetings when he came to Munich. He and Tina stayed at my house with me and my wife, and we had some photographs taken in the garden. Another time I came to London and we met up with the wives. We became very close friends.

People often compare the two of us. When they look back at our era, we went

the same way, chose the same course. Even though he was four years older than me, we played more or less at the same time. We both played in the '66 final, where the third English goal is still a great talking point in Germany. This is a shame because it reduces some of England's glory. We had been lucky with our second goal, to make it 2-2, but they were the better team throughout the game. There's no argument. England deserved the trophy.

I also remember playing against Bobby Moore in the European Championships in Italy in '68, and in a friendly game in Hanover later that year. We beat England by 1-0 – it was the first time a German national team had beaten an English team and I was lucky to score the only goal. And of course, there was the '70 World Cup when we played England in the quarter-finals and beat them 3-2 in a very exciting match that went to extra time. Where England maybe had a slice of luck in '66, we got our luck in the '70 match. England were leading 2-0 and we had not had a single shot on goal. After I scored a soft goal to make it 2-1, Alf Ramsey substituted Bobby Charlton, who we felt was the heart of the England team. We played better from that point and eventually Gerd Muller won us the match.

My favourite moment from when I have played against England and Bobby Moore was during the qualifiers for the '72 European Championships when Germany won for the first time at Wembley. Many people said it was the best game ever played between our two countries. Bobby came into our changing room after the match to congratulate us and wish us good luck for the remainder of the competition. This does not happen often in professional sport and it speaks volumes for Bobby's sportsmanship.

I was so proud that I could play against Bobby Moore. He was a true friend.

 # Moore tributes

As well as being a great man, he will always be a wonderful example for all sportsmen and sportswomen.
Eusebio

Chapter 7

Rivals with respect

Johnny Haynes

A prolific forward, Johnny started his career with Fulham in 1952. Appeared in some 600 League games and scored 145 goals. Also won 56 England caps and found the net on 18 occasions. Became Britain's first £100-a-week footballer when the maximum wage was abolished in 1961.

I played against Bobby in the First Division in the early 60s. Bobby got his first call-up to the England squad from Walter Winterbottom for the World Cup trip to Chile in 1962. He made his debut in our first warm-up game against Peru.

We knew all about Bobby. Everybody had been talking about him for a good few years. Even as a kid, everybody knew what a great player he was – it was just a question of when he was going to get a game for England and stay in the team. He was superb. We got on like a house on fire straight away and he was one of my really good mates. His death was very sad.

Bobby's career came along at the right time. There were big changes going on along with the abolition of the maximum wage. At that particular time, I was top of the tree, captain of England and my wages went from £20 a week to £100 a week overnight. Luckily there was interest from Italy which was a big thing in my favour because it convinced Fulham to stick my money up straight away.

I was captain for the '62 World Cup but early the following season I had a bad car crash in Blackpool. I didn't play for a year. I managed to play for Fulham for another seven years but I was never fit enough for international football.

Bobby became skipper in '63. He was the obvious choice and nobody else even came close. He was a great user of the ball, which became far more important than it had ever done before. It's important for a captain to be in the right sort of position on the field and he was perfect being in the middle at the back. He did the right thing, he was never too loud, but, nevertheless, there was a lot of authority about him. He was an outstanding captain.

In later years, I saw a lot of Bobby socially, especially once I got back from living in South Africa. I often used to bump into him and Stephanie on holiday because they would stay at Jimmy Tarbuck's villa outside Marbella and a mate of mine owns a place nearby. We used to have quite a few dinners together.

Bobby didn't change at all. Right from when he was playing. We would go out, have a few drinks together and he was great socially. I'm proud to say Bobby was a very good friend of mine.

Two of England's finest, Bobby and Johnny Haynes, face to face before Fulham v West Ham at Craven Cottage.

Bobby and Stephanie with their friends, Jane Benfield, Bobby and Jan Keetch.

Bobby Keetch

Starting his career at West Ham United in 1959, Bobby went on to play for both Fulham and QPR before retiring in 1968. He co-founded the London theme restaurant 'Football Football.' Sadly, he died suddenly in July 1996.

Bobby was always smiling. I was with him on the groundstaff at West Ham and we were together in England youth squads and he kept laughing right through his career, even after he became England captain. There was no flashiness about him, despite what he achieved.

Bobby was reserved. People came up to him and always asked all the usual questions. They weren't conversations as such, just Bobby responding to questioning. I've seen the same happen to George Best and when I moved from West Ham to Fulham people who grilled me just drove me around the bend – you didn't have conversations, just answered questions, which was very tiring. Even so, Bobby would just smile.

Lou Wade, who was one of the partners involved with Bobby in the Woolston Hall country club, once persuaded Bobby they needed to make the place more exotic so they put in a little pond and got some flamingoes. A heavy winter came down though and they found all the birds frozen into the ice. Then one night they were discussing whether they should chain the knives, forks and spoons to the tables like they do in transport cafes. The whole project backfired. It was just a series of disasters!

During the filming of the movie '*The Dirty Dozen*' I went with the actors Lee Marvin and Robert Webber to a party at Richard Harris' house in Belgravia and we met Bobby and Tina there. Robert Webber became a great Fulham fan and came to Craven Cottage a lot with me. We would go out socially as well with Lee Marvin and often bumped into Bobby in restaurants in the West End.

At the '66 World Cup final I had been given some incredible seats on the edge of the Royal Box and when the players came up to collect the trophy George Cohen looked across with Bobby Moore and pointed, shouting: 'Bloody hell! It's Keetchy!' Bobby said: 'How did you get seats in there?'

It was quite funny. There was the Queen waiting to present Bobby with the Jules Rimet trophy and the two of them had stopped at the top of the stairs and were shouting at me. You can see it on the film of the final before the bit where Bobby wipes his hands on the velvet drape of the table.

We opened a theme restaurant called 'Football Football' and got a marvellous waxwork model of Bobby, plus a stained-glass window of the Boys of '66. Our official charity is Bobby's Imperial Cancer Research Fund. More than anything, I would have loved to have offered Bobby a role there – he represented everything the idea stands for. At least the place is something that will reflect Bobby's status. We had a marvellous opening night with George Weah, Ferenc Puskas and Francisco Gento in attendance but it was tinged with sadness, too. I just wish Bobby could have been there.

Alan Hudson

One of the most talented midfielders of the 70s, Alan played over 300 games for Chelsea, Stoke City and Arsenal yet won just two England caps.

I was just 17 when I was called into my first England squad. It was during the home internationals and we'd just lost to Northern Ireland. We were at the hotel bar and went back to our rooms for curfew. Ramsey was downstairs as usual and the phone rang in the room about five minutes later. That was the signal, everyone synchronised their watches, and it was out the back staircase, all in Bobby's Jag and we were off roaring around the North Circular Road towards Jimmy Quill's pub: Bobby was driving and there was me, Ballie, Mick Summerbee and, I think, Rodney Marsh. What a bunch!

At Jimmy's pub, Bobby got out, took off his strides and threw them over his shoulder. He said: 'Come on boys, strides off!' and we walked into this party with our trousers over our shoulders. Just a bit of footballer fun. There we were in shirt, tie and jacket and underpants. I soon put mine back on, but three hours later Bobby still had his strides over his shoulder. It was his way of telling people to relax – 'I'm only Bobby Moore, don't make a fuss of me'.

He was always the boss, no matter what company we were in. Whatever Bobby said, went. There was something about his presence which I can't describe, but when George Best and Pele look up to you, that's something special. I went to a couple of shows with him: Phil Collins, Jack Jones, he loved those sort of concerts.

Bobby was the reason I had a successful time in America, playing for Seattle. I was out of work and he believed I'd love it. That was good enough, he swayed me. It was the greatest piece of advice anyone has ever given me. I had four years out there.

I ran an executive box at Chelsea for a year and Bobby would sometimes come in. It wasn't like meeting another footballer – he was the closest thing to Steve McQueen football has ever produced. He had charisma that would've made him a big film star and he was, in fact, the beginning of footballers having that film-star status in the media. He had been there and worn the t-shirt long before Bestie came along. Whereas George was all long hair, Bobby was grey suit, powder grey shirt, cufflinks, super smooth, like James Bond. He was in that class, wasn't he? Apart from his blond hair, if he had been in films it would have been in that role. You can imagine him sitting at the roulette table opposite Blofeld and saying: 'Moore...Bobby Moore.' Either that or one of the heroes in those early 70s TV series when they wore all those flowery shirts – he could've stepped straight into *The Saint* or *The Persuaders* or been Jason King in *Department S*. He had a quiet, Cockney accent instead of a marble in his mouth, but was unbelievably smooth nevertheless.

I get to West Ham a lot these days and seeing all that memorabilia there, the bronze bust, the stand, the stuff on the walls of the corridors, is the most justified thing I've ever seen. He was West Ham and it is fair reward for his loyalty.

Frank McLintock

Began his career with Leicester City before joining Arsenal in 1964, where he played 313 games and captained them to the coveted double in 1971. Capped nine times by Scotland, Frank is now a TV and radio analyst.

I t just seemed impossible he could die. It was just so unexpected. You hear of other people passing away but Bobby Moore doesn't die, you know? I'd worked with him at Capital Radio and he always looked so fit and healthy. But he kept his illness secret. I remember he asked me to take his place on a trip to America with Kenny Lynch and Peter Cook because he had to go to Scotland. It was only much later that I found out he was going there to have cancer treatment.

Bobby had a good understanding with Geoff Hurst. I would clatter Geoff from behind – that was when you could tackle from behind – so he would come short, then spin and go on a searching run. I used to run with him but Bobby would bend a pass that dropped over Geoff's left shoulder, on the opposite side to me. Bobby didn't just hit the ball in a team-mate's general direction, his delivery of passing always gave them a chance to do something with it.

When England beat Scotland 3-1 at Wembley in '71, they were going back to Hendon Hall. I lived in Winchmore Hill, which wasn't far from Hendon, so I said to Bobby: 'Can you give me a lift on the England team bus?' Bobby said: 'Of course.' So he put me at the back of the bus and I was drinking beer with the England lads. I had to duck down because if the Scottish supporters had seen me on the bus they would have ripped the bloody bus apart with their bare hands, especially since we had lost!

For ages, Jonathan Pearce, me and the rest of the Capital Radio guys would say we couldn't believe Bobby was dead. We'd go to Upton Park and he wasn't there anymore. It just didn't ring true or seem right.

I don't think people appreciated how nice Bobby was and how much they missed him until he died. It was something that hit me fairly hard after his death. I felt I'd never really expressed how much I enjoyed his company and how much I'd appreciated his football.

Mike Summerbee

Started with Burnley in 1959 but enjoyed most success with Manchester City where he made 355 appearances. Mike also played eight times for England during his 20-year career and also starred with Bobby in 'Escape to Victory.' Now runs his own shirt-making business.

Bobby Moore was every mother's idea of a perfect son. He was so slick and tidy. He was the only man I know who got out of a bath dry. I even used to joke with him that he ironed his money. He had everything the perfect English sportsman should have. Every professional footballer should learn about Bobby and his qualities if they want to make it.

I knew Bobby from when we were about 15, as we used to play pre-season games with Swindon Town and West Ham United. At one game, he came into the dressing room and just started talking to me and our friendship developed from there.

We had great fun making '*Escape to Victory.*' Bobby was invited to play a part in the film before me and they were still looking for a mixture of players who had a bit of personality and character. So Bobby rang me up and said: 'Miguelly, do you fancy being a film star?' I was slightly surprised. 'What do you mean?' I asked. He said: 'How would you like to appear in a war film and play a prisoner who escapes during a football match against the Germans?' I didn't regret saying yes. Bobby and I liked the same things, we had the same sense of humour, very alike in many ways. He was tidy and I was brought up that way too, so when we roomed together it was a fight to tidy up! We stayed in a nice hotel in Budapest – we weren't actually made to sleep in those prison camp huts we did the filming in! – and had room service. In the end, the waiter had to wear gloves because he was getting frostbite from carrying up the gin and tonics with ice. Bobby would be saying 'have a nice gin and tonic, Miguelly, and don't forget the lemon!' We were in bed late and up early for filming. Mooro always said: 'If you can't drink and get up in the morning, don't drink!'

There was fabulous camaraderie among the people on the set of the film, especially between the various international players, many of whom had played against each other in various World Cups, and the film stars. There were some famous faces there: Daniel Massey, Tim Piggott-Smith, Julian Curry, all famous Shakespearean actors. Then you had Michael Caine, Sylvester Stallone, Max Von Sydow, all directed by the great John Huston. It was funny, but all the footballers wanted to be actors and all the actors wanted to be footballers. But there was a great atmosphere on the set and we had a lot of fun, especially filming the match. Michael Caine was brilliant, coming out for drinks with Bobby and I, helping us with our lines. He looked after us, relaxed us when we had to do bits of the filming that were harder. Michael was just like Bobby was in the defence during a match – there to help out. It's weird, but given that everyone said Bobby had the grace and aura of a film star, how ironic that he finally got his chance on the big screen.

In the old days, I often spent time in London with Bobby when I played for England. The first time I was included in the squad I roomed with him because he wanted me to feel welcome. He told me I'd been picked to play before Sir Alf did. Alf must have told Bobby and he broke it to me. He was a person who very much encouraged people and gave them confidence.

He always had time for people, especially autograph hunters. It may sound like a small detail but he always had a good signature, not a rushed signature. I bet if anyone who's got a Bobby Moore autograph checks it out, you'll find that not only is it unhurriedly written but also clear enough to be identified by a complete stranger. It may sound mad but you can read the signatures of all the world-class players like Pele, Beckenbauer and Bobby Charlton. They have so much time on the pitch because they are so good, and its the same in life when their asked to write an autograph. How many of today's players' signatures are either illegible or they just do a quick squiggle like they're irritated you've asked them for a their autograph.

I used to speak to Bobby once or twice a week. We would regularly have social contact. Once, when he was doing a coaching course in Leeds, he phoned me and asked if he could stay at our house. Naturally I said he could and when he arrived we went over the road to my local pub for a drink. After a few gin and tonics Bobby was tired and decided to turn in. I told him what room we'd prepared for him and off he went. I think the landlord saw him over the road. Later, at closing time, my wife and I all went back home and when we checked on Bobby, the room he was supposed to be in was empty. So we searched around the house and when we checked my son's room – Nicky was about eight years old then – we found Bobby kipping in there, among all Nicky's toys. Apparently, Bobby found he couldn't sleep on his own and decided to sleep in with Nicky for company. Can't be bad, can it? You're eight-years-old and you go to school the next day and say to all your mates in the playground: 'Oh, by the way, the England captain slept in my room last night!'

Nicky remembers Bobby very well. Even in those days when he was very young, he still knew Bobby was really famous. After Bobby died, Nicky, who was at Swindon Town then, was fortunate enough to play in Bobby's memorial game – he came on as substitute in the second half and that really meant a lot to him.

I've got a shirt business and in the early 70s Bobby started up Bobby Moore Shirts. He introduced me to Morris Keston and all those people. We made the shirts to Bobby's orders, it was nice idea but it just didn't take off like it should have. The production difficulties

Mike Summerbee scrambling with Alan Stephenson.

could've caused a few problems between us and I certainly didn't want to spoil our great friendship with business problems.

A day doesn't go by without me thinking about him, because something always happens that reminds me. Like with Princess Diana's funeral service at Westminster Abbey. We had Bobby's memorial service there too, and it brought back fresh memories of the day and all the people who turned out for Bobby. The tributes and the things people said were so very much alike. Funnily enough, during Bobby's service there, I was looking up at the ceiling and right in the top of the Abbey was this bird, flapping about and hopping from perch to perch. When I asked around afterwards no one else had seen a bird, but I did. I like to think it was old Robert looking down on us, making sure I was dressed smart.

Terry Neill

Captain of both club and country, Terry played for Arsenal and Hull City, winning 59 Northern Ireland caps. Also managed at Highbury and Tottenham but now runs his own sports bar and is a radio analyst.

The man had guts. Look at the way he chested the ball down in the final seconds of the '66 final before launching that pass? I tell you what, my bottle would've gone and I would have definitely lumped it into the stand. If I'd been English instead of Irish and playing in that game, Geoff Hurst could've forgotten about his hat-trick – that ball would've been in the Wembley crowd. Geoff's definitely got Bobby to thank for being in the record books for that one.

There was always mutual respect between us. We grew up at West Ham and Arsenal, playing against each other initially in youth teams, then in first teams, and eventually for England and Northern Ireland. We were rival captains.

I got to know Bobby really well when I worked at Capital Radio. I probably saw as much of him as anybody else during the last three years of his life – he was in an office in Goswell Road and I was in an office in Clerkenwell Road, a few minutes walk away, so even when we weren't working we'd be on the phone talking. Bobby loved his commentary work. There was never any suggestion that he might refuse a wet night at Stockport because he was the great Bobby Moore. No, he would go where he was asked and there was never anything but enthusiasm and professionalism from him. Actually, we both enjoyed getting about to different grounds – we had to suffer one or two cramped commentary positions but that usually caused a laugh more than anything.

Bobby really could mix with kings and paupers. And whenever people brought up the subject of the FA not giving him a job he would dismiss it lightly. He looked for no favours, Bobby. He was just happy to do his thing.

The most time I ever spent with him were five marvellous weeks in Italy for Capital covering the '90 World Cup. My abiding vision of Bob was that I thought he had a bottle of wine stitched to his palm. At the Republic of Ireland v. Romania match in Genoa, Mick Lowes, Bobby and myself were doing the commentary for

Capital. We'd had a few drinks beforehand, nothing in excess, just something to wet our whistle, but the match was probably the hottest game of the lot and we were sweating buckets. We were sitting in shorts and T-shirts, Mick was doing most of the commentary and sweating onto all his notes so Bobby and I had to keep mopping he's brow.

We had a system whereby if you spotted something the other hadn't seen, you'd scribble it down and pass it to one another. Mick was doing the usual hundred miles an hour Capital-style commentary when I noticed Bobby slip a little note to Mick. I leaned over to see what it said, expecting to see something about the referee or a player, and written on it was: 'How do you fancy a large Remy?' Bobby and I were laughing and Mick, to his credit, kept a straight face and didn't break the flow of his commentary.

The Capital Gold radio team relaxing at their hotel between games at the '92 European Championships in Sweden. Bobby is joined by Mick Lowes, Jonathan Pearce and Terry Neill.

After the game, Mick, Bobby and myself returned to our room for a shower and a beer to watch an Italy match on TV. They won the game and all the locals spilled out into the streets afterwards, so we decided to have a stroll down to the seafront. We went into a restaurant and found most of the Romanian squad were in there with their coach, Emerich Jenei. It turned out his great hero was Bobby Moore and despite the fact they'd just been beaten and this guy had probably lost his job, for him to meet Bobby in person was his Christmas come early. We stayed there with them drinking and joking until the wee small hours – the owner of the place was more than happy to stay open because Italy had won. But, to me, the incident was reflective of the standing in which Bobby was held.

After such a long booze-up with the Romanians, we staggered, literally, all the way back to our room at what must have been virtually first light. I collapsed in the middle of the road and, a few yards ahead of me, Mick and Bobby had their arms around each other and were swearing undying drunken love like a pair of silly-arses. All three of us were giggling.

We had a very hectic month out there in the end. We covered some 15 games for Capital and there was only the three of us with Jonathan Pearce, who was based at the England camp. We had to move all over Italy. Initially, we were based in Sardinia, and flew or drove to Rome, Palermo, Genoa, Bologna and Naples. I remember Stephanie and Bobby would take time out on the beach occasionally and have some quiet moments, whenever Bobby had a free evening. On reflection, I'm really glad they had those moments together.

Bobby looked very fit in Italy. Strangely enough, we were both lucky in that respect, we didn't put too much weight on. Many people would remark how well we both looked, which was quite surprising given the volume of white wine we consumed! Stephanie quipped with me that I always had a glass in my hand and I replied that I was training to drink for Ireland, but, the irony of that was her husband Bobby could, and did, drink me under the table.

I realised something wasn't right with Bobby's health about a year after he joined us at Capital. He started losing weight and everyone at the radio station was concerned about him. Because he was such a quiet, private man I didn't enquire as to what it might be. Then, for a while, he seemed to be putting weight back on again. But then the last time I saw him was at Wembley at the San Marino game. I was chatting to someone when there was a tap on my shoulder. When I looked around it was Bobby. I hadn't seen him for a month so his jaundiced appearance was quite a shock. I couldn't help the look of surprise on my face and Bobby noticed this. What made his appearance more noticeable for me was that over Bobby's shoulder on the wall was the photograph of him holding the World Cup aloft in '66. I'm sure I'm not the only person to say this but he was so brave that night to make an appearance. The gesture summed Bobby up. It must have been a huge strain for him to make it to Wembley, but it just showed how much guts and determination the man had.

On the day of his memorial service at Westminster, we all came outside and some of them were coming to my Sports Bar in Holborn for a drink. We decided we would never get a cab with such a mob around so we were going to walk across Parliament Square. I noticed a police car on the pavement and the policeman driving obviously recognised me and waved. I went over to talk to the policeman. We had a little chat: 'Sad, isn't it', 'what a turnout', 'nice weather for it', 'dignified service', that sort of stuff, when I said: 'Any chance of a lift back to Holborn?' To my surprise, the policeman said: 'Yeah, sure, hop in.' So Don Howe, myself and some others who I can't recall, jumped into the police car and they gave us a ride to the door of the bar. They even put the siren on all the way to Holborn. I told them it's the sort of thing Bobby would've smiled at. A door-to-door taxi ride home from his memorial in a police car with its siren going! When we got to the bar, we cracked open a few bottles of champagne to toast Bobby's memory, but the policemen said: 'We'd love to have a drink for Bobby but we're on duty.' So, instead of a drink, they sped off in their car with their siren on again. Bob would've liked that.

Steve Kindon

Centre-forward for Burnley, Wolves and Huddersfield Town whose career was cut short by injury in 1982.

'm quite unusual because I'm a northerner who admired Moore. I played rugby as a kid and the '66 World Cup switched me to football. Eighteen months later I made my debut at seventeen for Burnley against West Ham at Upton Park. I was so proud my World Cup hero was going to be marking me.

I bought myself a new club tie and blazer with the Burnley crest on and took my autograph book with me. As soon as the coach pulled into Upton Park I saw Bobby outside signing autographs for the kids. I was first off the coach and I chased after him through the players' entrance, shouting: 'Bobby! Bobby! Can I have your autograph please?' He turned around, saw I was a Burnley player and, understandably, thought I was winding him up. I'll never forget the first two words Bobby Moore said to me. One began with 'f' and the other was 'off'.

Ralph Coates overheard what happened and said: 'It's okay, Bob, the kid means it. You're one of his heroes.' Bob immediately realised the mistake he had made and signed my book. Then, in an even nicer gesture, took me into the West Ham dressing room and asked the whole team to sign the book for me.

Bobby was three yards slower than me in running but I was four yards slower than Bobby in thinking. If he was ever caught out it was by a ricochet or spin of the ball. In athletics, everybody has to start when the gun goes off, but in football you have to use your judgement. They say strikers like Jimmy Greaves and Ian Rush got in the right place by luck. It's not luck, it's timing. It's a knack. And Bobby had that same knack on a football field.

He got booked for a foul on me. I'd knocked it twenty yards past him and he stuck out his leg and tripped me up. The referee ran over and said: 'Bobby! Bobby! Bobby Moore, come here! What's your name?' However daft it sounds, it was a ruling referees had to ask the player's name. When I tell that story, I always say the referee then said: 'Bobby, is that OBE or MBE?', but that's not true.

Usually, tales of old pros are exaggerated. When you talk to your dad, Stanley Matthews never got tackled and every time he crossed the ball, Stan Mortensen headed it into the net. But when I've watched the video of the '66 final and seen that documentary *'Goal!'* – the film of the tournament – my memories of Bobby are actually enhanced rather than diminished. He was faultless for the whole match. You look back at your memories and you remember a colossus. You watch that video and you realise he was better than that.

Norman Hunter

Joined Leeds United in 1959 and played 700 games. Won 28 caps for England, succeeding Bobby Moore in the number six shirt, retiring in '82

Bobby and I were candidates for the left-half position in the England team but Bobby had already made it his own by the time I joined the squad in 1965 and he got the nod virtually right through till around the end of Alf Ramsey's time in charge. I sat watching him for a few years. At times, I was a bit envious, but I admired the man. Some players, when they are vieing for the same position, might pick holes in their rival's ability and feel resentment, but I never felt that with Bobby. He was the best reader of the game I've ever seen.

My strength was my consistency at League level, probably more so than Bobby. But Leeds were a better side than West Ham at the time. But as far as class at international level goes, he was definitely the man. It would have been a good sprint race between Bobby and I because neither of us were very quick.

When he got back after being locked up in Bogota over the bracelet thing it was as if he'd been out for a day trip. The whole thing seemed to roll off his shoulders. It was quite fortunate it was Bobby Moore who was jailed rather than somebody else, because it never seemed to bother Bobby one bit and the way he coped with it gave the lads a feeling of raised spirits. They were trying to frame him for money or to undermine team spirit, but it had the opposite effect. In the end, we were unlucky in Mexico. We got beaten 3-2 by the Germans in extra time but we were a good side. Personally, I agree with those who say Bobby had a better World Cup in '70 than he did in '66.

I knew everything about his playing because that's all I seemed to do: watch him play. The better the opposition, the better he seemed to play.

Peter Shilton

One of the greatest goalkeepers, Peter started his career in 1966 with Leicester City, going on to play for Stoke City, Nottingham Forest, Southampton and Derby County. He gained a record 125 England caps.

Having Bobby in front of me in the England defence was reassuring because he was a good reader of the game and a sound tackler when he was left in one-on-one situations. He could hold up people, tackle, win the ball, and then be very cool when passing it out. A lot of players win the ball, panic and give it straight back to the opposition.

Bobby had a lot of strength to his character – you always felt he took much of the pressure and responsibility for the team upon himself. When Bobby Moore picked the ball up in the dressing room to go out you said to yourself: 'He could take the world on his shoulders.' He always looked as though he'd got everything under control and it made you feel so much better, so much more confident. If something went wrong, you had somebody with you who could handle the situation. He was never over-supportive, but you always knew he'd got his eye on you.

In '70 I went to the World Cup in the squad of 28 but I was one of six players who was left out. We trained at a posh members-only club and one night Sir Alf let us have a social night with the people of the club and a few beers, which was a rarity. But the lads set Bobby up by fixing a draw so he had to dance with this local girl – she wasn't ugly but she wasn't the best looking girl in the world! Bobby suspected he had been stitched up, but with his usual grace and charm, he got up, walked over and danced with her. All the players were creased up laughing, but he took it in great spirit.

The following season I made my full debut for England against East Germany. Sir Alf left Gordon Banks out and there was uproar in the press, but we won 3-1. One of the German guys hit a shot from about 20 yards and it deflected off Bobby and flew into the net. It was credited to their player but not many keepers can say Bobby Moore put an own goal past them in their first match.

I remember the Poland game in the World Cup qualifiers in June '73. The stadium in Katowice was packed with 100,000 people and the noise and atmosphere was very intimidating. They wouldn't even let us have any balls to kick about with before the start. In the first few minutes they got a free-kick and the guy bent it in to the near post and Bob was stretching for it with Gadocha, but the Pole got a touch on it and it went in past my shoulder. Just after half-time, Bob made the only bad mistake I can ever remember him making for England when, as the last line of defence, he pulled the ball across Lubanksi's path who just got a touch on the ball and it went under Bobby's foot. Lubanksi came through and hit it. I thought I'd done everything right to narrow his target, but the ball crept inside the post. Later on Alan Ball got sent off rushing to defend Martin Peters after an incident. For England to lose 2-0 was a massive thing and Bobby knew he would get slaughtered in the newspapers at home.

A couple of us went to Bobby and Alan Ball's room with Sir Alf and had a drink to console Bobby. We were up 'till the early hours. Alf even insisted on taking the blame for the first goal because he hadn't warned us how Poland took kicks from wide positions. But Bobby never moaned about it – he knew he would be criticised although he was conscious his mood shouldn't get through to the other players. He never shirked responsibility for anything.

When we played Poland in the return game, Bobby was dropped and people remember Norman Hunter, Bobby's replacement, making the mistake that let

A rare long-range effort from Bobby beats Leicester City's Peter Shilton in a 5-2 victory for West Ham at Upton Park in August 1972.

117

Poland score. Tony Currie lost the ball, but Norman should've flattened the fellow. However, he missed him and I should've saved it. I suppose you could blame all three of us. But just like in Katowice, it was one of those nights when we knew everything was going against us.

With 125 caps I'm the only player who has beaten Bobby's remarkable England appearances record of 108, but being a goalkeeper makes that easier than an out-field player because we go on forever!

In 1970 the squad got together for the song *Back Home*. I remember going on *Top of the Pops*. We all wore dinner suits and it was really good fun. We got to number one in the charts and Bobby was in his element with that – I think he quite fancied himself as a pop star! I was also involved in the song *World In Motion* in 1990 with the band New Order but I was the only one who sang on both of those England records.

I met Bobby many times over the years and I always found him a person that spoke to you. He had an unfortunate distant exterior, but deep down he was a warm fellow. He had so much class.

 # Moore tributes

Bobby had a wicked sense of humour. Many is the time he went along the England team deliberately introducing the players by the wrong name. Ray Wilson would be George Cohen, I'd be Roger Hunt. Mooro would be winking at me while I was shaking hands with an FA dignitary and with a straight face he'd be saying: 'This is Roger Hunt.' And they wouldn't know.
I think Bobby got me into more trouble than any other footballer I've ever known. On the '64 tour when we went to New York we were staying at the Waldorf Astoria. It was about 11.45pm and Alf had put a curfew on the lads going out. Mooro said: 'Come on, we're going out,' and I said: 'Where are we going?' He said: 'I want to see Ella Fitzgerald.' When you're room-mates, you have to go along. Down in the lift we go and we get to this bar where Ella Fitzgerald is per-forming – we couldn't get in, the place was packed. So we poked our heads around the door so we could say we've seen her sing. We were back within an hour. But that wasn't the best thing to do and Alf got to know about it and wasn't happy. But Mooro got me into a lot of scrapes.
One of the reasons for me going to West Ham was because Mooro was there. There wasn't a lot for me to go to West Ham for – the main reason I left Tottenham was because Bill Nicholson didn't want me. I was privileged to be a friend of Mooro's. He was one of my greatest pals. We had great trips, great times. I tend to remember that, more than the football. The football speaks for itself.
Jimmy Greaves speaking on *A Tribute To Bobby Moore* video

Chapter 8
Cottage comrades

George Best

One of the greatest players of all time, George made his debut for Manchester United at 17 and played his first game for Northern Ireland just before his 18th birthday. Best had spells at Fulham and Bournemouth before playing in the American League.

I was completely unprepared for my reaction when I attended Bobby's memorial service because I didn't realise how much he meant to me. I was sad because a pal had died, but during the service, I burst into tears. I was standing there wiping my eyes with my sleeve because I hadn't brought any tissues. Only Sir Matt Busby's death had affected me like that.

Bobby and I had become close friends over those last few years from sitting in press boxes together for our radio work, but there were people at the service saying they had known him for 25 years, but had never got close to him. I suddenly realised what a lovely man Bobby was. Few people in life cheer you up and I couldn't wait to see him at the games. When he walked in a room he lit it up. You knew you were in the presence of someone a little bit special.

> **"Few people in life cheer you up and I couldn't wait to see him at games. When he walked into a room he lit it up"**

There was a big contrast between us in the 60s. I was the hairy one and he was the clean-cut one. We were chalk and cheese in so many ways, yet we forged this friendship. If there was a reason for our closeness, it was mutual respect. The first time I played opposite Bobby was in the semi-final of the FA Cup in '64. Everybody wanted a West Ham v Man United final, but we were drawn against each other in the semi-final. West Ham beat us 3-1, but had United got through instead of Preston I would have beaten Howard Kendall to the record of youngest player in an FA Cup final.

All through the 60s and 70s, I played against Bobby many times.

And I hated playing against him. He was one of the very few defenders who never committed himself and my forte was making players sell themselves. I used to draw players in, play it off their legs, but Bobby didn't dive in. He waited and waited and followed me for yards, backing off until we ran out of pitch. We almost ended up in the crowd sometimes. He held you up and waited for you to make a mistake. He made very few himself and never gave the ball away either. I look at defenders today, ones who are supposed to be world class, and it's fifty-fifty where the ball goes.

We bumped into each other at functions but when we played together at Fulham I got to know him better. The match finished and all he wanted to do was go out and have a lager with the boys. We had a great laugh at Craven Cottage because there was constant mickey-taking going on. Bobby was such an easy-going, happy-go-lucky, sort of bloke.

I was on holiday in Spain when England won the World Cup. Being Irish, I didn't really give a toss whether they won or not, but I was chuffed for him. I watched it in a bar full of Brits. I was screaming at the telly with them, so I suppose I wanted England to win, sort of!

I played in the greatest decade for British football there's ever been. All the other stuff was incredible. It was a time of flower power and hippies and the Chelsea scene and music and The Beatles and The Rolling Stones. If you weren't a footballer, you wanted to be a rock musician, and if you weren't a rock musician, you wanted to be a footballer.

Mooro was a legend of the 60s, even more so after the World Cup. United would play the London teams and have thirty thousand people locked out. Now, with some teams, there's more people on the pitch than in the stand. Every team had five or six crazy characters. I can still name every line-up in the first division, from goalkeeper to outside left. There was no violence because the fans didn't have time to fight. They wanted to watch the characters on the field. In those days, it was fun. Nowadays football has taken a serious turn.

In the mid-70s Bobby opened the first Mooro's Bar and I got invited. Some local lads were there who looked a bit dubious, but they treated me with the same respect they gave to Mooro. It was identical when I took Bobby along to the opening of a bar in Belfast. You would think an Englishman in Belfast wouldn't get a warm reception, but they treated him to drinks all night. It showed how much people felt about him, even outside England.

A few years ago we were doing commentary on a match at Chelsea and he said: 'Bestie, do you fancy something to eat?' and I thought he'd buy me a meat pie, but he was gone for ages. I thought where on earth is he? He came back with fish and chips, salt, vinegar, everything. He actually left the stadium and queued in some chippie in the King's Road. I thought this guy lifted the World Cup and he's gone and got me fish and chips.

Rodney Marsh

Started his career in 1962, playing for Fulham (twice), QPR and Manchester City before managing Tampa Bay Rowdies.

People always thought I started at Fulham but I started at West Ham United. I was there in 1959 as a 15 year-old training on Tuesday and Thursday nights with Malcolm Allison. Bobby was about three years older than me and he was in the Under-18s.

A Fulham scout recruited me when I was 16. He went to my father and said they wanted me, so my dad said: 'Do you want to play for West Ham or Fulham?' and I said: 'West Ham'. My dad went to the West Ham scout at the time, Wally St Pier, and asked if they were going to sign me and he said there was no guarantee, so I signed for Fulham.

I think the '66 final was better than great. When you've seen it so many times over the last 30 years it doesn't do justice to the enormity of the event. England had never been in a World Cup final, let alone won it and I always said Bobby was the catalyst behind the victory. Everybody responded to him.

I used to see Bobby at the Anglo-American Sporting Club and at different functions, but we never said more than a passing hello. Around '71 we played five times for England together and that's when our friendship started.

In '76-77 we all came back from America and played together at Fulham. George Best was in Los Angeles, I was at Tampa Bay and Bobby was at San Antonio. It's only in retrospect that I realise what priceless times they were at Fulham. Crowds went from 3,000 to 25,000 and again, Bobby was the catalyst. He drew people towards him. He was unique, unlike me and Bestie who are, for want of a better word, mavericks. The main reason I went to Fulham was because Bobby was there.

I would say that Bobby was one of the greatest players I played with, and one of the greatest drinkers. If there was a team for drinking, Bestie would be the vice-captain and Bobby would be the captain!

I've not had the opportunity to say this really but he was such a delightful human being. Somehow he touched the lives of everyone who met him and I would like to think we were friends.

Alan Mullery

Between 1958-75 Alan played for Fulham over two periods separated by eight years with Spurs. He won 35 England caps.

People who supported Fulham when Bobby and I played there always knew they would never win anything but they were a club that enjoyed their football. The first time I was at Craven Cottage, before I went to Tottenham, we won our first game of the season and one of the staff said: 'Well, lads, only another 34 points and we'll avoid relegation.' Each season we remained in the first division, we used to have a 'Staying up party' with a 40-piece orchestra and bubbly flowing all night.

During my second spell there, Alec Stock, the Fulham manager, came to see me in 1974 and the conversation went something like this.

Alec: 'How well do you get on with Bobby Moore?'

Me: 'I roomed with him on England get-togethers for four years.'

Alec: 'Would you have any fear of him coming to Fulham?'

Me: 'No, none at all.'

League Cup action from 1974 as Bobby closes down Trevor Brooking at Craven Cottage.

Alec: 'Okay, go to West Ham and convince him to sign then.'

So I grabbed the forms, got in a mini-cab, went over to West Ham and persuaded Bobby to sign. Bobby thought the time might be right to leave and I was saying: 'It's great at Fulham, come and join us.' Bobby signed on the Friday and played his first game on the Tuesday night and a huge crowd turned out to see him. We were playing Middlesbrough, who won the championship that season, and we were 4-0 down after twenty minutes. After picking the fourth one out of the net I was walking back to the centre spot and Bob said quietly, 'I think I might have made a mistake coming here.' I burst out laughing. The irony was, by the end of the season, we were in the FA Cup final.

We played eleven games to get to Wembley, including four matches against Nottingham Forest, home and away and neutral grounds – the last one was in front of a bloke and his dog in Hull. We beat Everton 2-1 in front of 45,000 and defended for 89 minutes against Carlisle before sneaking a 1-0 with our only shot of the match. In the semi-final against Birmingham, the ball hit John Mitchell on the knee and went in – it was the worst goal 'Mitch' ever scored. Mooro was 34, I was 33, and we were going to Wembley again. We should never have been there – the team was nowhere near good enough.

We had writs served on us about boot contracts the day before the final and the court said we could wear any boots but we had to paint over them so the makes were obscured. But after the first ten minutes of the match the paint wore off and everyone was running round with Puma, Adidas and everything. It was farcical.

The final was our worst performance of the whole tournament but the best party I've ever been to was our 'losers' party at the Savoy. The West Ham team even came to our party, that's how good it was!

Bobby couldn't go anywhere without somebody recognising him and he presented an image of being very staid and he looked as though he didn't talk or laugh much, but that wasn't him. He had a wicked sense of humour and he was one of the nicest, most polite men I've ever met in football.

My admiration for him increased tenfold when he came back from house arrest after being accused of stealing the bracelet to perform as he did in the World Cup in '70. Everybody admired him more after that. He acted like nothing had happened, just got straight into the training, the competition started and he was outstanding, easily our best player in Mexico.

Four weeks before the tournament started, we were going to play in Colombia and Ecuador. We stayed at altitude in Mexico at 7,000 feet, did two weeks training, and then went to play Ecuador and Colombia. We were sitting in the huge Hotel Tequendama in Bogota wearing our presentation track suits and Mooro and Bobby

Charlton had gone into this jewellery shop, came out and sat down with us on the settee to relax and chat. The next minute police poured in from nowhere and pointed guns at the four of us sitting on the settee. It was like something from the movie *Butch Cassidy and the Sundance Kid*. I had never seen so many guns. The girl from the shop, Clara Padilla, was pointing at Mooro. They were all speaking in Spanish, we didn't understand a word. They gestured for us to stand up, which we did, and they searched us and, obviously, found nothing. In the meantime, somebody had rushed to Alf and said we were all being held at gunpoint. He came in, tried to communicate with the policemen, couldn't, and they just grabbed Bobby and took him away with Alf screaming blue murder, despite the fact none of them could understand him. It was the most frightening thing I've ever been involved in.

Somebody with the England party phoned the British consulate and they got Mooro released because the Colombians couldn't prove he'd stolen anything or even that there was anything missing – there was nothing on us and nothing in the settee. In the meantime, we played a game, beating Colombia 4-0 and then went to Ecuador and beat them 2-0. On the way back, we landed in Bogota to catch another flight and there was a delay of about eight hours, so we went back to the Hotel Tequendama. Bobby Charlton, Mooro, all of us, sat watching the James Stewart western film *Shenandoah* in the basement to occupy us during the wait. But the police arrived and took Mooro, ostensibly for him to

> "The shop girl claimed he put the bracelet in his pocket – but the England tracksuit didn't have pockets"

make a statement. Shortly afterwards, we had to get on the plane. Alf wanted to stay but inside a week we were playing in the World Cup, so Alf left two English FA people behind, Dr Andrew Stephen and Denis Follows, and the squad got on the plane and went back to Guadalajara, in Mexico .

By now, the whole nonsense was rife throughout the world that Bobby had been accused of stealing a bracelet. He was held in the British Embassy in Colombia where he had a dreadful time and wasn't allowed to leave until it was proven or otherwise – the accusation was plain daft because with Mooro's money he could've bought the entire shop, not just one stingy bracelet. Diplomatic negotiations were going on all over the place from England, to put pressure on the authorities to release him. We were all worried about him because you know what happens in South America – people can disappear without trace, can't they?

Consequently, about three days before we played the opening game, they released him and Bobby arrived back in Guadalajara. He'd even been forced cross-examine his accusers in court and had exposed the whole thing as lies. The shop girl claimed he put the bracelet in his left pocket but the England tracksuit didn't have pockets. I was rooming with Bobby and Peter Thompson and I was going downstairs to post some letters home when he came out of the lift. I gave him a big hug because I was so relieved to see him, but he had lost at least a stone in weight that week. He'd lost muscle and everything from not eating properly and from the sheer worry he was never going to get away from that place. He had been locked up wearing this track suit all week, with no change of clothes, and as we went into our room he ripped it off and threw it out the window, saying: 'I never want to see that bloody thing again!' Down below about 40 Mexicans were fighting over it. I phoned Alf and said: 'Bob's back!' He said: 'Order some champagne!' and Peter, myself, Bob and Alf sat in the room and drank a few glasses.

We played our first game and beat Romania 1-0 and he was absolutely fantastic. Just a few days later we played Brazil and although we lost 1-0, the team gave a great performance. We all lost a stone in the Brazil game because of the heat but Bob had lost all that weight on top. I don't think I've ever seen anyone play as well as he did that day.

In our last game, we beat Czechoslovakia 1-0 with a penalty. We were runners-up in the group, Brazil won it, so they stayed in Guadalajara, we went off to Leon where we played West Germany in the quarter-final. I didn't realise how well we

played against Brazil until I saw the video a few years later and I don't think I've ever seen an England team play so well against a top side on form.'

For an hour against the Germans it was just a continuation of the Brazil match - we tore them to pieces and we were 2-0 up. We were absolutely murdering them. Geoff had a couple of chances, and I think there was also one disallowed goal, and a few penalty claims.

At that point, the one thing everyone remembers, of course, is Bobby Charlton and Martin Peters being substituted by Sir Alf Ramsey.

It was such a tremendous performance, Alf and everyone else was looking forward to the semi-finals and I think Alf must have said, 'You're strolling it lads, off you come, Bobby Charlton, Martin.' People say Alf made a mistake by taking Charlton off and resting him against Germany, but he had substituted him in the other three group games because he felt Bobby was the oldest player and he might suffer in the conditions. If anything, he was probably as fit as anyone. We weren't going to give anything away because on came Norman Hunter and Colin Bell and you couldn't pick two lads with more energy for the last half hour of a match. Consequently, we conceded two goals. The first a shot by Beckenbauer, who now without his marking responsibilities, had come more into the game. People forget how much England were dominating that game and Peter Bonetti had nothing to do and when it came to the first real save he had to make it flew right under his body. There were still 25 minutes to go, we still fancied ourselves strongly but they put on Grabowski who gave Terry Cooper a dreadful time. The Germans got the equaliser through Uwe Seeler. In extra time they began to tear us to pieces and eventually Muller got their winner. Everybody was shocked to go out because we fancied ourselves very strongly to meet Brazil in the final.

There were some eerie similarities and differences in '70 from '66. The weirdest one was at the end of the '70 match with the Germans the TV commentator said, 'Some photographers are on the pitch!' In many respects, some of the things that were advantages in '66 were reversed in '70. Instead of a home crowd, it was a partisan Mexico crowd who were anti-England. On the eve of the Brazil match samba bands were playing outside the hotel on loudspeakers from about nine o'clock. We walked to the door of the Guadalajara Hilton Hotel to see all these people in the street, it was as though the Rio carnival had come to Guadalajara. These bands were lovely and we watched them for a while from the hotel thinking what a great atmosphere there was going to be at the match but you could hear this racket everywhere you went in the hotel. About 10.30pm we went up to bed and on the top floor where our bedrooms were the noise was about 25 times louder. They had plugged in to big loud speakers and had great drums banging. Because no one could get any sleep, at about three o'clock we moved to rooms at the back of the hotel but it didn't help at all. Nobody got much sleep. We were up by eight o'clock preparing for the match at midday. They were very clever in the way they did it. Funny thing was, the police allowed them to do it. So there was a very anti-British atmosphere, they disliked us immensely.

Alf was worried about the food out there, even in the top hotels, so he arranged to take our own chef and everything else. We'd even been sponsored by a British beef company who were sending us sides of beef and steaks, but the Mexicans impounded all our food. In the end, we had to eat frozen fish fingers and chips. Pretty much whatever we needed, they wouldn't provide.

Alf had a whole range of checks set up for us. We had to weigh ourselves as soon as we got up and had to take pills for all sorts of things – although most of them were probably bromide! But we had to take them in front of the doctor. We weren't allowed to wash our hands in anything other than special anti-bacteria solution because if you washed your hands in the water there it made your fingers drop off! We had to wash our hands before and after everything, before meals, when we went to the toilet, the lot. It was very strict. After every game we had to drink eight pints of liquid like orange juice, water, anything but beer, to replenish the water we had lost. We were restricted never to sit in the sun for more than five minutes on our front, five minutes on our back and five minitues in the pool per day. Alf blew a whistle and everybody would tear off their track suits to reveal their swimming trunks which they'd put on underneath to save time. We would lay on our fronts for five minutes until Alf blew another whistle and we would all dive in the pool. He blew another whistle and we would all lay on our backs. It was like Colditz. It was very strict, but to be fair, it worked. Alf and his crew were meticulous. We had Doctor Phillips, who was at Middlesbrough supervising the medical side, with Harold Shepherdson and Les Cocker, who was the coach and kit man at Leeds United. To walk anywhere you just shed water, so they even arranged for us all to wear these towelling wrist bands, which helped.

The tactics Alf used in '70 were pretty much the same as his system in '66, with one or two changes of faces. We had two lynchpins in that England side: Bobby Moore and Bobby Charlton. Mooro was the king at the back, starting attacks and covering for everyone, and Bobby Charlton who was king of the middle of the park.

Bobby Moore was a special man. It was a privilege to know him, a privilege to play with him and a privilege to be his friend. A great, great footballer.

Les Strong

During a career which lasted from 1972-84, Les played for a number of clubs including Fulham, Rochdale and Crystal Palace.

We used to play terrible pranks on Bobby when he came to play for Fulham. He was this great superstar yet we treated him as one of the lads and he liked that. Whenever he saw me he would sigh and say: 'Oh, no! Not you? What do you want? Leave me alone!'.

Bobby folded everything up neatly and the moment his back was turned I would tie his socks in knots and hide them and fold his trousers and shirts crooked so they creased. It drove him mad!

On coach journeys I would point out of the window, he would look out and I would put a pen up to his face so when he turned back he got an ink mark on his cheek. Or I would sit behind him and tear up bits of paper and put them on his head. The crowd would be waving to him and he would be waving back with this pile of paper on his head!

The team were sitting down for a meal in a hotel restaurant the night before a match and we pretended there was a phone call for him. When he went to reception to get the phone we picked up his place setting and moved it to a little table in the corner and then moved our chairs together so there was nowhere for him to sit when he came back.

If we played golf, I'd always cough or drop my club as Bobby was about to putt or tee-off. When we went for a drink, Bobby would regularly get surrounded by idiots. One by one we would slip away and leave him alone with these wallies. We would be further down the bar making faces at him and he would be trying to politely chat away to them and not laugh.

To lighten things on the coach when we were going to games I used to point at Bobby and shout: 'Look at the old boy, don't you think he looks nervous?' The truth was exactly the opposite though. We were the nervous ones.

Bob often got his own back. When we roomed together I would be in the bathroom shaving and he would lock the door from the outside, go down to the bar and come back an hour later and let me out. Or if I was getting something out of the wardrobe he would push me inside and shut the door.

He invited me to a formal black-tie dinner suit function and agreed to leave my ticket on the door. I arrived with the full monkey suit on, bow-tie, the works, and when I walked into this big room full of people everyone was in casual dress, including Mooro. 'I meant to tell you,' he said. 'It was changed to casual attire.' Everyone was looking at me and I felt a right prat!

It wasn't all pranks, though and he helped me considerably with my football. I was left-back and when Bobby got the ball I stood by the half-way line. With anyone else you would have to drop back and cover in case they made a mistake. One pass from him and I was attacking. Everyone used to think I was an attacking left-back but it was only because he made it possible.

When games finish players usually drift off in different directions but at Fulham the whole team would go to The Duke of Wellington pub in Sloane Square. Teams rarely stick together like that. It was what got us to Wembley. We were never the same after Mooro and Alan Mullery left.

One day in a cup match, we were leading Bolton 1-0, no stoppages, but we were still playing in the ninety-eighth minute when Bolton equalised. The referee blew the whistle, which meant extra time. Bobby argued with him and got sent off. Back in the dressing room we said it was disgraceful and we wouldn't go back out. Alec Stock said: 'If that's how you feel, I'm with you.' So the crowd were waiting for us to come back out while some of the lads got in the bath. In the end the referee warned if we didn't go back out, we would forfeit the match.' We decided we might as well go out and have a go and ended up drawing 2-2.

In 1990, just before the World Cup in Italy, I saw Bobby in the bar at Heathrow airport. I crept up behind him and tapped him on the shoulder, then ducked out of sight. A few moments later I tapped him on the other shoulder and had him turning in circles. When he finally saw me he did his usual sigh and said 'Oh, no! Not you? If I'd have known you'd be here I wouldn't have come. Go away, leave me alone!'

I miss him desperately. The impression of Mooro is so strong that even now I think of him at least once a week. About a week before he died somebody tipped me off how seriously ill he was. I was in Anguilla, in the Caribbean, training the national team, so I rang him. Stephanie answered and I said: 'I'm Les Strong, I used to play with Bobby, can I speak to him?' Bobby came on the phone and he said 'Oh, no! Not you? What do you want? I thought I'd got rid of you. Why don't you leave me alone?' The geezer was dying yet he was cracking jokes. It was good to hear his voice.

I told Bobby that one of the hotels on the island had asked me to offer him a room free of charge if he wanted to convalesce for a few weeks. He said: 'I've just come back from Young Island and if I had known I was so near you I would have come home sooner!' I was really pleased I got the chance to talk to him.

There's a Bette Midler song from the film *Beaches* where she sings the words 'Did you ever know you're my hero?' Every time I hear it I nearly burst into tears. I didn't tell him he was my hero but I wish I had.

John Mitchell

Played for Fulham and Millwall during his eight-year career. John now runs a promotions company, Mitchell Marketing Associates, which he started with Bobby Moore.

Like any other kid in the country, Bobby was my idol. At the time of the '66 final, I was fourteen and I was in a barn in Wales with the scouts. I recall it very vividly. Ironically, there were some German kids there and we all wanted to watch the World Cup so the farmer set a telly up in the barn. When West Germany scored first the German kids were jumping about and we were booing them. When England won, the German kids crawled away very quietly! There are three moments you never forget where you were: Kennedy being shot, Neil Armstrong walking on the moon and Bobby Moore lifting the World Cup.

The first time I met Bobby was when he signed for Fulham and walked into the dressing room. Fulham was a warm club, lovely people, and Bobby was ideal for us. We all had this image of what he was like: Bobby Moore - the man the Germans couldn't ruffle. But there he was, changing next to us in the dressing room. We were surprised by his warmth and sincerity.

During Bobby's time at Fulham dressing room banter was rife and myself and Les Strong were the worst jokers of the lot. We'd give stick to anyone and everyone, it didn't matter if you were Moore, Mullery or Best, you got your share. But Mooro gave as good as he got. It was unbelievably silly stuff, wind-ups, jokes, like schoolkids larking about. Mooro would be having a hot cup of tea and stirring his cup, Strongy would be looking the other way and Mooro would put the hot spoon on Strongy's hand. But it seemed funnier because Bobby was once the captain of England.

He was a terrible insomniac. If you shared a room with Mooro, he'd get up in the middle of the night and make himself a cup of tea. You'd be dozing when suddenly you would hear the kettle click on. It's probably why he had more time than anyone else because he would plan his days at night, when everyone else was asleep.

Bobby loved golf although he played conservative and simple golf. Short swing, quick, but hit it straight down the middle. Never erratic. On the Wednesday before the West Ham v Fulham FA Cup final, we went to play golf at Maldon. I was partnering Les Strong and Mooro was with Alan Mullery. Bobby and Alan teed off with good shots. Strongy went next and made a real mess of it. His first ball sliced out of bounds on the right, so he hit a second ball and that sliced off to the right, hit a tree,

Playing the captain's role again. Bobby at the helm of Peter De Savary's sponsored yacht, Blue Arrow.

went up in the air and landed in some horrendous rough ten feet further back from the tee. He had two further swipes and the ball eventually came out of the rough but he was still no further forward than the tee.

By this time Mooro and Mullers had walked off down the fairway. I stood on the tee, trying to play my shot, but I was holding the club and laughing because I couldn't stop thinking about Strongy messing up all his shots. Because I was laughing, I caught my shot on the heel of the ball and it went down the fairway, heading straight for Mullers. Before you could say 'Fore!' it's smashed him straight in the hand, his arms went up in the air and he disappeared down this verge. I knew there was a river there so we all went running over. Of course, I'm thinking Oh no! The Cup final skipper, we're supposed to be preparing and I've busted his hand playing golf! We got to the top of this verge and looked down and Mullers is there at the bottom of this ditch on his knees with his hand thrust into the stream. He had a big bump on his hand, but thankfully it wasn't broken. I can remember we had to go back to the clubhouse and once we knew Mullers would be okay, we were cracking jokes all the time. Mooro was hilarious. He was saying that Mullers had let him down, that he could've played one-handed, that he wasn't offering enough team effort and that kind of thing.

Fulham went on a trip to Sweden and we were about 5-0 up against a local side and, for the crowd's entertainment, Marshy caught a cross in the middle of the box, bent over and placed the ball on the penalty spot, so they could score a goal. The crowd loved it. The reception afterwards was first-class, champagne, fine food, and magnificent hospitality.

At about 3am, there were no cabs about so Strongy and myself strolled back to our hotel, which was about two miles away. We went down a quiet side street and saw somebody sitting in the middle of the road. It was Mooro, sitting with a bottle of champagne and a glass. We walked up to him and he looked up, his eyes glazed: 'Hello Mitch! Hello Strongy! Pull up a chair!' I said: 'You're in the middle of the bloody road, Mooro!' and he replied: 'Have...have a glass.' So we sat down and had a drink with him. After a while we said: 'Come on, we've got to get back', and the three of us eventually got back to the hotel. We had all had a few, but he was absolutely lovely with it.

We reached the hotel at 5am but we had to be up at 7am because we had to catch the hydrofoil. We virtually carried him upstairs, opened the door to his room and laughingly shoved him in. In the morning, we were waiting downstairs and all the press were there, ready to take pictures of the players. Strongy

"No one wants the Bobby Moore stickers, they keep sending them back!"

and myself were laughing to ourselves and saying there was no chance Mooro would be down. But bang on seven o'clock, his door opened – the hotel had a big open reception area where you could see up the different floors – and Mooro came walking out, absolutely upright, suit on, tie straight, shoes polished, hair brushed, immaculate. He came down the stairs, all the press were taking pictures, and Bobby said 'Morning, Gentlemen! How are we today? Fine, lovely, wonderful, super, nice to see you all,' and went straight past us, out of the reception door and got into the coach.

We all piled on the coach after him and as the coach drove off, it hadn't gone 50 yards up the road and out of sight before Mooro's head lolled back and he went straight to sleep. He was hilarious.

Fulham wasn't a club geared for on-going success, but it was a good, decent club and you looked forward to going there. We played together for three or four years and the day Bobby retired I scored four goals in a 6-1 win over Leyton Orient.

After Fulham, Bobby and I went different ways and I didn't see him for for a good few years. I went to Millwall, busted my ankle, retired, had my own business then joined Blue Arrow, which in those days was relatively unknown. We won an industry award in our first year and I went to The Dorchester to collect the prize. I walked in and there was Mooro. He said 'What are you doing here?' and I said:

'Receiving an award. What are you doing here?' and he laughed and said: 'I'm presenting it!'

The following week, I called Bobby and asked if an opportunity existed to join us, what would he be looking for. Bobby, being a modest man, suggested an equally modest sum. I added a bit on top of Bobby's amount and submitted it to Tony Berry, our chairman. His immediate reaction was 'I can't employ Bobby Moore for that amount. It's not enough!' In the end, the Chairman topped it up further so Mooro got quite a bit more than he asked for. Bobby worked there for about three years.

Our part of the company came under Blue Arrow Business Travel and Bobby's role took him across the whole group. He worked hard, got involved in various promotions, sports functions, organised golf days and arranged hospitality. He was very good at it. Conscientious and particular to detail.

His desk was always orderly and neat, not a scrap of paper out of place. He had lists of how and when to do things. As a player he organised the back four, read situations, never panicked and those aspects of his character he carried into his business work.

I later left Blue Arrow and joined Panini, the sticker company, where, with Bobby, I set up a company within it called Challenge Group. It had the basis to be very successful until a change of direction at the top of the group meant they withdrew our funding mechanism and we had to wind that part of it up.

One of the Panini collections was a World Cup stars selection of stickers, one of which was Mooro. We used to play tricks on him by leaving loads of the Bobby Moore stickers laying around. We'd hide them in books and in drawers and when he uncovered them we'd say 'Oh, look, no one wants the Bobby Moore ones. They keep sending them back!' He used to laugh.

Bobby and I decided to start our own business called Mitchell Moore Associates. It was a shame Bobby had been tarnished by rumours that he was a bad businessman. My experience of working with Bobby proved to me that this was both untrue and unfair. If people could have seen the work he put in, the things he attended, coupled with all the money he raised for charity, they would have thought differently.

He was so genuine. Bobby was equally at home with the tea lady at Fulham as he was with managing directors and chairmen. There are not too many people you can say that about.

Bobby had a saying: Work hard, play hard. But the Bobby I knew only played hard if it didn't stop him working hard.

On the Friday before he died, he called in to the office. To me, here was a guy who knew he was dying and over the last few weeks he visited everybody and everything special to him to say goodbye. He did Wembley stadium, the offices at Capital Radio and phoned everyone he needed to phone. I've got one or two people who I'm close with, on a par with Bobby, but given his background, given who he was, no one could touch him. We had a talk and he said one thing that will be with me for the rest of my life. I tend to be a workaholic, up early, late in at night, working weekends, taking stuff home, it's my nature. And Bobby said: 'Mitch, it's the quality of life, son. Think about your family and behave yourself. Quality of life.' He walked out the door and I never saw him again.

I will always miss him. Every moment you had with Bobby was a special one. Thankfully, I had a lot of special moments with him.

Peter Mellor

A goalkeeper for a number of different sides between 1969-80, Peter's clubs included Burnley, Portsmouth and Fulham.

In 1969 I came out of non-League football to play in goal for Burnley in the First Division. I had always looked upon Bobby Moore as a class act and suddenly I was playing against my idol. When I talked to him in the players lounge, I wondered whether I had the right to be in the same room as him. Thankfully, everything I assumed about him being a great guy proved to be true.

I went to Fulham in '72 and after he arrived we played over 100 games together. He always made himself available for a throw-out. I don't think I have ever distributed the ball by hand better than I did during my time at Fulham. Bobby saw the ball coming to me and the moment I recovered from the catch or save, he would be in space wanting the ball. It helped me because I wasn't too bloody good at kicking.

I asked Bobby one day: 'What made you such a great passer of the ball?' and he explained he'd been given some advice: 'Wherever you are on the field, programme your mind to think if the ball came to me now, who would I pass to?' That, Bobby said, was what he had based his game on. Bobby's rule lives on because I pass on that tip when I coach players.

I copied things Bobby did, as you do with people you admire. He had the initials BM on his shirts, so I started getting PM put on mine. That's the influence he had on many of us.

He would go quiet prior to a game, certainly for the last thirty minutes before kick-off. He would sometimes give quiet motivational talks, just a short word in your ear. 'Come for those crosses' and 'Look for me', that sort of thing. He would certainly put any youngsters in the team at ease. He was very good at remembering who put penalties where. He would say: 'He always puts it right,' or 'left' or 'high' or 'low'. At no time did Bobby use his greatness to get one over on you. Some superstars will belittle the apprentices or the youth players, but Bobby was always thinking of how he could help others.

He was no pushover on the field though. I've seen him sort a few people. He would maim anyone or go over the top, but if people kicked him, they got a whack back at some point. He was a great deal stronger than people thought and if he ever got bundled off a ball, he would invariably get a free-kick for a foul.

The '75 FA Cup run was the greatest time of my career. We weren't the best team in the world but we did have a sprinkling of quality and experience like Bobby and Alan Mullery that helped us bread and butter players. We had that bit of luck as well.

The night we got through at Maine Road against Birmingham in the semi-final replay we stayed up all night sitting around a big table in the hotel foyer and drinking champagne. The next thing we knew the morning receptionist came round shaking us all. We were all stirring and Bobby sat up and said: 'I think it's time to start celebrating!'

Bobby was so consistent with his game. Having said that, I remember one league game at Craven Cottage where Bobby put two own goals past me. Both identical headers. The ball was whipped in to the near post, Bobby tried to head it clear and both times it came off the side of his head and into the net. After the second one I bloody glared at him, but he just gave me an embarrassed grin. Sometimes he would duck a cross because he knew I was behind him. He'd joke by saying something like 'I've forgotten my shampoo today so heading is definitely out!'

After a Fulham away game one night, Alec Stock, the manager, let five of us go out to a club: Viv Busby, Barry Lloyd, Strongy, Bobby and me. A guy came up to Bobby at the bar and said: 'You're Bobby Moore, aren't you? Did you really take that bracelet?' Bobby looked at him in that usual resigned way of his, but I said: 'You shouldn't say things like that. I think it's in your best interest to clear off.' So the guy walked away, but a few minutes later, he came back and asked the same question. Bobby was still calm, but I snapped and started to wrestle with the guy. Two bouncers grabbed him, pushed me to one side and literally dragged the guy out of the club. Afterwards I said: 'I'm sorry, Bob'. He said: 'That's fine, Pete, thanks. I could never have done that, but I'm glad you did.'

Bobby gave me a signed copy of his book, which I've kept to this day. In it, he mentions about those two goals I let in at Wembley. A while later he said: 'What did you think when you read it?' I said: 'We're all human, aren't we? You want to hear what I bloody said about you when you lost that ball to Lubanksi in the World Cup qualifier in '73!' Bobby grinned. But it was all in jest.

Years after we left Fulham he bought a car from me with the money he got for making *Escape to Victory*. I won a black BMW for being Player of the Year, which I was then allowed to buy for a knock-down price. Bobby loved it. I was going out to America to live, so he gave me the dollars and I gave him the car. I heard he took it abroad somewhere and had the wheels stolen off it!

Bobby's last cup final appearance ended in defeat – by his former club. Peter Mellor can't prevent Alan Taylor scoring his second in Hammers' 2-0 victory.

In the 60s everything started to stabilize and get back on its feet, whereas during the 50s my parents were just trying to put food on the table and survive. In the 60s, football crowds returned, there were more characters in the game, more self-expression on the field and we were hungrier for it because there was little TV coverage then. But people relaxed properly. It wasn't materialistic relaxing with a computer game or a video, it was relaxing with the family and friends and going down the park and doing things together. Materialistic things have become more important than conversation in the home and love and stuff like that. Our values were better then and have become somewhat lost.

Bobby had style, on and off the field. He was the greatest professional I ever played with. He knew about values.

John Lacy

Signed for Fulham in 1972. John moved on to Tottenham Hotspur and Crystal Palace before entering non-League management.

I was only young when I played alongside Bobby at the back for Fulham. It was a great privilege. Everything he did, especially from the football point of view, was a lesson to be learned. He'd been there, seen it and done it by the time he came to Craven Cottage and what he didn't know about the game would've filled half a postage stamp.

He was always very collected, like Prince Charles. The only time I ever saw him really let go on a football pitch was when we scored our goal in the last minute of extra time in the FA Cup semi-final. Because of his age it was his last chance of playing in a cup final. We were all looking at him saying: 'What's up with Bob?' because he always kept his emotions under control. But when the ball went in he was leaping about and screaming just like our fans behind the goal. It was such a strange sight, and a reassuring one, seeing him let go.

 Moore tributes

Bobby was the perfect professional: never late for training, never moaned about aches or pains or feeling tired. He only ever wanted to do one thing: play football. For me, he did better than any Englishman has ever done before.
Alec Stock, former Fulham manager

Chapter 9
Moore respect

Jamie Redknapp

Began his career playing for Bournemouth. He was sold to Liverpool where he has since become an England international.

Bobby Moore was a close friend of my dad, Harry, and we spent our summers with him in America when I was about five. He was like 'Uncle Bob' to me. I was always having pictures taken with him. I've got one of me sitting on his knee during one of those summers in America.

He knew I loved to play football and he would often have a kickabout with me, giving me tips. Once we were at a Mike England Soccer School and a few players were taking penalties against Mike. Bobby said to me: 'Go on, Jamie, have a go.' I ran up to the ball and pointed where I was going to put it then kicked the ball. Bobby said: 'Don't tell him what corner you're going to put it in!' So next time I stuck it in the opposite corner.

I was at Tottenham as a schoolboy when I was about fourteen and one night I saw Bobby at a game. I hadn't seen him for about four years and didn't want to go over and bother him in case he didn't remember me. But he came over and started talking to me, he even remembered my name. 'Hello, Jamie,' he said. 'How you doing? How's your dad?' The other schoolboys there couldn't believe Bobby Moore knew me. I was really proud.

He had that bit of magic about him. He lifted the World Cup for England, no one had ever done that before, and who knows whether anyone will do it again?

Alvin Martin

An England central defender, Alvin played 582 games for West Ham between 1977-96.

Iwas having a meeting with Ron Greenwood and John Lyall in an hotel when I was fourteen, to discuss signing for West Ham, and Bobby came down the steps into reception. It was the first time I had ever seen him and you could tell he had something about him. I signed for West Ham as an apprentice in '74, six months after Bobby left, but no one ever missed an opportunity of using a Mooro example to show you the right way to do something. Some people try to become charismatic or make out they've got it. Bobby didn't have to. He just had it.

Ron Greenwood, Geoff Hurst and Martin Peters carry the floral wreath of the famous number six shirt before the home game against Wolves on March 6, 1993.

Tony Gale

At Fulham from 1976-1984, Tony played 359 matches for West Ham.

I took over from Bob at Fulham when he retired. When I first signed apprentice forms as a sixteen year-old, I played two games against Leyton Orient and Norwich because Bobby was playing in America and he missed pre-season. When he returned I went back to the reserves after filling in for him. We played only one game together, against Bristol City in a reserve match to get Bobby warmed-up. It was boiling hot and everyone was doing their stretching in a group out in the sunshine but the stand by the riverside cast a shadow over some of the pitch and Mooro warmed up in the shade. I remember thinking it typified him that he was shrewd and professional, even about things like that *before* the game.

Bob and I liked to play sweeper, behind an attacking centre-back, and I remember saying: 'Who is gonna attack the ball?' and Bob said: "Don't worry about it, I'll attack the ball, son, you just stay behind me.' Amazingly people said he could never head a ball, but I can never recall him losing a header. And even in a crappy game like that against Bristol City reserves, I can't remember him misplacing a pass or missing a tackle. And he wasn't really trying – it was just a run-out for someone of his calibre and he breezed through, barely breaking sweat, just loosening his legs for his initial first team game. The geezer was a class act.

I played in the reserves for a whole season and the following year Bobby retired. I took over from him in the first team at the age of seventeen.

Bob was a big face at Fulham, along with Alan Mullery, the year they got through to the FA Cup final against West Ham. The following year Fulham made the signings of George Best and Rodney Marsh. Oddly enough, I was Bobby and Rodney's boot boy – it was my job to scrub their boots after every game. I made a fatal error with Bob at the beginning because I threw away his tie-ups. Bob would use the same tie-ups all season – it was a ritual that had become a superstition with him. When I first cleaned his boots I put my hand inside them and found these soggy, crepe bandages in the bottom, so I chucked them in the bin. The next game came along and he called me into the dressing room when he was putting on his boots and said: 'Where's my tie-ups?' I pointed to the table in the middle of the room where there were about 1,000 new tie-ups in a pile. 'No, son,' he said, 'where's the tie-ups that were in my boots?' I felt terrible and didn't know what to say. 'I use the same tie-ups all season,' he explained, so I replied: 'I'm sorry, Bob, I chucked them.' I felt like crying. He just smiled and said: 'Just get me another pair and I'll use the same pair from now on, okay?' He didn't scold me or anything. I thought he was going to be angry but he just explained what he wanted.

My first tour with Fulham was to Copenhagen. The first thing Best, Marsh and Mooro did when we got there was to find the bar. They sat there all night with hundreds of women – who they weren't interested in – crowding around their table. The three of them just sat around drinking and singing to Tom Jones music all night. Every time I hear a Tom Jones record nowadays I think of those three sitting in this bar in Copenhagen getting slowly legless surrounded by admiring totty. Unbelievable old smoothies, they were.

Some years later, when Bobby worked for the *Sunday Sport*, he did a review of West Ham's game against Wimbledon, which we won 1-0. He wrote that I was the nearest thing he had seen to himself, that I had a great game, that I should already be playing for England and one day I would. For me it was the greatest praise anyone could ask for and I've kept the cutting to this day … although I'm still waiting for my first call-up!

I was really shocked when I heard the press release about his illness and then, shortly after, even more stunned by the news of his death. We played a fund-raiser match in 1995 – a rematch of the Fulham v West Ham Cup final in aid of Fulham 2000 – and I took Mooro's place for Fulham in the number six shirt. I also played in the Bobby Moore memorial game for Cancer Research after he died. Both occasions were quite moving. Everyone who played in the Bobby match got a special West Ham kit with Bobby Moore badges on the shirts and shorts, which I've kept to this day. Afterwards, Stephanie, his wife, sent me a hand-written note to thank me for playing. I think she wrote to everybody who turned out.

When I was at West Ham, just before John Lyall left, in about 1988, I was sitting in the dressing room before a game with Alvin Martin. The press had always been fond of labelling new centre-halves at West Ham the 'new Bobby Moore' and Alvin and I had been the club's central defensive partnership for a few years. Mick McGiven, who played centre-half for West Ham after Mooro left in '74, was pottering about in front of us sorting out kit. I was winding him up over something or other and Alvin was laughing at him when I said: 'Look at you, Mick, they brought you in to replace Bobby Moore and look what happened there!' Alvin was laughing about too and nearly fell of the bench. Mick threw the tracksuits he was holding into the kit skip, turned around and put us both down with one wicked line: 'Galey...' he said, 'they 'ain't never f****** replaced Bobby Moore...!'

Tony Cottee

Scored 146 goals during two spells at West Ham in the 80s and 90s.

I only met Moore twice, both times while I was at Everton. He was doing his radio work. At Goodison Park, you come out of the tunnel and have to go across the pitch to the players' car park. Bobby was sitting in the press box with his headphones and that cap on and he waved and called out. The second time he actually went out of his way to come over and shake hands, which was a nice gesture because a lot of the old pro's don't take any time to talk. He said: 'How you doing?' I think I had just scored a hat-trick against Spurs and he said: 'Nice to see you doing so well. Are you enjoying it here?. Have you settled on Merseyside?' that sort of thing. After I had finished speaking to him I thought, blimey, I've just been talking to Bobby Moore. He was that much of a star.

He was a legend to everyone, especially in the West Ham area. Recently my wife Lorraine and I moved to Chigwell and we hadn't been there two days when the milkman said: 'Bobby Moore used to live around the corner, you know?'

Steve Potts

Long-serving defender who started playing for West Ham in 1985.

I can identify with Bobby Moore because he played in a similar position to me and he had weaknesses he compensated for. I was only three years-old in 1970 but someone handed me a video of the Brazil match from that World Cup and he showed brilliant timing for some of those amazing tackles. There was the Jairzinho tackle where he was running at Moore and Bobby just stuck out a leg and took it off him, no trouble. It wasn't just that tackle, Moore did about three or four similar tackles in the same game. I can only wish for one tackle like that a season.

Steve Jones

Formerly West Ham and now playing for Charlton Athletic.

It was a big buzz for me to play for West Ham, the team I followed as a kid, but there was no greater occasion than when I played in the Bobby Moore memorial match. My most treasured shirt is the one I got from playing in that game because it has a special Bobby Moore crest on it. I have it framed in a picture in my lounge. Also, Stephanie Moore, his widow, wrote to all of us afterwards to express her thanks. It was an amazing night. Stephanie unveiled a bust of Bobby and they got all the players from the '64 and '65 West Ham teams to cut a ribbon to open the new Bobby Moore Stand that replaced the old South Bank terrace. They did some memorable team photographs out on the pitch.

I went to the gates to see all the tributes. It gave me a real lump in my throat. There was one I read that really made me think. It said: 'Dear Bobby, You will never be forgotten. Your memory and presence will always be with me.' and it was signed 'Darren, West Ham under-16s.' I know how he felt. You couldn't put that West Ham shirt on, go down that tunnel, emerge onto the pitch, without thinking about Bobby and players who had gone before.

Rio Ferdinand

Promising young defender who made his West Ham debut in 1996.

It's very flattering to have people say I'm the new Bobby Moore at West Ham, but I think it's going a bit overboard. He was a legend at West Ham. He won the World Cup, he was England captain and he proved he was the best, whereas I've only just started my career. It's going quite well at the moment but it will be a long time before people might be able to say things like that about me. I don't think there will ever be another Bobby Moore. There can't be. He was just the ultimate player. There can only be one Bobby Moore and there will only be one Rio Ferdinand. There have been some good players play for England, but not many of them have won a World Cup medal. Not only did Bobby get one, he lifted the trophy as well. 'Good' is one thing, but you only do that if you're a 'great'.

Julian Dicks

Played for West Ham from 1988-1993. After a spell at Liverpool he returned in 1994.

Bobby wrote a few articles about me but there was never any criticism, just advice and encouragement. I spoke to him on three occasions and his words gave me a lift at an important time when everyone else was putting the boot in on me. He was Mister West Ham and he never had a bad word to say about me.

Gary Mabbutt

Joined Tottenham Hotspur from Bristol Rovers in 1982 where he became captain and has played 16 times for England

I never saw Bobby Moore play live but when I was a kid living in Bristol he was my total idol. I only ever saw him on television on *The Big Match* on Sundays or *Match of the Day* on Saturday nights. I was always a West Ham fan and had pictures of Bobby around the walls of my bedroom.

The first time I ever met him in person was quite an incredible experience. I'd been at Tottenham six years and after a game I was walking through the directors' lounge when a voice said: 'Oi, Gary!' I turned around and it was Bobby. By that time I was captain of Tottenham and had played for England, yet I was totally starstruck. He said: 'Gary, I just wanted to say I've watched you playing well for Tottenham for some time and you're doing a good job. Today's game was great and you played well as usual.' I was gobsmacked. Here was my superhero saying all this to me.

I remember being virtually in tears when he made that drag-back slip against Poland that time in '73. I was devastated for him. All of a sudden my hero was public enemy number one in the playground at school. He didn't deserve to get so much stick for that one mistake.

Bobby made the number six on the back of his shirt famous. I guess it's no surprise for people to discover that's the reason I've always played in a number six shirt through most of my career.

Chapter 10

From the bench to the boardroom

Terry Venables

Trained at West Ham under Malcolm Allison, played at four London clubs, then managed Crystal Palace, QPR, Spurs, Barcelona and England.

Bobby was a couple of years older than me and already breaking into the first team when I met him at West Ham – I was a fourteen year-old schoolboy there for coaching. He was so friendly and welcoming, you knew he was a warm person straight away. He called everybody 'son' and he was only about nineteen himself. He took me to Cassettari's restaurant and paid for my lunch. That surprised me and I looked up to him from then on.

Later on, I played for England when he was captain and we became closer friends over the years. He was always aware of his conduct, his position, but when he let his hair down he was a funny guy – there were many sides to him. Ron Greenwood said his ideal player was an extrovert on the pitch and and introvert off it, and that was a little like Bobby, although he wasn't introvert. He had a good personality, but a quiet, calm one. Maybe the people who knew him saw more sides to him than the outside world did. Maybe he seemed untouchable but, in reality, he was one of the boys. Good company.

One New Year's eve, Malcolm Allison suggested I pack up playing and concentrate on coaching. I stood with Bobby and Frank McLintock at a party of a friend of ours and told them my predicament. They were very supportive and said I should keep playing but I was saying: 'I'm not going to get any better at football but I can get better at coaching.' They liked playing in front of people but my feeling was I could still play in a track suit on the training ground. We were talking in the corner for hours so we can't have been much fun at the party!

When Bobby didn't get the Watford job, I thought it was a waste of his talent, so I was the first to get him involved. I took him to Palace as youth team coach. I

think sometimes people are a bit nervous of big characters but they have so much to offer. The time Bobby was about the place was great – he had so much charisma. He got snapped up very quickly after that, moving on to Oxford City and then Southend.

The Sunday before he died, he and Stephanie were due to attend a meal with me, Bobby Keetch, Jeff Powell and our wives. But Steph rang up and said he was too weak to make it. Bobby had been saying right up to the last minute he wanted to go for the 'meal with the chaps',

Take your pick! Bobby with Terry Venables and Lawrie McMenemy.

but he couldn't make it. So we had a particularly awful night really, a very sad evening. We talked about the old days but we just didn't know what to do with ourselves. We all wished Bobby could've been there with us. Two days later, he had died.

Brian Clough

As a player, Brian scored 251 goals from 274 games at Middlesbrough and Sunderland before injury cut short his playing career. He became one of Britain's most successful managers, guiding Derby County and Nottingham Forest to the First Division championship, and Forest to two European Cup victories before retiring in May 1994.

I was a fan of Bobby Moore, the same as everyone else. You couldn't find a better role model for any footballer. Alf Ramsey liked him, so he must have been good. Alf was from the old school of managers – if Alf liked him, that's good enough for me.

When I was manager at Derby County I tried to get him away from West Ham. I met Bobby in Churchills bar in London. It's already come out that it wasn't a casual meeting. I'd talked to Ron Greenwood because I also had an interest in Martin Peters and Geoff Hurst, but Ron was adamant that none of them were going anywhere.

When we met I asked him if he was interested in winning a League championship medal. Bobby said: 'Who wouldn't?' I asked him if he'd play for Derby County and he replied: 'Why not?' When we moved to the restaurant for lunch the maitre d'hotel refused Bobby entrance because he was dressed casually. So I told them if my player can't sit in this restaurant my team would never stay there again! Did it work? Well, it must have made a difference because we ate in the restaurant. But Ron wouldn't part with him so Bobby playing for Derby County wasn't to be.

The story of the tablecloth is true. Some years later when I was at Nottingham Forest, we played Bobby's new team Fulham in the cup and I gave him a Nottingham lace tablecloth for his wife, Tina. It was a tragedy the two of us weren't able to work together and the note I wrote with the tablecloth said exactly that.

It was barmy that we didn't get him to Derby. We saw him as one of the final pieces of our jigsaw. He would have played sweeper. In that role, Moore was as good as, if not better on occasions, than the man who introduced it, Franz Beckenbauer. We would have put Colin Todd at right-back and told him to learn from the master. Colin was a player in his own right but I wanted that bit of finesse at the back. Age came into it as well – Colin could have gone on for ten years but Bobby probably had two years left at the top level.

When you're a Football League manager, irrespective of who you've got playing for you, if you see somebody of Bobby Moore's rare calibre then you pursue it and try to get him. I had a young side then, Roy McFarland was no more than 20, Todd was in his teens, so Bobby Moore's experience would have been invaluable and would have rubbed off on all of them.

Bobby was special because of this: he could intercept a football and give it to a colleague. That sounds far too simplistic, but you'd be amazed at how many people can't get the ball for a start, and, if they get it, they don't know what to do with it. Bobby Moore was one of the few players who knew what he was going to do with the ball before he even got it. He wasn't the best in the world at getting possession, but the side I had at that particular time were all 'getters' of the ball. So I didn't need Bobby to be a tackler – I had plenty of those. What I needed was for the getters to win the ball then give it to somebody who could utilise it. Bobby Moore would have fitted into our set-up like a hand into a glove.

He would have brought many strengths to Derby, mainly on two fronts. First, he would have brought special qualities to the pitch and second, his stature would have rubbed off on everybody off the field. So when we were running around chasing a game – I was a young manager and the players I had in my team were even younger – his calm assurance and approach to the game would have given us an edge and the young lads would have developed so much quicker.

I was at a learning stage at the time and some of his guile and ability would have rubbed off on me as a manager, not just the players. So instead of becoming the best in the business as a manager as quickly as I did, I would have done it a bit faster with the help of Bobby Moore.

In any given situation in a match, Bobby Moore would have known what to do and he would have known straight away. That's the ability I wanted from him. To see things others could not. It's like when you bake a Christmas cake, you put the icing on last. The icing is no good without the cake foundation and the cake isn't always as good without the icing. Bobby Moore would have been Derby County's icing.

If I'd have stayed at Derby with Peter Taylor instead of leaving, we would have 'done a Liverpool'. We won the championship when nobody thought we could, we got into the semi-finals of the European Cup, which was unheard of, and we were taking everyone by surprise because half the country still hadn't heard of us. I'll tell you what, they would have known all about us over the next five years. We were building for it and that's where Bobby Moore came in. We were preparing for the long term, not just the short term.

During the time I was at Derby, I worked for a chairman called Sam Longton, who has been dead for many years now. We were in Germany for a pre-season tour and West Ham were playing out there in a tournament, so Sam and I went to watch them. At that time West Ham were the so-and-so's of everything and their team that day was studded with stars – Peters, Hurst, Moore, and the rest. Sam tapped me on the shoulder and said: 'Will you do me a favour? Will you introduce me to Bobby Moore?' I said: 'Of course!' So we went down to the dressing room – they had great big corridors in those days and were much more advanced than our little grounds. Bobby Moore was warming up with a couple of other players so I introduced him to Sam and left them chatting for a few minutes before taking Sam back to his seat. That shows the esteem in which people held Bobby. There was Sam Longton, millionaire, chairman of a club on the up, so to speak, and he didn't want to meet anybody else but Bobby Moore. And I would've thought meeting me was enough for him!

So that's Bobby Moore. I was sad not to have worked with him. Good luck, I hope the book goes well for you, young man.

George Graham

Spent most of his playing career at Arsenal before managing Millwall, Arsenal and Leeds United

I played against Bobby when he played for West Ham. I don't know anyone who doesn't have a soft spot for the Hammers and the way they play. People think it started with the 60s Academy and their European win, but it began when they had a team of characters with Malcolm Allison, Noel Cantwell, Dave Sexton, Malcolm Musgrove and their crowd. They were all great thinkers and Bobby passed through that. It was an incredible amount of good influence. He followed in the tradition but became a far superior footballer to any of his predecessors.

People go on about Bobby being a nice man, but it was true. He was great socially and I see an image of him standing, very relaxed, with a lager in his hand. Terry Venables and I both sang at Bobby's 50th birthday party. We both wrestle for the mike at a karaoke! I think we sang a Tony Bennett number or one of the Frank Sinatra songs.

Bobby epitomised England's finest hour. They won the World Cup on home soil, so everyone could appreciate it and savour it better. Can you imagine him lifting it today? Moore would be a multi-millionaire and he could have got advertising and PR jobs for the rest of his life. Then, they were earning peanuts by comparison. He would have got the financial reward he deserved but he could not have been loved anymore by the nation. The world had him on a pedestal, including me.

For his memorial match, I was really chuffed when the FA asked me to be manager of the Premier League side. It was a lovely idea to have a player from each club represented to play West Ham. I have a lovely team photograph from that night.

When you get to the end of your career as a footballer, you realise when the fleeting glory has passed and the adulation has died down, the friends you've made in the game are one of the most important things. And Bobby had retained friendships with so many people. That says a lot about him.

It was nice to have known Bobby Moore.

Alex Ferguson

Manager of Aberdeen before taking over at Old Trafford, Alex led Manchester United to all major domestic honours, including four Premier League championships and two FA Cups between 1993 and '97.

Moore was the best defender I have ever seen. He was also a very nice man. The first time I ever spoke to him on a one-on-one situation was on a plane to Aberdeen in 1991. We sat beside each other on the flight so we had quite a long chat and he was stimulating company. I was really surprised at his affection for Manchester United. He said it was because they've always tried to play football the right way. I thought that was fantastic.

He was working for Capital so he was part of the media, yet there was none of the usual questions a journalist might ask you in a situation like that. Most would take advantage of the situation and ask me all manner of questions. For instance, we'd just drawn 1-1 with Luton but there was no: 'Oh, Alex, do you think you've thrown the League away?' questions. He was interested in me as a person, just talked football and never even mentioned whether we were going to win or lose. Not once did he talk about himself. That was refreshing.

I only ever played against him once for a Scottish League XI at Hampden – they beat us 3-0. I was centre-forward and it was a horrible, sleety night in Glasgow but playing against him I remember I didn't get kicked. A lot of people in our game criticise failures and weaknesses. The favourite one is: 'All he can do is score goals.' My opinion is forget what he can't do and celebrate what he can do. And Bobby Moore could do most things right. As I said, people criticised him for not being the biggest central defender in the world and having no pace but his timing made up for that. And Bobby's timing was impeccable. For instance, Bryan Robson's greatest asset was to be in the right place at the right time – he was last in the box but first to get the ball.

But, in Bobby's case, despite his weaknesses, he was the best centre-half England ever had, and one of the best I have ever seen. He was world-class. Those little chips he used to put up to his front players were marvellous.

In later years I saw Bobby a few times, when I was in London and he was doing the radio work. At the time, we thought he had overcome the cancer. But he always said: 'I'm fine', whether he was or not.

Gerry Francis

Played for eight clubs, captained England and won twelve international caps. His managerial career took in Bristol Rovers and QPR before he became manager at Tottenham Hotspur in November 1994.

Like many people, I was surprised Bobby did not get more involved with the management and coaching side of football when he finished playing. However, having been in management myself I know how difficult it can be and there is a lot more to it than people appreciate. Some like it but some prefer playing. From my own point of view, I'd go back to playing tomorrow if I could. It's a lot easier and less hassle. Management is a lonely job. You've got forty-odd players and you can only pick eleven, so you've got thirty players not happy with you and some people dislike that side of the job.

I was about fourteen when Bobby lifted the World Cup and I'd been on holiday to Clacton with my parents. We'd watched all the games at the camp and we were dashing back to our pre-fab in Chiswick to see the final. We got terribly held up on the way back and got home as the Germans scored their late equaliser. Bobby was a great England captain and, in later years, I was lucky enough to be skipper after him.

I've got some very cherished photographs of some events I did with Bobby. I have one taken at the launch of Bobby's biography with all the big names who came along to promote it: George Best, Jimmy Tarbuck, Elton John, Kenny Lynch, Bill Shankly, even Joe Bugner, the boxer. Another one I've kept is of all the lads at the launch of Bobby Moore Soccer Schools one year. Bobby had so much clout that when he requested your help on something, you went, no matter who you were.

I also have two photographs from Team America v England in 1976. In the first one, I'm leading out England and Bobby is leading out Team America and the second one shows me in the middle of Pele and Bobby, two of my greatest heroes. I scored that day and the pictures are something I really do treasure.

Alan Smith

After playing for Wimbledon from 1974 to '76, Alan became manager of Dulwich Hamlet. He joined Crystal Palace in '81 and was made manager in '93. Since leaving Palace, Alan has managed Wycombe, worked for BBC Radio Five live and was appointed Fulham Youth Coach in October 1997.

I was manager of Dulwich Hamlet when Bobby Moore was just made manager of Oxford City. It was horrendous really that the great man should end up being manager of Oxford. Dulwich were top of the League, going for the championship and we were his first opponents.

The television cameras were at the game, making it a real big thing that Bobby had become a manager. Before the game I milked the situation more than I should have done, winding my players up about beating Bobby Moore. We won 2-1 and I was so chuffed. I was thinking this is the only time Alan Smith is ever going to beat Bobby Moore because I was never going to do it on the field.

Directly after the game I felt terrible. Bobby came over and showed an incredible amount of humility by saying: 'Well played. I was really worried about the game, it's my first match in charge and you really played well.' Here was a guy who had won the World Cup and done everything and he was congratulating me. I was so embarrassed that I had wanted to win it so desperately just because he was the manager. I wasn't very pleased with myself, in fact, it made me feel very small. Bobby made me realise that wasn't what it was all about.

On every occasion you met him, he never spoke down to you. He listened to what you said and genuinely treated you with respect.

Some years later, when I was manager of Crystal Palace, he came to do his work with Capital Radio and I mentioned that incident to him and apologised and he said: 'Not to worry, it doesn't matter now, it wasn't important.'

Fred Street

An England physiotherapist from 1973 to 1994, Fred served under five England managers from Joe Mercer to Graham Taylor.

Bobby visited my physiotherapy clinic for a few sessions around 1990. He had sustained a routine knee injury playing for a Pele XI – the veterans often played testimonials. Bobby never looked much different from the day he raised the World Cup, he was always in good trim. One day, one of my nurses said: 'Is that really Bobby Moore with you?' and I said: 'Of course it is!' She said: 'I've always wanted to meet him,' and I replied: 'Sure, I'll ask him.' So I asked Bobby if the girl could meet him and, naturally, Bobby said he'd be happy to. When she came in she walked right up and said: 'It's lovely to finally meet you, Mr Moore, I was at school with your daughter!' He looked at me and laughed and said that had made him feel much better.

I missed out on working with Bobby during his playing days as he had finished when I started my duty as England physio. In later years, though, Bobby travelled in the press bus with Capital Radio, so I got to see him more often.

One story I heard about Bobby was from during the latter stages of his career with Fulham. He and Alan Mullery were coming off the pitch having lost and were exhausted. 'I'm bloody knackered!' said Mullery, and Bobby replied: 'Knackered? We should be grateful to even be here!'

Bobby was, undoubtedly, one of the last great captains. So many of them just spin the coin now.

Vic Jobson

Chairman of Southend United since 1984.

Bobby Moore saved Southend United Football Club. No question about it. I paid off the club's debts of £1.2m because Bobby agreed to take the manager's job. I get very angry when I hear people say he was a failure as a manager. It depends if you measure success purely on immediate results. Sometimes you can't see success as easily as that, it takes time to show up.

Bobby was one of the finest managers I've come across and my personal opinion is he would have made a very good England manager. His coaching ability was out of this world. We were in the Fourth Division and Bobby did marvels with players who were barely Fourth Division standard. We were expected to apply for re-election to the Football League but he stabilized the team and kept us off the bottom.

He used to amaze everybody at the club. Each morning he would run to the ground from his house in Eastwood and he would have a different tracksuit on every day. He'd get to the office about eight or nine o'clock, change and be immaculately dressed – he even used to wear blue socks to match his blue tie.

He'd open his mail, go through the commercial aspects of his work and then he would get Harry Cripps, his assistant, to collect the players and the balls, and find a place to train. They never had a training ground, so they used one of the school grounds or whatever place Bobby could arrange. He would coach the team, have an apple or orange for lunch and then coach the apprentices.

He would come back to his office with the balls and do some more work. Most days we would have a board meeting, sometimes until two in the morning and he would still be here for them, then run home. But he'd be back here again the following morning, as immaculate as ever in a different tracksuit.

Bob came here as commercial manager after six months working in Hong Kong where, I believe, he didn't get paid. But he wouldn't ask for money. If he got a cheque for appearance work, he gave it to the club or to charity, yet he needed it as much as anybody. When I joined I found Bob hadn't been paid for his work at Southend either and when I raised it he said: 'That's all right, I can manage.' I made sure he got his wages. Bob did the job of three men. He worked like no one else I've ever seen. It's the only way this club survived.

There were some people here who couldn't wait to get home. Five minutes after training they would be gone. But Bob never said a word, he never complained that others didn't put in as much as him. He felt they had their way of doing things and he had his.

Bob was older than all the players, but he was still easily the best player at the club. There was one frustrating problem for him. We'd be watching a player do something stupid and he'd say to me: 'Vic, why did he do that?' and I'd say: 'Because he's a Fourth Division player, Bob.'

Towards the end of the season Bobby needed to move back to London. Stephanie was working for British Airways and was flying out of Heathrow. It was a long trip to the airport. He said: 'I'll travel by train and finish the season, but I would like to leave.' I begged him to stay but he said: 'I had one marriage fail because of football, and I don't want to lose another one.' But all the press put it out that he was fired. Bob wasn't fired. I wanted him here for 20 years.

As a compromise, I made him director of football. It's a popular title these days, but he was the first. Bob had good experience and sound judgment, so why shouldn't I have used it? He came to board meetings from London and I didn't buy or sell a player or make a decison about the club without consulting Bob first. He was still on the board as director of football when he died.

I don't know of any time when he was wrong, even though his opinion may not have seemed right at the time. There were only two occasions when I went against his advice, and he was proved right on the people he warned me about over the course of time. He was a lot sharper than people gave him credit for.

Bobby did well to maintain our League position. We moved forward but not in an obvious way. Bob set the foundation for our days in the First Division. He brought in players that did well or reaped an excellent return when we sold them on. Dean Austin, Justin Edinburgh, Dean Neal, Shane Westley. I didn't touch Stan Collymore until I'd spoken to Bobby. Bob set the tone and David Webb added to it. After Bobby left, we got promoted, relegated and promoted before we reached the First Division. We did it in three years and we should have done it in two.

You can't replace someone like Bob. We'd known each other since he played for Woodford Youth and I played for Woodford Town. As chairman of Southend, I learned from the fellow and I tried to find someone I thought was the same to replace him. But they're not the same. He wasn't a saint and he wouldn't want you to call him one, but he was a very good man. I never heard him say anything bad about anyone.

Bobby's house was broken into once. He went upstairs and saw a Tesco bag in the bedroom the burglar was using to collect the gear in, but the guy had done a runner, but not before he nicked a thick gold bracelet of Bobby's. He came in next day and he said: 'Can you believe it, some sod has gone in there and nicked my bracelet?' So, for a joke, Brian Dear made a quip about the Bogota incident. 'Never mind, Bob. That's how you got it!' he jested. Bobby just laughed.

I remember when he got home one night just after moving into a new house and Tina said: 'I've let the repair people take the television.' Bobby said: 'What repair people?' and she said: 'Three blokes in white coats came and said you'd told them the TV wasn't working, so I let them take it.' Bobby said: 'What? There's nothing wrong with our TV.' He thought it was

"This tiny boy, who was holding Bob's hand, tugged on it and said: Did you ever play football?"

Kenny Lynch playing a prank but when Bobby questioned him he knew nothing about it. Three blokes had actually had the front to come and nick his telly!

At the memorial service Franz Beckenbauer was sitting at the back of the hall on his own. He'd come all the way from Germany just to pay his respects. He spoke a few words but there aren't many places where someone that great could be in the background.

Bobby was very close to his mum. She had a place in Barking and we used to call in there sometimes and have a cup of tea and a bun. A lovely little lady. She'd say: 'Have you got your vest on, son? It's cold outside, you know?' and he'd say: 'Mum, leave it out.' His mum would just tell him: 'You're still my son.' Bobby was very sad when she died, but he didn't show sadness. He would laugh in company, but he wouldn't cry.

When Bobby got his problem, we all kept it quiet because we thought that was right. He fought for three months longer than he was told. The reason he didn't want to let it out was because it would put too much pressure on his friends. Can you imagine that? He was worried about us. He took Stephanie away for a fortnight to America before he died. He wanted to have a holiday with her. It's so hard to face something like that and he had months to face it.

On school holidays we ran soccer schools where all the junior blues came along with their parents. Bobby loved getting involved with those. One day he had kicked around with the little kids and we were coming off – I was walking along behind Bobby – and this tiny boy, who was holding Bob's hand, tugged on it and said: 'Mr Moore, did you ever play football?' You might think Bobby would tell him about being England captain and the World Cup but he just smiled and said: 'Yes, I enjoyed it too.'

Bobby's integrity was beyond reproach. He played his football and lived his life in honesty. I hope people say that about me, but it is definitely something you can say about Bob.

Do you know, I named my son Robert after him?

Peter Storrie

A lifelong supporter of West Ham who became managing director in 1991.

Everyone in the East End wanted to be Bobby Moore. We wanted number six on our backs and we wanted to kick the ball over the park and play like him. I watched Bobby from the terraces and felt privileged when I got to know him in later years. He was a very ordinary chap, but with some very extraordinary qualities.

Bobby made you feel as if you had known him forever. When I became managing director at West Ham he used to ring me up quite a lot. Who am I? I'm nobody, but he's Bobby Moore. That was wonderful, to have the man I wanted to be when I grew up ring me for chats.

I went up with my dad on the supporters' train to the Manchester United semi-final in '64 and it was absolutely packed. He had warned me not to be too disappointed because we were playing United and he didn't think we would win. But we did win, 3-1, and Bobby was outstanding.

One night my parents had allowed me to go to a night game on the assurance I would be in by half-past nine. But I stayed on to get Bobby's autograph and got a good whacking when I got in late. I was saying: 'But dad, I got Bobby Moore's autograph!' It didn't make any difference. Years later I told Bobby I'd got ten of the best because of him. He thought it was hilarious.

His death was a total shock to me. First of all, when I started getting phone calls from the press that morning, I thought it was a sick wind-up, but then I just went numb. It was the same for everyone at the club.

We took some solace from being able to name the new South Stand after him. The timing of the rebuilding meant we were able to make the gesture. A few people asked why we didn't name the Centenary Stand after this player or that player but, we at the club, were opposed to naming it after another player because it would undermine the significance of naming a stand after Bobby.

I'd love to be able to say there will be another local lad out there who will become the next Bobby Moore, but I don't think there ever will be another West Ham centre-back playing over a hundred games for England and raising the World Cup. Bobby's name was known in every corner of the globe.

My proudest possession, which I've had for some years, is a picture of Bobby in different strips that I've got hanging on the wall of my office. It is a nice reminder. Some of the tributes left by the gates when he died were burned and the ashes laid under the stand but we've kept a lot of the items and eventually they will be displayed down the corridors within the stadium.

Bobby meant so much to everyone in this area. We had fifty schoolkids, aged around eleven, from St Edwards School next door come in for a tour of the ground. I led them out on to the pitch area and said: 'This is the Bobby Moore stand and we forget because it was a long while since he played,' but virtually every child knew who Bobby Moore was. So it goes on. And I think it will continue.

Ken Bates

Chairman of Chelsea since 1982.

Bobby will never grow old in people's minds, in the same way that President Kennedy won't. Camelot, the name given to Kennedy's era, has always seemed real because we remember Kennedy as a young man and it will always be the same with Bobby. 1966 has become football's Camelot because all the photographs and memories of Bobby show him as we want to remember him – a young hero.

It was a very dramatic game, what with the disputed goal and the late 'They think it's over' effort. I know where I was - in the Bahamas. I'd seen every England game up to the final and then had to take the kids on holiday. Of course, in '66 you didn't have all the televisions you have now, so I think there was a little paragraph about it in the local paper in the Bahamas with: 'England beat Germany 4-2 in the World Cup final last night'. So I went and had another drink to celebrate.

It was clearly the highlight of Bobby's career and he'll be remembered as this blond adonis holding up the World Cup. People remember him in his prime, the boyish figure, never a hair out of place, fit, slim, handsome and athletic.

I never knew much about him, because he was a private person. But he was also very dignified. I only really met him once in his playing days, when he was captain of West Ham and I was chairman of Oldham.

Displaying the Charity Shield which Hammers shared with Liverpool in 1964.

In the game, Oldham got a penalty and Bobby Moore stood behind the penalty taker and signalled to the West Ham goalkeeper which way he was going to shoot, and, sure enough, he shot the way Bobby pointed and the goalkeeper saved it. Oldham got an equaliser eventually but we lost the replay at Upton Park.

I went into the West Ham dressing room and said: 'Good luck in the Cup!' Bobby Moore looked round, as he was tying his tie, and said: 'Thank you very much, Mr Chairman, and good luck to you too.' He was very gracious.

People will talk about what he did in that Brazil game in the '70 World Cup and, to my mind, he played some of the most elegant and effective football I have ever seen in the game. But equally he should be credited with his behaviour outside of football, after he finished playing. Whatever the temptation, he never knocked the sport in that period, he never used the things he knew to settle scores or make easy cash. I think he was a man who could not hurt people, either on or off the field.

Reg Burr

Chairman of Millwall from 1986 to '95, now a director and life-president

This might sound jingoistic, but I'm not ashamed to say it because it's the truth. 1966 meant the final chapter of World War Two could be closed. We had beaten the Germans twice at their game and once at ours. And we did it at Wembley, in the final of the World Cup. It was wonderful.

It was like VE day all over again. In fact, it was better because on VE day I was injured after the war. As a country, we had been going through a bit of a tough time and it was something we could all latch onto and feel proud of again. And Bobby's type of Englishness drew on the better side of our national character, on our sense of fair play and of dignity and determination in the face of overwhelming odds.

Bobby was a man of the 50s, stuck in the 60s. In fact, all of Sir Alf's players were like that. Well-turned out and disciplined. A team reflects the manager and Alf was a pre-war player, short back and sides, no nonsense.

If we're honest, in the decades after the war, there was still a lot of left-overs from it, feelings and suchlike. It was still very fresh in people's minds because, other than the very young, they had all experienced it. A lot of people have forgotten now, we are a few generations further on, but we had something like six million casualties.

Winning the war made us quietly pleased with ourselves and '66 became a reminder some years afterwards that we could still win things. I suppose Bobby reminded people of an era when, by and large, they were better behaved towards each other. The 40s and 50s may not have been like that, but it didn't matter: Bobby Moore showed us that football could be like that and if football could, well, so could life.

I think people like Bobby often find football management impossible because it is very hard for great players to understand why people can't do what they find so easy. When I first went down to Luton in the Fourth Division the football was joke. I said to the manager: 'That player can't play!' and the manager said: 'I know but he kicks everything and that's what you need in this division.' He was right, but I couldn't see Bobby tolerating that level of football.

What stunned me at the time of Bobby's death was the reaction of younger people. Our players at Millwall were very upset. Some very great footballers have died in the past and you might have expected our lads to say: 'Oh yeah, he's dead,' but they treated it very seriously. People of all ages felt we had lost a link to a better, more decent, time and I think they were right. Bobby was a guy who never looked out of breath and never ill-treated the ball like they do nowadays. He always stroked it around the pitch magnificently. There are some players who have one or two of Bobby's attributes, very few have several and none have all.

Two goal hero Alan Sealey celebrates with Bobby and Ronnie Boyce after winning the European Cup Winners' Cup at Wembley in 1965

Chapter 11
Whistle blowers

Jim Finney

A Football League referee from 1959 to 1971

In all the West Ham games I refereed during my career, I never booked Bobby, and I only admonished him once. That was when Graham Leggat of Fulham clattered into him. Bobby waited his turn and a little later, when his opponent was on one leg, he belted him back. Bob didn't kick him, he just hit him with his shoulder and Leggat was sent flying five yards on to his backside. I said: 'Bob, that's the first time I've had to give a free-kick against you. I know you did him because he got you earlier, so let's have no more of this nonsense.' He replied: 'Fair enough, Jim.'

In the 1966 World Cup tournament I refereed a couple of games in the northeast with Russia, North Korea, Italy and Chile. I did the quarter-final between West Germany and Uruguay in Sheffield and was more or less nominated to referee the final until England got there. During the final I was sat in front of the Royal Box with the other referees and Rudolf Kreitlein, the German official, was filming the match with his own cine camera. He wasn't too pleased when we scored in extra time. We all went to the banquet afterwards and I can remember the MP George Brown standing outside on a car and conducting the crowd in community singing.

I nearly got arrested with Bobby once. I spent seven weeks in America with

Jim Finney (centre), refereeing Bobby's testimonial against Billy McNeill's Celtic

the West Ham squad in 1963 and six of us went down to Coney Island beach one day and all we had on were our swimming trunks. It was quiet on the beach so we walked up to the boardwalk for a drink. I was standing a few feet from where the lads were drinking, looking out to sea, when a fellow came up and said: 'I'm a detective, you're not allowed to be on the boardwalk in trunks, so if you don't move on, you'll be arrested.' He told us we could only wear longer shorts, so I said: 'Quick, lads, you've got to cover up or we'll finish up in the bloody nick!' We all drank up and went back to the beach.

I refereed Bobby's West Ham testimonial, against Celtic in 1970, when Jock Stein was their manager. Bobby gave us all a cigarette lighter in the shape of a World Cup. It still takes pride of place on my coffee table to this day.

Jack Taylor

Began refereeing in 1955 and was in charge of the 1974 World Cup final between West Germany and Holland. He retired in 1978.

I came across Bobby Moore in the late 50s. He had enthusiasm and a will to win, but he also had respect for the officials. He didn't argue. Even when he became a household name, his attitude didn't change.

Sadly, in today's society, people want to hear about misdemeanours. You remember the ones who were trouble, but not the ones who were no trouble at all. West Ham were a club who traditionally produced well-disciplined players and young referees starting out would often be assigned to Upton Park matches because they would get respect there.

Bobby would always see fair play and we would usually have a chat when he came up to toss the coin. I didn't know him well but a referee seldom does. He was the ideal choice for England captain. He gained respect without bullying players.

In the '66 World Cup I was refereeing matches for countries like Korea and Italy, who played their games in the north of England, but I was at Wembley for the final. There were 30 referees from all over the world and we had a table at the banquet after the match. I remember going out on to the balcony and looking at the huge crowds outside. We were united through sport. For everyone there, it was a night we will never forget.

After the final, I recall Bobby going round and congratulating the team, thanking Alf Ramsey, always giving the praise to others.

Of course, the other decision that went their way was the crossbar goal in the final. All the referees had stayed together in the same hotel for the tournament and Tofik Bakhramov, the Russian linesman who gave the decision for that Hurst goal, was in the next room to me. Tofik didn't speak any English at all, although his French was good so I'm told. The Swiss referee, Gottfried Dienst, spoke reasonably good English and German, but there's no way the two of them could have communicated!

Afterwards, through interpreters, I remember asking Bakhramov if it was in but

I was never convinced. Bakhramov was situated somewhere between the six and eighteen yard mark, he certainly wasn't on the goal-line. Of course, it is hypothetical because the referee's decision is final anyway.

In '70 I was refereeing in Mexico City and England were in the Guadalajara area. The only time I saw England play was when they were defeated in Leon by West Germany. I actually believe that England '70 side was the best England side we have ever produced.

When England were knocked out, most of the squad went straight home or on holiday, but Bobby stayed on to work for television and moved up to Mexico City. I saw quite a lot of him in the last part of the tournament and often found myself sitting with him or watching training together.

When I retired from refereeing in 1977-78, I received the players' merit award, which is the only time a referee has ever won it. Everybody thinks that referees are bastards. By voting for me, the players were saying I was still a bastard, but at least they were saying I was a fair one!

Among others, I remember getting a letter from Bobby. It said: 'Congratulations and well done'. Coming from him it was an especially nice touch.

For a few years after that I was commercial manager at Wolverhampton Wanderers. I saw Bobby only fleetingly, but there would always be a polite hello. I worked for the Football League as co-ordinator for the sponsors and had a lot to do with the Rumbelows Cup. Bobby, myself and Denis Law recorded a television advert for the Rumbelows Cup. All three of us just spent three days joking and reminiscing about the old days.

There are people I've got respect for in football, but I can't think of anyone I've had more respect for than Bobby Moore.

Chapter 12
Moore than a mate

Michael Caine

Michael's acting career took off with his first major role in 'Zulu' in 1963. By the time he had played secret agent Harry Palmer in 'The Ipcress File' ('64) and 'Alfie' ('66), he was a big star. He also appeared with Bobby in the film 'Escape To Victory'.

I met Bobby during the filming of the movie *Escape to Victory* in 1981 and saw very little of him after that film. I hardly knew him but I have especially firm impressions of him.

I find it ironic that having lived in London at the same time as Bobby for forty years, we never came across one another, yet met in Hungary for the first time. We came back to London where we both lived and hardly saw each other again. When you're an actor, you're always travelling so I was always off on some movie or other and I didn't even get to see friends I've known for years.

At the time of *Victory*, I was quite a heavy drinker but he and Mike Summerbee used to leave me sprawled under the tables somewhere in Budapest and had to find my own way home, I'm afraid! Unfortunately, I didn't spend a lot of time socially with Bobby and the one or two evenings I did spend with him I have absolutely no recollection of at all. We really cut a swathe through Budapest, I must say.

I have always been, and still am, a big football fan, so I was aware of Bobby for nearly all his footballing career – right from when he was playing in his early days for West Ham. I was a Millwall fan when I was young because I came from South London, but everyone was aware of Bobby. I put him on the same level as Sir Stanley Matthews – a great footballing gentleman. In some ways, it goes along with the movie stardom rule that the bigger the star, the nicer they are. Bobby was a supreme example of that.

Victory was a lot of fun to make. Incredible. People say the reason the Germans didn't score was because the Allies had Rambo in goal. It's all so long ago and lost in the dim recesses of my mind, but Bobby was always very quiet as far as the film-making was concerned. He watched it very closely and his main concern was to get what he did right. He took it very seriously indeed. As far as the football was concerned, he was consulted but, then, of course, we were inundated with football specialists with Pele and all the other senior players.

Sadly, I met Bobby on the set of *Victory* and virtually said goodbye to him on the set of *Victory*. I also saw him in Langans restaurant and had coffee with him once or twice, but he was usually with company.

I remember '66 though. I was working on a film in America. I never saw the final but heard it on the radio. The Americans didn't cover it on television so I used to listen to the BBC World Service. I always travelled everywhere with a shortwave radio, even to this day. I know I didn't get home, I think I was in Los Angeles, so the time difference was vast, but I did manage to see the match about three days later because they showed it on one of the sports stations in the States. A marvellous game.

Apart from the World Cup win, the 60s themselves were a bit special. In any field of endeavour that you care to think about, people started to excel. It wasn't just a few actors becoming famous or a couple of rock n' roll groups, it was all over the place: writers, playwrights, artists, sportsmen, musicians, hairdressers, photographers - everyone. It all went through the roof. It happened for Bobby in much the same way. He started playing football and became world famous. Everyone was doing their own thing and it was a great time.

He was revered because of his position as the captain of the team that won the World Cup. He was almost revered as 'Saint Bobby'. It was a reverence which could go to the head of someone with an ego, but he didn't seem to have that kind of ego. He had the normal ego we all have - for instance, he was always very smartly turned out and had a great taste in clothes, so he had enough ego to do that, but he did not consider himself better than anybody else because of his position. He merely regarded it as his job, the thing he did, and he was grateful for his good fortune.

Bobby was the greatest gentleman in football. He stood out. I'm not saying most footballers are ruffians, but he did stand head and shoulders above the rest as both a gentleman and as a gentle human being.

Kenny Lynch

Kenny met Bobby at the Ilford Palais dance hall when they were local East End celebrities. He was singing in the local pubs and clubs and Bobby was captain of England schoolboys. Their close friendship spanned some 38 years and they had their own company, Lynch-Moore Associates

Bobby never told me about his first bout of cancer. I asked him about it and he said:'Oh, what difference does it make? That was ages ago,' so I never brought it up again. Bobby always had an unselfish reason for doing things and you could guarantee it was in your interests.

The night before he died, Bobby phoned at eleven o'clock. Unusually, I hadn't spoken to him for a week, since the England v. San Marino game at Wembley, and he didn't look too bad that night. I didn't recognise the voice at the other end of the phone. 'Who's that?' I asked.

'It's me!' he said. 'Who do you think it is?', but his voice was very weak. Then he said: 'I was worried about *you*.'

I'd had a bypass operation some eight weeks before. 'Never mind *me*, I was worried about you.'

He said: 'I'll tell you what we'll do . . . you worry about me, I'll worry about you, and I'll speak to you tomorrow.'

So I said: 'Okay, that's a deal,' and he put the phone down. That was the last thing he ever said to me.

He died at six o'clock the following morning. Stephanie, his wife, phoned at ten o'clock, as I was about to go off to appear on *The Gloria Hunniford Show*. She said: 'Bobby died at six o'clock.'

I was like . . . gutted. I wasn't expecting it because Bobby was . . . invincible. I was sitting on my bed and I didn't know whether to shoot myself or disappear up my own backside. I thought, sod the TV show, so I rang the director and said: 'I can't come in.' I walked about my house in a daze all day. I went to bed early, at eleven o'clock, which is unlike me. I was crying – I didn't even cry when my parents died.

I had been crying for about an hour when I started to think about the things Bobby and I had done together. By three o'clock I was creased up in bed with laughter, thinking about a trip we took to Brazil for a celebrity golf tournament. I suggested Bobby came along and he said: 'I'd love to but I don't really play golf.' So he went out on the driving range and after four days was hitting the ball well

> "He had set lines: 'All right? How's your family?' – they were probably bloody orphans, he didn't know!"

enough, although he never got as far as hitting woods – he used a four iron for everything, even to tee-off, and I almost had to stop him putting with the bloody thing!

The first day in Rio we played a few holes and we were eating our meal in the hotel restaurant when Ronnie Biggs walked in with five huge geezers – the ones who kidnapped him. They told us they were working on the James Bond movie and had returned to do some stunts for inserts, which was quite feasible. We had a drink with Ronnie and these guys and that was that. Later, when the kidnap story came out, one of the tabloids did a feature claiming: 'Bobby Moore and Kenny Lynch involved in kidknapping Ronnie Biggs from Brazil', which made us laugh.

The next day, we went out to the course on our own because Bobby didn't want people watching him scuff his four iron down the fairway, but there was a guy following us. Bobby said: 'Who's that bloody geezer? Find out who he is! I can't concentrate with him watching us!' We asked the guy and he explained he was from the Brazilian Football Association and they wanted Bobby to present Pele with a pennant at an Old Brazil v. New Brazil charity match at the Maracana stadium. Bobby wanted to decline the offer – it wasn't his scene to present things in front of 200,000 people. As a joke, I said: 'If you do it, I'll come on with you!' But Bobby took me seriously and asked if I could come on with him. The Brazilian guy agreed, so Bobby said he would do it.

We went to the Maracana, which is enormous, and Pele even gave us a tour of the stadium beforehand. They introduced Mooro over the tannoy and the crowd booed him, although they were laughing. Mooro and I walked out, handed over the pennant, Pele said: 'Thank you,' shook hands with Mooro and also shook hands with me. The referee and linesman shook hands with Mooro and me and I could see they were all bemused, thinking: 'Who the hell is this guy with Bobby Moore?'

As we came off the pitch the crowd threw a barrage of rubbish at us: eggs, tomatoes, fruit, vegetables, the lot. Bobby was dressed immaculately, like David Niven: new slacks, new shirt, jumper draped over his shoulders, and we were being pelted with all this muck. I spotted two tomatoes hadn't burst, so I threw them back at the crowd. Bobby shouted: 'Stop that, you dozy sod!' He was looking down at his messed-up outfit and more tomatoes were hitting his clothes. 'Look at the bloody state of me! This is a brand new jumper!' he shouted. 'It's all your fault – if you hadn't thrown those tomatoes, they wouldn't have thrown stuff at us!', and I replied: 'But they threw 'em first!' I can't explain how funny and ludicrous it was, but I was laughing – he was convinced we got covered because I threw the tomatoes back. I was thinking about this in bed on the night he died and I couldn't stop giggling.

During that Brazil trip, we went to a party whose host had a beautiful Swedish wife. As soon as we arrived she nabbed Bobby and I for a drink and introduced us to her friend. We were chatting when Brian Close, the cricketer, came up and asked if we wanted drinks. We'd seen him sitting by the pool wearing a handkerchief with four knots on his head and a pair of army shorts. He looked at the two girls and, in his broad Yorkshire accent, said: 'By 'eck, if you were racehorse, you'd win f****** Derby!' Bobby and I laughed out loud it was so funny. From then on, the 'racehorse' line became a running joke between us, right up to when he died.

Bobby had this annoying habit of ringing every day to ask how I was. He would say: 'Hello, Ken? You all right? I just wanted to see how you are, you all right?' I'd say: 'Of course, I'm all right! Why are you asking me if I'm bloody all right? I left you only a few hours ago!' He did it with everybody. If we were going out, I'd ring and say: 'I'll pick you up at six-thirty, okay?' When I got there, I'd get out of the car and he'd say: 'Hello, Ken? How are you? You okay?', and I'd say, 'You just asked me that on the bloody phone!'

Bobby liked people. He would stop and talk to anyone, sign autographs, and he would never say no, unless he had to genuinely go somewhere. Jimmy Tarbuck was forever saying: 'Come on, don't yak to them forever, we've got to go.' But Bobby would chat for hours, even to ones he didn't know. He always remembered people. In fact, I've never met anyone in the public eye who had so much time and energy for everyone like Bobby did. Personally, I never once saw him be rude. Bobby sensed when people were in awe and he went out of his way to put them at ease. He had set lines: 'All right? How's your family?' – they were probably bloody orphans, he didn't know – but when people left him they felt a million dollars.

You learn what to expect from people and I never expected Bobby to do anything bad to me. Most people have some kind of fault. They put themselves first, for instance, but Bobby didn't do that. I've got friends who would stand in front of a bullet for me, but if you had a nice woman you'd turn your back and they would be

Bobby with Kenny Lynch and George Best. Kenny named his second daughter, Bobbie, after Bobby. She was born just a few months after Moore died. Stephanie Moore is Bobbie's godmother.

asking for her number. But not Bobby.

Bobby hated the thought of someone saying bad stuff about him. It hurt him to be disliked. He wouldn't do anything sly or snide to anybody. The worst thing Bobby did was drink with the lads. He might get told off by the club, but it wouldn't occur to him to be nasty. He thought everyone was a nice guy.

Bobby preferred people to be themselves and when he was drinking with the lads there wasn't any pressure on him. When we got together, we were footballers or showbusiness people and we didn't think about being famous – it's just another bunch of mates out on the town. The sanctuary of a relaxed drink with the lads was very important to Bobby.

I was forever ribbing him about things like his pace: 'You're not fit, you tart, you're just slow,' I'd say to him. 'Of course you can play for 90 minutes – at your pace you could play for four hours!' Bobby got quite good at golf and was on a few winning teams, so I would say: 'How come you won? Let me check that bloody score!', and I would regularly wind him up about the tickets he got me for the '66 final: 'What about them sodding tickets? Right at the bloody back, the very last row, it was like watching Subbuteo, I couldn't see a bloody thing!' Bobby would reply: 'Sorry, Ken, I didn't know, we just got given them.' He apologised, even before he had heard what I was going to say.

Bobby liked being with people he knew. Trouble was, everybody thought they knew him. I think he got blindsided by people's intentions or capabilities. He always believed everyone was honourable. So maybe he was a bit gullible out of his own niceness. And because he wouldn't dream of behaving badly to others, he never suspected for a moment people might do things to him. Bobby knew football inside out but he was on uncharted territory in business. He had to find alternative sources of income. Some people dabble and get lucky, but Bobby wasn't. And everything that could go wrong in these ventures, unfortunately did go wrong.

Seven of us were supposed to put money into the Woolston Hall Country Club. The original idea was that we would each do one night a week – celebrity faces to bring in the crowds. I went on a trip and when I came back they had got someone else in. They spent a fortune, but it was a big disaster. Before they could open there was a fire and one of the partners had a shotgun fired at his house. The debts mounted, the profits were non-existent so the bank finally called in the loan and Bobby had to pay a lot. He didn't say much about it, but he took his knocks that way.

Bobby had quite a successful leather goods business with Freddie Harrison and Morris Keston, called Harrison-Moore. They made all sorts of leather and suede stuff and I had a lot of gear from them, we all did, at trade prices as well. I had a beautiful suede trenchcoat, but I left it at a party or something. Tarby, Mooro and I went to a Billy Eckstine concert at The Talk of the Town and Billy announced we were sitting in the audience. Afterwards we were invited backstage to meet Billy and when we got into his dressing room he was wearing one of Mooro's suede jackets. Bobby was really chuffed.

Through the 60s Bobby and I spent a lot of time together. We would go out after matches for a drink to The Black Lion in Plaistow or for a meal with Tina and my girlfriend, Dorothy. Bobby loved music: James Taylor, Michael McDonald, Doobie Brothers, Stevie Wonder, those kind of singers, and we went to a few concerts. Bobby and I were always up to something. We sang in the car driving home at night and Bobby couldn't sing a note, flat as a pancake, but we'd be laughing all the time.

> **"I was forever ribbing him about things like his pace. You're not fit, you tart, you're too slow, I'd say to him"**

Bobby and I did a scene in an Alf Garnett film called *The Garnett Saga*. In the scene we go to The Black Lion for a drink -- we did that virtually every week so I suggested to Johnny Speight, the writer, he put it in the script so we didn't change our routine! Bobby and I were drinking and Alf wandered over drunk, shouting: 'Oh, look, it's our Bobby, the captain of England! And look! He's with the coon singer!' I had to say: 'Tell him to p*** off!' We did about 30 takes of this scene because Bobby and I kept giggling. It took hours. The problem got worse because I was topping up my pint, but the moment you put a lager in Bobby's hand it was gone! I was saying: 'Will you stop drinking that stuff!'

The Mayor of Margate asked Tarby to get a side to play a Sunday match, but in the 60s players got pulled up by the union for playing celebrity matches. But we got Mooro, Brian Dear, Frank Lampard and West Ham's black defender, Johnny Charles. As they couldn't play as themselves, Tarby suggested we introduce them as showbiz stars. We announced Bobby as the 'Bass player for The Kinks' and Frank Lampard was 'Backing vocals for The Drifters!'

Afterwards we were getting changed and I was sitting next to John Charles and I said: 'Will you sit over there because I keep washing your bloody leg!' I couldn't believe it, but Charlo went and sat with Mooro. We were all in stitches.

When Bobby got arrested over the bracelet nonsense, I telephoned the consul in Bogota hoping to speak to him. They said: 'Only his family can speak to him.' To which I said: 'I *am* family.'

'But you said your name was Mr Lynch?' the guy said.

MOORE **than a legend**

Thinking on my feet, I replied: 'Yes, that's my stage name. My real name is actually Kenny Moore.'

'Ah,' said the geezer, 'Kenneth More? The film star?'

'No,' I said, 'same name, different guy.'

He finally put me through and said: 'Mr Moore, it's your brother Kenny on the phone,' and I thought, I hope the soppy sod doesn't say: 'I haven't got a brother called Kenny,' but he came to the phone and asked: 'Who is this?'

'It's me, yer schmuck!' I said.

Bobby was surprised: 'How did you get through?'

'I lied and said I was your brother,' I explained. I told Bobby to wait there, that everything would be all right and that I was on my way to Bogota.

'Don't you dare come here!' he said. 'If you turn up, I'll get four f***** years!'

After a match West Ham played in Belgium, Ron Greenwood said to the team: 'Go and enjoy yourselves!' and had gone to bed as usual. Mooro, Johnny Byrne and I went to this quaint little bar and Johnny bet us twenty five quid he could drink a measure from every bottle behind the bar – this was before we'd heard of alcoholic poisoning. The drinks had dust on them and were some sickly colours, but Budgie started drinking. The barman was begging: 'No, no!,' with Budgie saying: 'Keep 'em coming!' He got through about 20 measures, so we said: 'You've got our money.' After some arguing, Budgie reluctantly called it a day. 'All right, but I'll finish off this last one,' and he picked up this drink of green muck, knocked it back in one go, fell straight on the floor and never woke up for eleven hours. I thought he was dead! Me and Mooro carried this big lump up to the room. We couldn't wake him up, we poured coffee down him, he was groaning, and finally we got him on the plane. I always shiver when I think about it.

> **"Don't you dare come to Bogota! If you turn up I'll get four f****** years!"**

After Bobby's spell as manager at Oxford City, Lawrie McMenemy asked him to work with the kids at Southampton. Weeks later, I asked Lawrie how Bobby was getting on and he said: 'It was weird. Bobby only did one day, the kids loved him, but he never came back.' Whether Mooro didn't like the long trip to Southampton or what, I don't know. Bobby was lost after he stopped playing. He did apply for the England manager's job once after Don Revie left but he never got a reply from the Football Association.

Bobby was often asked to name his favourite footballer and he would say: 'I've played against too many great players to choose one.' I asked him once and he said: 'It's difficult, but I have to say Pele. The others – Cruyff, Best, Beckenbauer – were all great, but when Pele first came on the scene, he did things I'd never seen before. He caught the ball on his thigh and volleyed it.' Beckenbauer was Bobby's hero, but Pele was his idol.

In the 80s, Bobby, Martin Peters, Geoff Hurst and myself did a football cabaret event at Gatwick - it was a forerunner to the *Sport in Question* format Jimmy Greaves and Ian St John use on the television, with a panel answering questions from the audience. The master of ceremonies was stuck in traffic, so I did it. I said to Mooro: 'We should do this and earn a few quid.' So we started Lynch-Moore Associates, began The Bobby Moore World of Soccer roadshow and we dragged in our mates – Malcolm Allison, George Best, Steve Perryman, Alan Ball and Jimmy Greaves. I was master of ceremonies and the audience asked questions.

When we did that roadshow, we might have drunk lager 'till six in the morning, then drive from Leicester to Bristol next day. When I got up I felt really rough but Mooro looked like he'd come out of a bloody sauna! Worse still, no matter how drunk he got, he would fold his clothes up before we went to bed. It drove me mad. When you're pissed and someone's doing that, it's like a work of art, you can't stop watching them, can you? He sat on the bed folding everything up and laying it out symmetrically.

We gave Bobby Moore's World of Soccer the elbow after five years when the work dried up. We bought some shares in it for 11 pence: the first day the price went up a penny, then next day they sank to about four bloody pence and stayed down ever since. Bobby was a great picker of shares!

Bobby and I drove up to the gates of Upton Park where a bloke was selling *Bulldog,* the National Front magazine. I said: 'Look at that schmuck!' and Bobby said: 'What do you mean?' I said: 'That bloke is selling the National Front paper.' The window on the car was open and the seller said: 'Wotcha, Mooro!' and when he caught sight of me in the passenger seat, added: 'What are you doing with that black bastard?' Bobby didn't say anything. He just shot the geezer a long look, wound up the window, drove through the gates and never said a word.

Bobby was always coming out with dry one-liners. We went to the 1988 FA Cup final between Liverpool and Wimbledon. Vinnie Jones was having a nightmare. He was tackling well but every time he passed it went to a Liverpool player. Bobby said: 'If we go out tonight, remind me not to take Vinnie because he'll be passing the drinks to the wrong people!'

The night he passed away I realised my memories of him wouldn't die, because I have so many. I kept finding photographs of him in my house, so I made a scrapbook. There was one of us in Spain, one in Portugal and some I didn't even remember where they were taken.

Bobby Moore was a great pal and barely a day goes by when I don't think about him. He was a really unbelievable man.

Michael Parkinson

Michael is a journalist and broadcaster who currently presents shows on Radio Five live and is a columnist with The Daily Telegraph.

I was a friend of Bobby's, but not a close one, although I was a great admirer of his. I first met him in 1970 when we played in a charity football match in Harlow New Town against a local side. Our forward line was: myself, Elton John and Rod Stewart, and in defence were Bobby, George Cohen and Jack Charlton.

MOORE **than a legend**

The local centre-half thought he was a hard man and he knocked Elton John down in the first few seconds. Elton's glasses came off and the guy trampled on his glasses and broke them. Of course, you might as well have taken Elton's left leg off – he can't see a thing without his glasses.

The man who fouled Elton was a lunatic. In fact, their whole team were mad – they acted like they were playing professionals and were kicking us. Rod Stewart went for the guy who kicked Elton and Bobby intervened, saying:'No, no, son, leave it out, it'll be all right.'Three minutes later, however, they found the guy who broke Elton's glasses face down in the mud and had to carry him off. Nobody saw what happened, but he had been attended to by Bobby.

I was playing on the right wing and Bobby said:'Michael, watch me.When I get the ball, I'll point where you should go.' So he pointed, I ran and he would send an inch-perfect pass inside the full-back, but right down into the far corner of the ground. It was a terrible thing to do to someone of my poor physical condition. It meant I had to run about 100 yards further than I'd done in my bloody life and after the third time of chasing his passes I fell down and was sick on the spot. Bobby thought it was hugely funny. In those days they used to have a cuttings service and my favourite cutting of all time said: 'On the right wing, Parkinson responded to the expert prompting of Bobby Moore.' I showed it to Bobby who thought it was hilarious.

I never had Bobby on my TV show, although I did a couple of interviews with him. We did a film called *The Boys of 66* twenty years after the World Cup, by which time I'd got to know him better and we did the interview in the royal box at Wembley, which was a nice touch given his memorable encounter with the Queen that day. He wasn't the greatest talker. He was funny when he relaxed with you, when he could trust you and talk football, but it wasn't his forte doing talk shows.

He was a very engaging companion. My wife Mary and I often went to dinner with him. Nice is a horrible word, but it suited him down to the ground.

Mike Summerbee told me a marvellous story. Mike was playing for Manchester City against West Ham and committed a dreadful foul on Frank Lampard, a grotesque foul, and no sooner had Mike kicked him up in the air he thought:'Oh Christ, what have I done?'As he turned away, Bobby came up, eyeball to eyeball. He didn't shout, but just said:'Now, Mike, that wasn't a very nice thing to do, was it?' Mike said he felt terribly guilty. That was Bobby's charm, he wasn't demonstrative, but he had his way of making it known when he disapproved.

Bobby Moore was a proper hero. In '66 he was that slender boy holding up the World Cup in his red England shirt with three lions on his chest without any sponsors' name on it. If you think about what has happened in the years since, there has been a loss of innocence, the game has changed, it has got more glitzy. It has changed at its soul, and it has changed for the worst. But Bobby represented what everyone thinks of as the best. Football was nicer then, with real heroes.You went to a match and you didn't get your head kicked in and people didn't scream and swear and abuse players in the way they do now.

Bobby was a lovely, lovely man. Impeccably behaved, on and off the field.When people have long forgotten some of today's spitting, snarling footballers, people will still talk of Bobby Moore.

Jimmy Tarbuck

Comedian and TV personality who has known Bobby since the early 60s.

Bobby Moore was one of the great companions of life. You always had a good time with him. He had a very unique sense of humour. He was a national hero with film star looks. A very well-dressed fellow indeed and the world's greatest lager-drinking champion.

We played in many celebrity matches. In one big game we were in the dressing room, I was captaining the side, and Bobby said to me: 'I have to tell you Jimbo, this is the first time I haven't led the team out in ten years.' I said: 'I'm ever so sorry Bob, I didn't know, do you want to?' He replied: 'No, no, I just wanted you to know.' The ground was packed to capacity and we're walking down the tunnel. I've got the ball and I strode out with the great Moore behind me. I was talking over my shoulder to Bob saying: 'Look at this crowd, it's fantastic! Of course, you're used to all this.' I got to the centre circle and turned round and they'd all stayed down the tunnel while I walked out on my own. There was Bob roaring with laughter and I was standing there in the middle of the bloody pitch with a ball and no team. Afterwards, he said with a grin: 'Sorry Jimbo, my lace broke.'

David Frost rang me one day and asked if I'd play in a fund-raiser at Wembley before the Cup final. If I could get a team to play his team, they'd raise £50,000. So I put the phone down to David Frost and rang Bobby. I asked if he'd play and he said: 'Certainly!' Bobby's next phone call thirty seconds later was from David Frost. 'Hello, Bobby, it's David Frost here, I'm getting a team together to play against Tarby's team at Wembley, can you play?' Bobby said to him: 'Sorry David, I'm already playing for Tarby's team!'

During the match, I was playing at the back with Bobby and suddenly I got a second wind and went on a run. I tried to cross the ball and he jogged up behind me. 'Here Jimbo! Inside! Give it here!' he said. But I didn't listen. I kicked it and it never went anywhere near where it was supposed to and he just looked at me for a long moment and as I went past he said: 'Long way, ain't it?' I just roared with laughter and said: 'Yes, Bob, I understand.'

We got a penalty and the kid from Coronation Street, Chris Quentin, grabbed the ball and said: 'I'll take it!' But I was the captain, 100,000 people at Wembley and I said: 'No, I'll take it!' and snatched the ball from him, put it down on the spot, took a quick run-up and put it away. As we're walking back to our own half Mooro quipped: 'No dispute about who was taking it there, Jim?' I looked at him and he just laughed at me.

We went to a great deal of sportsmen's dinners and one day we were entering the main hall of the Hilton in our dinner suits when walking ahead of us was a woman athlete – a very attractive lady – and Mooro, being the gentleman, opened the door to let her pass through. 'Thank you,' she said. He joked: 'What would you do if I ran after you?' and she replied: 'I'd slow down for you, Mr Moore!' We roared at that and then Bobby said: 'She must have seen me play, eh Jimbo?' He could take a joke at his own expense.

I was guest of honour with him at the West Ham table at the Footballer of the

Year dinner, and it looked like he might win it. There were twelve of us, the chairman, directors, players – I was the only non-West Ham person on the table. A director said: 'Bobby, perhaps you'd order the wine please?' Mooro said to the waiter: 'Yes, we'll have a crate of Chablis.' So the director queried it: 'Don't you mean a bottle of Chablis?' 'No,' said Bob. 'A crate.' The waiter brought this crate of wine and Mooro said: 'Open them.' The waiter didn't understand. 'What? All of them?' he said. Mooro replied: 'Yeah, one each!' We all had a bottle each and I was laughing because you should have seen the directors' faces – slightly miffed would have been an understatement!

He cared so much for others. The charity Dreamflight, which takes kiddies who are not very well to Disneyworld, was very important to Mooro. I can see him now, carrying a child who couldn't walk up the steps into a plane. He was teasing this little lad who was squealing with laughter. He had such a rapport with kids but he always thought it was so unfair that they should be so ill. He was a magnificent man. So unselfish.

Mooro did this thing when he talked where he repeated words. He'd say: 'How you been, how you been? Yeah, yeah, what you been up to? What you been up to? seen so and so? Have you seen him? Have you seen him?' Also, my experience was that Mooro was the worst bloody businessman in the world because he believed everyone at face value. Some people jumped on his coat tails with promises of what they could do. I'd say to him: 'Hang on, I'm not sure about this,' and he'd be saying: 'No, no, Jimbo, it'll be fine, it'll be fine.' We had this leather company called Harrison-Moore. We made fantastic leather overcoats, everyone had them, but no-one paid for them. We gave them away to everyone and all we got out of it, Me, Mooro, Freddie Harrison and Morris Keston, was a leather overcoat each! Mooro made shirts as well. My nephew in Liverpool has got one of these Bobby Moore shirts and it's his prized possession to this day.

It's a crime the FA didn't offer him something. My belief is there was a certain amount of jealousy there because Mooro got all the limelight. Bobby would have been sensational as Sports Minister. I'd moan at Mooro about it and he'd say: 'It's okay, don't go on, don't go on,' but it wasn't okay. And there are some people out there who should look at themselves in the mirror. I've seen the very same people come up to Mooro after a game and shake his hand and put their arm around him. I had to turn away. 'I'll get a lager,' I'd say. 'Only one?' quipped Mooro.

He was never violent or unsportsmanlike. Watching him on the pitch emerge from a tangle of players with the ball was a thrill to me. There was my mate beating them all. We would have loved to have been out there

Jimmy Tarbuck interviews Bobby at another '66 reunion, with Alf Ramsey in the background.

doing that, but never could. It was like he was on that pitch doing it for me.

He kept his illness a secret and never divulged it to me until just before it was in the newspapers. It didn't surprise me that he didn't tell me – he wouldn't have wanted to burden me.

Pele said Moore wasn't a player or just a friend, he was a brother. The hardest thing I've ever had to do in my public appearances was to speak at Westminster Abbey for his memorial service. I said: 'I usually open my appearances with 'It's nice to be here!' but today it's not nice to be here because it's not fair.' And it wasn't fair what happened to him. It's terrible that a boy of 51 who achieved so much and gave so much to the nation should not be able to get some reward by enjoying the precious years with Stephanie, his children and his grandchildren. He was some fella.

I miss the phone going. I can hear him now: 'Hello Jimbo! All's well? How's things? How's Pauline and the kids? Yeah, yeah, good, good, fine, fine…' Then after all this rigmarole he'd say: 'I just wanted to ask you something…' You knew it was coming after everything he said. He was always a good audience for me because we'd see each other and he'd roar. He had an amazing presence, wherever he walked, heads turned. Whenever we poshed up you would be in your best gear and look sharp, and Mooro would walk in and make you look scruffy.

I often think about him and I just choke up.

Doug Hayward

Doug started his own tailoring company in 1963 and moved to his current premises in Mount Street in 1967.

Bobby Moore first came to my shop for his suits in about '68. It was a pleasure to make for someone with such a trim figure. My clothes were very expensive. It always costs that bit extra to go first class, as they say, and Bobby was very dapper. He reminded me of the East End dockers when they dressed up for their Friday night out in the old days. It was the way they were brought up, part of their ritual. Overalls for work, yet there was never anyone smarter when they went out.

When you met Bobby, you knew he was one of the greatest footballers you've ever seen, so you wanted to like him. He was a very reliable, honourable, decent man and, unlike some players, he never let you down. That was also true on the pitch: when you watched him, he never disappointed you.

There was a football obsession in the 60s. Twelve of us had season tickets, I held them here and if people couldn't turn up they'd call me and we had people on the subs' bench, so to speak, waiting to go along. We went to Chelsea one week, Fulham the next. When it all started we went to Alvaro's Restaurant in the King's Road – he said bring your friends and eat here for a quid. The group was always changing, but there was Tommy Steele; Tony Charles, the TV producer; Herbert Kretzmer, the writer and lyricist, Tony Richmond, a director and lighting cameraman; the actors Terence Stamp and David Hemmings and others.

There was a whole buzz about working class people making lots of money and they all liked football. All of a sudden there was this great explosion of hairdressers, photographers, TV people, all working class boys doing very well for themselves. Cockney actors I knew who would usually be killed in the first scene of a war film became stars and they dragged everyone else along with them.

I went to the '66 final with Terence Stamp. We went on the train. A wonderful day. I felt deep disappointment when the Germans scored first. I thought That's it! The buggers have done us. It was a very traumatic game. Alan Ball ran and ran, even in extra time, and when Geoff Hurst's shot hit the bar, everyone was willing it over the line.

It's very difficult to imagine the atmosphere. Every single person in England was watching the game on black and white television, but 100,000 of us felt very privileged to be there. It was the last final you needed to go to because watching on TV became so good after that, what with colour and everything. I think Rank did a film of it in colour. It sold very well in Europe, I believe.

There was dancing in the street afterwards. We all went down to Jerry's drinking club in Shaftesbury Avenue that evening. It was an extraordinary night, people driving blew their horns, everybody was out in the streets going totally nuts. A great wave of nationalism went rushing through everybody for weeks after that final. In those days, they even sang God Save The Queen without jeering.

Bobby was a customer for five years. He was a giant on the field, an extraordinary authority, controlling everything and everyone, if he pointed and said: 'Get after it!' players did. But there was none of that off the field. He was a very quiet person and he went along with things.

In his heyday, Bobby was quite easily the most adored man in England and it's not difficult to see why. A fair player and a wonderful person.

Johnny Speight

Johnny was the TV scriptwriter for The Arthur Haines Show and the very popular long-running comedy series Till Death Us Do Part with West Ham fanatic Alf Garnett, played by Warren Mitchell.

I met Bobby through my friend Johnny Haynes and later from doing *Till Death Us Do Part* when I wrote Bobby into the show several times. On the show, Bobby was Alf Garnett's hero. Alf regularly ranted that 'Bobby Moore, captain of West Ham and England, was clean and that the only time he'd ever had his name taken was by the Queen, when she pinned the OBE on his chest'. And Bobby's picture was always in the Garnett's living room, along with Churchill. They were his heroes: Bobby Moore and Winston Churchill.

We filmed many scenes at Upton Park and once filmed Alf going up to Anfield to watch West Ham play Liverpool with his son-in-law, 'the Scouse git', as Alf used to call him. We had to film in the stadium and were worried when Alf appeared in the stand. The Kop would start chanting 'Alf Garnett' but they were marvellous. They knew he was there, they could see him, but they understood we were filming and never said a word. Liverpool won, and Bill Shankly, the Liverpool manager, said: 'I hope we haven't ruined your filming?'

We filmed Bobby running to catch the train home at Lime Street Station. Alf was there to see his hero and tried to grab him. Bobby was supposed to shut the door on Alf as the train pulled out. But Bobby was behaving too politely and treating Alf as Warren Mitchell. I took Bobby aside and said: 'Look, you're doing it all too nice. You've got to forget it's Warren. It's Alf Garnett, this drunken, awful boor who stinks of booze and is pulling at your new

TV character Alf Garnett, one of Bobby's biggest fans.

suit. Try and get in a temper with him.' Bobby said: 'Okay, I'll have a go.'

Bobby did it, and it was almost too real. He slammed the door and fortunately Warren was quick-witted and got his hands out of the way in time, otherwise he would have had his fingers crushed in the door! Bobby played it marvellously the second time and luckily no one was hurt.

Bobby couldn't run fast, although it was difficult to beat him because he would cut an opponent off before he had a whiff of an option. Bobby told me the only person to ever embarrass him was Georgie Best – he was harder to contain than Pele because not even George knew what he was going to do. Not only did Best have tremendous pace, but he could stop dead and make space for himself by stopping so that you'd run past him, by which time he had switched direction. Bobby told me that he was almost impossible to contain.

"Bobby wrote: The only time I've ever seen Best completely beaten was by Sam Booka"

Bobby played the ball out from defence. It was wonderful to watch. All the great continentals play it out, they don't just boot it. Bobby told me he often argued with big Jack Charlton because 'Jacko's idea was to get the ball up the other end and they can't score when it's up there.' But Bobby's attitude was, 'Yeah, but while we keep giving them possession, we can't score either.'

Not enough players bring the ball out of defence anymore. If you can come out of defence, beat a man, or certainly draw someone out of position, you've got the edge. If you watched Bobby, he would take the ball off the full-back, draw the marker, then set the full-back free into space with a pass down the wing. Before the opposition knew it, there was a man with the ball ready to cross into the danger area, all due to Bobby's movement and skill.

MOORE **than a legend**

Ron Greenwood told me that Bobby went to Fulham because the West Ham players had got into the habit of always giving Bobby the ball – whether he wanted it or not – and didn't play their own game.

By the time '66 came round, I'd done the *Comedy Playhouse*, which was the first episode of Garnett. Before Alf I'd done *The Arthur Haines Show*, who was a stroppy socialist. Alf was an evolution of Arthur.

Alf was born one day when I was selling insurance around Custom House. In those days there was a road called Draughtboard Alley, because it was the only street with black and whites in it. I was walking past a house which had broken windows, a real slum, yet it had a Tory poster in the window. I found many of the working classes, even ones voting Labour, are more Tory, morally, in some of their ideas, than Tories are.

We had Alf brought up in Wapping. He believed people were born to rule, the Queen was an Empress and the King an Emperor. The East End was full of myths and we used them in the show. There was one about Jim Barrett who played for West Ham. We had Alf saying Barrett would go in the Boleyn Arms before the game and drink ten pints then go out and play a blinder. But football is a big village, almost nothing to do with the rest of the world. Everyone knows each other and myths start up worse than chattering housewives.

But *Till Death Us Do Part* was the first television show to bring football into the context of the comedy. I'd hear people arguing about football and it was like a religion. So I thought if we had the son-in-law being Scouse, a Liverpool fan, and Alf being West Ham, it would work to have them bickering about it.

I was at many of the '66 games. About 12 of us got a block of tickets: Eric Sykes, Stanley Baker, Sean Connery, Richard Harris, Jimmy Tarbuck, all that lot. We had tickets for White City and Wembley and the deal included tickets for the final, fortunately England got through. Eric Sykes organised it all and after the final we all went back to Sean's place for a drink - he had a flat in Chiswick.

England played really well that day. Marvellous. We brought the '66 final into the film version of *Till Death Us Do Part*. They wanted a movie and I couldn't think of a plot, so we came up with this idea of the war years, when Alf was younger and what led up to him becoming the Alf Garnett everyone was so familiar with. We had Alf's daughter Rita as a baby and the Scouse git coming on the scene, Rita's wedding, all that. We got Alf and the Scouse git to go to the final and filmed them in what was supposed to be the crowd at Wembley, standing amongst some German fans.

The first time Bobby and Tina came to dinner when I lived in Northwood they couldn't find my house so they asked in the local pub where I lived. Bobby caused quite a stir - it wasn't long after the '66 victory and the whole pub was in uproar. When they finally made it to the house my kids were upstairs and they jumped out of bed and were on top of the stairs shouting 'England! England!'

I was at a dinner party with Bobby and Tina and my wife Connie at Ned Sherrin's house, the producer of the Garnett show. We were expecting Georgie Best and he arrived late, drunk, missed most of the dinner and he was drinking that Xambucca - the stuff where you set fire to the glass. We all had a good share of booze that night, but it hit George faster and he ended up falling asleep. I said: 'Look at George, all the players in the world couldn't stop him, but Xambucca left him for dead.' Bobby, who had a column in the *Daily Mirror* at the time, said, 'That's a marvellous story for the column!' So he wrote 'The only time I've ever seen Best completely beaten was by Sam Booka.' The next thing the bloody press are asking around about Sam Booka and who does he play for!

I saw Georgie Best and Bobby playing against Chelsea during their time at Fulham and they were playing marvellously. Butch Wilkins was having a nightmare trying to contain them and George sold him a dummy which left him for dead. They had both lost a bit of pace, but they had great football brains. Take Frank Sinatra, his voice is nowhere near as strong as his early records but his phrasing and timing is better. If you're clever enough, you can adjust when you lose some of your strengths.

Kevin Keegan told me a story how Shankly used the psychological advantage to help him play against Bobby Moore. One of Kevin's first games for Liverpool was against West Ham. Shanks came into the dressing room and said: 'Don't worry about Bobby Moore. I've just seen them coming in and they all look knackered. It's all them night clubs down in London. That Bobby Moore has got bags under his eyes.' Kevin told me he had a good game but Bobby played like a master. After the game Shanks said, 'Well done, young Kevin, you were up against the greatest half-back in the world this afternoon and you did very well.' Shanks had conned him.

Bobby was playing in one of those charity matches down in the East End and the changing room was just a shed, very dodgy. Bobby got changed and said: 'Oi, Speighty!' – he used to call me Johnno or Speighty - 'Will you look after my watch, mate? I don't like to leave it in the changing room.' So he strapped the watch on my wrist. I was standing there talking while the game was on and I felt fingers on it. I looked down and there was this little kid trying to nick it. I said: 'Go on, piss off out of it, you little sod!' and he ran off.

The last time I saw Bobby was at a Variety Club golf day. He looked quite well. I was chatting to him for about an hour and he was off to do a radio thing, but he never said anything was wrong with his health. I can't think of anything we spoke about, just chat, golf, football, that sort of stuff. He walked off towards his car and that was the last time I saw him. I was shocked when he died. It came right out of the blue. I hadn't heard a whisper he was ill. On the day he passed away, I got a phone call from the press to ask me if I knew Bobby had died.

It was terrible. I can't explain the feelings.

Bob Bevan

'The Cat' has become a major name on the after-dinner speaking circuit, relating tales of his hopeless goalkeeping in the Old Wilsonians 6th XI

Whatever else Mr and Mrs Moore did when they brought up their only son, Bobby, they taught him incredibly good manners. One story Bobby did impart to me, which highlights his good manners, was the day he travelled to Upton Park from his home in Barking for his debut against Manchester United. 'I hadn't reckoned on such a big crowd,' he told me. 'I got on the bus from Barking but when I went to change buses there was an enormous queue. I had to let three buses go, they were full, and it was getting worryingly closer to kick-off.' He didn't even think, as some might, to say to the fans in the queue: 'Look, I'm playing today, do you mind if I go in front?' When he finally got a bus to the ground, the gates were locked and it took him ten minutes to convince a steward and a police-man he was a player and that he was late to get changed for the match. He nearly missed his debut!

Bobby put together quite a nice 20-minute speech for the after-dinner circuit with some rather amusing stories, but he would only talk about himself when pressed and, even then, reluctantly. I lost count of the times I told him to bring the World Cup success into his speech but he regarded it as immodest. I'd say: 'It's what people want to hear, Bob. Jack Charlton brings it into his act and it's never boastful.' But Mooro would give me one of his enigmatic smiles and I knew to leave the subject alone. He was too good-mannered to disagree.

Whenever we spoke he was always more interested in hearing about my game the previous Saturday. It did not matter what level I played at, Bobby insisted he knew my game was as important to me as his professional matches were to him when he played. You knew you were one of Mooro's friends when he began to have friendly digs at you. Once, when I told him I was to captain a side, he wanted to know if I could catch the coin. And when he learned I was to keep goal against him in a charity game at Wembley, he said: 'Excellent, Cat. I've never scored at Wembley before!'

He was always slightly embarrassed by any fuss, especially when asked to sign autographs by an excited mob – a betrayal of confidence which he never allowed to show up on the field. When I asked him about being known as ice-cool, he replied: 'Ice-cool? Images are something other people create for you. You can only be yourself.'

He had great respect for the views of others. When he was doing his foot-ball forum roadshows with Jimmy Greaves and George Best he found the audience soon ignored the speakers and started to argue among them-selves. 'Why not?' he'd say: 'Everyone's got opinions. It's what the game is all about. Even the England manager should lis-ten to opinions.'

"He learned I was to keep goal against him in a charity game at Wembley. He said: Excellent, Cat, I've never scored at Wembley before!"

For me his best line came at a Footballer of the Year dinner. He hated public speaking and was only supposed to hand over the trophy to Kenny Dalgish. But the journalist, Bob Cass, had made a highly-amusing speech giving useful phrases for the press when covering the forthcoming Mexican World Cup in 1986. Things like 'Hombre loco' was 'here comes Jeff Powell' – that sort of thing. Amazingly, Mooro grabbed the microphone. 'Another useful phrase for South America...' he said... 'Braceleto gonno!' The room was in uproar.

I can't count the number of times he played in charity games for me or found me jobs when he worked for Blue Arrow, but I can count the number of times he ever asked me for something – just the once. I spoke for him at a dinner at St Albans City. Bobby dragged me into a corner afterwards and said: 'I've got your money here.' I

argued with him about it but there was a point at which you stopped arguing with Mooro. It's hard to define, he didn't lose his temper, and it wasn't even a look, it was just that I realised he was going to make me take the cheque. There was a steel in him, yet I can't think of a nicer bloke. In a way, he could have done with a manager but he wouldn't have wanted to admit he needed one. Not a money-making machine agent, but someone who would have been sensitive of his image. You couldn't have made him nicer but a good agent could've made him hang on to his money a bit better. I think Stephanie helped get his affairs in order in that respect.

We ran one charity match at Palace where I managed to get nine of the original '66 team to play and about 4,500 people turned up. I remember Jack Charlton coming by train – he got off at Norwood Junction and walked to the ground with his boots in a Safeway's bag!

I watched the '66 tournament on television in Catford – Bobby Charlton says I'm the only person he knows who doesn't claim to have been at Wembley. I always thought the best game was England v. Portugal. The thing I recall vividly was that my parents weren't interested in football at all but we sat and watched the semi-final in the lounge. Near the end Gordon Banks pushed a save over the bar and my mum dropped her knitting. I looked at her and said: 'You're actually watching this, aren't you?' and she replied: 'Oh yes, it's quite exciting!' Winning the World Cup was a fantastic feeling, but it dulls with age. If you're into football, it's one of the greatest days of your life.

I'm always the last to know anything and I didn't know about Bobby's illness 'till very late. I found out Bobby was in hospital so I rang up Stephanie to ask if I could see him. She explained he wasn't having visitors, only family, but that it was kind of me to call and she would pass on my respects to Bobby. So I sent a card instead. A few weeks later he rang to thank me for enquiring after him. He didn't actually say the word cancer but he didn't have to. Then I saw him a few times after that and he looked in very good nick, so we assumed everything was okay.

The last time I saw him was after a League Cup match where my team, Crystal Palace, had beaten Chelsea - the weather was awful, peeing down, muddy pitch. I was walking across the car park when I heard a voice call out: 'Cat!' Peering through the rain, I could see a figure in a funny cap but couldn't make out who it was. 'Who's that?' I said, and he replied: 'It's Mooro!' When I realised who it was, I said: 'Hello, Mooro! How are you doing? What did you think of the Palace tonight, then?' I knew he wasn't a huge fan of my team and he said: 'Yeah, I thought your boys played well.' I didn't know then that he wasn't so well, it was so dark with the rain and everything. I wrote in the programme the following week: 'Even Mooro thought we played well and he's not our greatest fan.' Not knowing, I made some remark about his silly cap. When someone told me about the cancer I felt terribly embarrassed. Anyway, I left a message for him and sent him a letter but it clearly arrived the morning after he died. I was at Fulham Broadway when I heard he'd died. A friend rang me to tell me the news. I felt a bit close to weeping and I remember getting the other half to give me a hug. Suddenly it hit me how close I felt to him and I'd hardly claim to be one his bosom pals. I'm sure other people felt that way.

Terry Venables is a mate of mine so I went down to his bar, Scribes, for a drink. The barman said Terry wasn't expected so I just started talking to someone else there when, suddenly, Terry walked in. And we stood there chatting about Mooro for about an hour. I think we both needed to be around someone in football. It's hard to explain.

On the railings at Upton Park, a fan hung a card. It said: 'I wanted to be like you.' I think we all wanted to be like him. He had so many qualities as a player but he had even more as a man and a friend. He's certainly a bloke I miss seeing about. It's like you've lost one of a set, because the others are all still there. I don't know if it's the right thing to say but it's like ... the most important one has gone – not that I wanted any of the others to go in his place, but it's almost like a ship without a rudder now.

I used to do a gag about Bobby which stemmed from a real incident. I was put next to him for the first time at a match at Crystal Palace and we mostly sat in silence, with me making the odd bit of small talk, trying not to make a nuisance of myself. In reality I was shocked to be sitting next to a man who, the only time I'd ever seen before, was beating the Germans on black and white television. He must have realised I was a bit nervous so he leaned over and asked: 'What do you make of it so far then, Cat?' This led to me doing a routine where I claim I was sitting next to Bobby Moore and he says: 'Pardon me, Cat?' and I reply: 'What do you want now?' It always got a big laugh, especially if Bobby was in the audience. Mooro used to say to me afterwards: 'I remember the incident, Cat, but you said something like: 'It's a bit f***** cold...!' "

Over the years it had become a ritual for me to wave to Mooro from my seat at Crystal Palace whenever Bobby was in the Selhurst Park press box. It was six weeks after he died before I was free to go to a game and I was looking up at the press box searching for a BBC colleague. 'Looking for Mooro, Cat?' a friend next to me enquired. 'No,' I replied, 'but I don't suppose I'll ever be able to come here without thinking about him ...'

Michael Henry

For 17 years, Michael has been the Maitre 'd for Langans Restaurant in London, where Bobby was a regular customer.

What can one say about a bloke of his talent? Langan's Restaurant has been open 20 years and Bobby had been coming in ever since I started. We used to have friendly banter about football, Bobby being West Ham and me a Chelsea supporter. We used to give each other some stick. He was an extremely pleasant man and very easy to talk to.

In '66, I was in the stand at Wembley, cheering them on. I was working at the Royal Gardens in those days and it was the centre of the world's press, so there were loads of tickets going. I was in the £5 seats. It was the greatest day ever. I was hoarse and could barely speak when I came out. The present England team needs a person of Bobby's leadership and authority. It would make the difference between a good side and winning the World Cup.

He would always help you out. A few years ago I went to see the First Division play-off final at Wembley, when Blackburn beat Leicester, and was stranded outside a lounge, unable to get in. Kenny Dalglish had invited me but I couldn't find him. I met Roberta, Bobby's daughter, in the corridor. I explained why I was stuck outside and she went into the main lounge, told Bobby about my plight and he came straight out and took me in. I was relieved to be able to pay my respects to him at his memorial service. Bobby was a different class.

Henry Cooper

'Our Enery's' professional boxing career stretched over 17 years, from 1954 to 1971. He held the British, European and Commonwealth titles.

I got to know Bobby very well because we were from the same era. We attended all the big sporting functions, Sportsman of the Year and suchlike. While I was top of the boxing world, Bobby was at the top of football.

He was a bit reserved but that was a nice trait. He wasn't a big mouth and let his boots do the talking. A blooming great footballer. I was always keen on football and if I hadn't made it in boxing, I would have hoped to have made it in football. I used to play in goal as a kid, but as I got better in boxing, I gave up the football.

I remember the '66 World Cup final very well indeed. Three years before, in a ring on the very pitch where Bobby was carried on his team mates' shoulders, I fought Cassius Clay for the World Heavyweight title. If only I could have seen off Clay like Bobby did the Germans, I'd have been all right!

I went on holiday to Bermuda straight after that, to spend some time with Bill Tucker, the orthopaedic surgeon. While I was there he offered me a batch of tickets for the World Cup finals. On my return home, I gave the tickets to my brother and friends and we went as a group to Wembley for all the games. Ironically enough, as well as me, Clay was in the crowd for the final as he was there to fight Brian London a week later – and he knocked him out in the third round.

Bobby came to a lot of my fights. He was keen on boxing. Once I remember him coming into the dressing room to wish me luck. I got to know him much better in later years because he used to play in the Variety Club Golf Society. We played together many times, helping to raise money for the mentally and physically handicapped kids.

It's such a shame the good guys always seem to die young.

Ray Winstone

Made his name in the borstal film 'Scum'. Ray also appeared in the ITV series 'Fox'. His latest movie releases are 'Face' and 'Nil By Mouth'.

I've always been a mad West Ham fan, brought up in Plaistow. Any time I go back to Upton Park, the moment I turn the corner and face the main stand, I get a feeling like 'I'm home!' I get a real shiver up my back. And a warm feeling at the same time. I can't explain it, you know? It's where I come from. My roots. I love it to bits. Even if I go there and I've got the hump, regardless if West Ham win or lose, I see my mates, talk about the old days, and I feel better.

Moore was a super-human. I can remember standing on the corner of a street near West Ham park in '64 and watching the bus come past with all the West Ham team sitting on top: Moore, Hurst, Sealey, Sissons, that lot. I was with a load of other kids and we were all armed with those tubes of bubbles – the ones you blow?

In '66 I went with my dad to all the games: Uruguay, France, Mexico, Argentina, Portugal and the final. He wasn't that mad on football, but in those days, West Ham had a team to be proud of, didn't they? Especially after winning the FA Cup and in Europe ... then we won the World Cup! Just like the song we used to sing on the North Bank: 'I remember Wemberlee; when West Ham beat West Ger-many; Martin one, and Geoffrey three; And Bobby won the OBE...'

When I heard about the bracelet business in Colombia I was disgusted. That's the sort of thing you expect in those sort of countries, isn't it? I think I'd turn down any acting jobs out there.

I saw Bobby the evening of the San Marino game at the Hilton Hotel afterwards. It was sad to see him, you could tell he was ill, but he was still smiling away. Cancer is terrible – I've seen it in my family – but Bobby kept his dignity. I've always been a forward when I've played football, so someone like Hurst would usually be my favourite sort of player, but Bobby was the all-time greatest. A defender isn't a glamorous role, but some of the things Bobby did were about as glamorous as a defender can get. When you watch the Preston North End video again, the balls he was floating around, the passes, were wonderful. The dead ball stuff was out of this world. Many times I saw him pick up the ball and turn in a 360 degree circle over the ball, like a ballet dancer, and wrong foot the whole of the opposite team.

The West Ham v. Fulham final caused me some very strange feelings. I didn't want to see Bobby do badly and didn't really want him to lose either. Nobody minded Fulham, they were a little club and it almost didn't matter if West Ham lost, just to see Bobby lift the Cup again. I think most of West Ham would've cheered just as loudly if Bobby had lifted the Cup rather than Bonds. When Moore left West Ham it was like losing your right arm. West Ham lost something when he moved on, and they didn't recover for a long time. I know we had class of Brooking and Devonshire, and we won the FA Cup in 1980, but it still wasn't right. Probably not until '86, when we came third in the League.

Oddly enough, I played against Bobby. I've played six times at Wembley in charity games and Bobby was playing for the opposition in the celebrity warm up match before the '87 FA Cup final between Tottenham and Coventry. There were all the usual suspects playing: David Frost, Mick Channon, Daley Thompson, Lloyd Honeyghan. It was 20 minutes each way, and I played up front with Bobby Moore marking me.

Right from the kick-off, I've gone forward with the ball and Bobby has loomed up in front of me, so I've dropped my shoulder, flicked the ball ahead and gone round him. It must have been five or six yards further on before I glanced down to find out I didn't have the ball anymore. When I turned around, Bobby was playing it out to the wing. They said he was the pickpocket but I never even realised he'd nicked the ball off me. F*** knows how he did it. You've got to remember, he wasn't a young man then, he was only a few years off 50.

I'm not a brilliant footballer but I can play. I can hit a ball, and I remember one moment in the game when the ball came over to me from Mick Channon. I shaped to hit a volley and was about to connect really sweetly. I could tell it was heading towards the top corner and I expected to see it hit the net, but no sooner had I made contact with the ball than Bobby casually stuck out a foot and took it off my toe. It was really spooky having this guy read what I was going to do. Now I know how Pele and all those wingers felt. It was like playing chess with someone who not only knew what moves you were going to make but was setting you up to make them in the first place.

All the way through the game, while he was marking me, he was talking. He was saying things like:'Hold it, wait for it, now, go on, have a run,' and he'd step up and let me run on to a pass to make me look good. I read a book recently about Muhammed Ali and how he loves nothing more than to let other people look good in public or lets them win or allows people to be themselves and be successful. And Bobby Moore was like that, too. He was big enough to make himself look bad just so you could have your moment of glory. You've got to have certain great gifts to truly be a great. Playing against 'God' was one of the highlights of my life.

When Moore died, I went down to Upton Park. I live in Enfield now, so I drove down there in the car. I didn't get out - just drove past. That was enough for me. People grieve in different ways and, for me, the journey was enough. It wasn't anything to do with trying to be hard or anything, I knew how much he had affected everybody and just didn't fancy standing there with upset people all around mc. Bcing back in the area brought back all the memories I needed, so I called in to a mate's house and we had a beer while chatting about Mooro. That was enough for me.

Bobby Moore has become folklore in the East End. A bit like Robin Hood. Living in Enfield, my little girl – she's nine years-old – was starting to show an interest in Arsenal, so that was it: I bought her the West Ham shirt, the book, the video, the lot, straight away, no messing about, and she's been hooked on West Ham ever since. I take her to home games and not long ago we were sitting next to Martin Peters and he was chatting to her during the game. 'Who's that nice man, daddy?' she asked me afterwards. So I explained who he was, moved on to Bobby Moore, Hurst, '64, '65, '66, '75, '80, '86 – the full monty West Ham history lesson – and she was as enthralled as she would be for any bedtime fairytale. It was amazing.

The people around Enfield now are a different breed from what I'm used to in East London. They're not like the neighbours I had during my childhood. People say all that close community stuff is finished in the East End but that's not true. I recently filmed a series in the area called *Our Boys*, about a family who lose their son. My character dreams of his son playing for West Ham and I had to learn all these West Ham songs for the part. We did scenes in the Boleyn pub and I was shocked how much of the area hasn't changed since I was a kid: the streets, certain buildings, the look of the houses. People say it's all gone, but bits remain. There are pockets of families still around the Custom House and Silvertown areas who've been there all their lives, since the days of the dockers.

It's amazing, in my game, how many people are West Ham. I've always been curi-ous how it's happened. People go on about Manchester United fans everywhere but there's a silent army of West Ham in all corners of the globe. For instance, I was filming in Edinburgh not that long ago and discovered this pub full of Scottish West Ham fans. Then, years ago, I was at a West Ham game once and there was this German flag behind the goal. It was a group of West Ham Germans over for the weekend. That could only come from '65 and watching Moore against Munich 1860, couldn't it? It's so weird. But then football is weird.

Moore was just such a top geezer. What about the way he used to look upfield for a pass? If you said to someone that Bobby Moore had the front, in the middle of the match, to stand on the ball with one foot, bring his hand up to his forehead and stare upfield like a geezer shouting 'land-ho!' on a crow's nest, people would say you're winding them up. But it was true. I've seen it with my own eyes.

Terry Creasey

A West Ham fan, Terry met Bobby around 1964 when they drank at the same pubs in the East End. They became friends and spent time together socially, even going on family holidays.

When I was out drinking with Bob, I'd come home at different hours, could-n't stand up, and Diane, my wife, would say: 'I suppose you've been with Bobby again?' and my answer would always be: 'Well, yeah, how did you know?'

It didn't matter who we met, Bobby would introduce me and say: 'This is my pal,

Terry Creasey.' I felt so proud to be his mate. I was introduced to all the stars: Jimmy Tarbuck, Kenny Lynch, Reg Varney, Max Bygraves, Johnny Speight and some footballers like Jimmy Greaves. It was a regular occurrence after a game on a Saturday. We didn't know where we were going to end up and what time we got home, I'd never know. This went on for years.

I was going to West Ham regularly when I first met Bobby and we would go in the Harlene Motel, have a dinner, a dance, a cabaret, Saturday night affair, the usual stuff. It was a meeting place for all the footballers and I got talking to John Bond, Peter Brabrook and Ronnie Boyce. We would also go in the Moby Dick pub in Chadwell Heath with our wives.

Later, Bobby had some pubs with Jimmy Quill: 'Mooro's' in Stratford, 'Tipples' on the corner of Bethnal Green Road, and 'Woody's' in Chigwell, which was next to Woodford Town Football Club whose chairman, Bill Larkin, was a friend of ours. I even became a partner with Frank Lampard and we had a pub called 'The Brittannia' in Plaistow. Bobby was always in there.

One Christmas Eve we went drinking and in the back of Bobby's car was the family's Christmas turkey, but we had to leave the car because we were all incapable of driving. Of course, on Christmas day the car wasn't outside the house and when Tina came to cook the Christmas dinner there was no turkey – it was still in the boot of the car!

I was with Bobby, Alan Ball and our wives when we went to watch Gene Barry at the *Talk of the Town,* when he was a song and dance man. We went backstage to meet him and took him to Tramp. A nice man. One other occasion, Bobby, Alan Sealey and I visited Gene at the studios when he was making *The Adventurer* and he introduced us to Barry Morse from *The Fugitive* and Robert Vaughan and David McCallum. They all wanted to meet Bobby.

Bobby could always find where the drinks bar would be hidden in hotel rooms, even if it was disguised behind a wall panel. He would walk in and say: 'Tel, fancy a tipple?' and I'd say: 'Yeah, but where?' He'd go right to it, open up a bit of wall and there it would be. It was like he could almost smell it.

Bobby wasn't a big eater. We often went to steak houses with the family and I would say: 'Mooro, don't you want something to eat? How about a nice juicy steak?' and he'd just have cheese and biscuits. He watched his weight and was always doing extra training.

He would often invite me back on a Sunday. We'd have a drink with friends: Terry Clements, Bob Stirley, Mick O'Shea, business pals, and afterwards we'd often go to Bobby's because he had a little room with a bar and we'd sit down, tell a few jokes, have a few tipples and Bobby was in his element.

We had a party after he came back from the Mexico World Cup

Enjoying a night out with (left to right) Terry Creasey, Bill Larkin and Brian Dear.

MOORE **than a legend**

and I was a bit concerned because he had a pain in his chest. I thought it was a heart attack. He had a check up and it turned out to be nothing. But he kept everything to himself. On his 50th birthday party in Putney, my wife Diane remarked how slim he was. I never for one minute sussed anything was wrong and the next day I found out he was going into hospital. I phoned him and said:'You're a lad, you don't say nothing?' and he always replied with something like:'Well Tel, you know?'

And he never nicked that bracelet, by the way. Bobby wouldn't even pinch a box of matches. He was very generous. You get a lot of mean players who think they've got a licence not to buy a drink. But Bobby was the opposite – you almost had to stop him buying everything. I'd say:'Turn it in, Bob!', but he'd never listen.

If you were in a restaurant or a pub, there was often some wally giving Bobby lip. Sometimes people would be commenting on a game, but some were nasty, yet he never turned a hair.'All right, me old son?' he would say, as though nothing had happened. I never once saw him react violently, despite people being really nasty. Once or twice I thought:'I'll have to sort them out for him,' but Bob always said: 'No, no, it's okay.'

Bobby got involved in making made-to-measure shirts in the 70s with Mike Summerbee. Bob had me measured up and several weeks later the shirts arrived, different materials, different patterns, but there was a balls-up because the shirts were miles too small. I said they must have got my measurements mixed up with Ronnie Corbett's, because there were about two inches of shirt to tuck in, so the moment I moved it came out! Bobby was hysterical with laughter. I don't know whether he did it on purpose, but I never paid for the shirts, which was a shame because there were about half a dozen that went to waste and they were made from good material. I loved to see Mooro laugh. I can see him now, laughing at me in this shirt.

One Sunday morning I went running with Bobby around the pitch at the ground – people say Bobby wasn't fast but he was a lot bloody faster than me! Afterwards I jumped in the bath and got soap suds right up to my neck. Fortunately Ron Greenwood never used to go in on a Sunday so the lads never minded me joining in. But John Cushley, the Scottish centre-half, kept crying wolf and shouting

> **"He never nicked that bracelet, by the way. Bobby wouldn't even pinch a box of matches"**

'Creasey! There's Greenwood!' and 'Creasey! Quick! The Guv'nor is here!' and I'd jump out of the bath and run and hide in the toilet. I always felt Mr Greenwood might think I was intruding, even though I was Bobby's guest. I was soaking in the bath, smothered in soap, when Ron Greenwood did in fact walk in one Sunday. He knew who I was because he'd seen me at the games with Bobby, but he said: 'Who's this?' and Bobby replied:'It's all right, he's been training with me.' Mr Greenwood seemed satisfied and carried on as normal.

A crowd of us went up on a coach to Blackburn to see Bobby's last game for Fulham. It was quite sentimental because I'd seen him play so many times for West

184

Ham, Fulham and England, you never thought it would end. He was a thoroughbred. I called him 'The Maestro'. I would say to people: 'Seen The Maestro lately?'

If anyone asked Bobby a favour, nothing was too much trouble. He didn't do it for gain either, helpfulness was his natural way. I don't think I would ever ring him in the middle of the night, nor would I ask him for money or anything like that, but I felt he had a lot of time for people. He felt comfortable whether he was talking to the Queen in Buckingham Palace or some old boy nursing his pint in a little pub in the East End.

I was just so pleased and proud to have been a very good friend of his. Bobby was a bit special. I really mean that. It's just a crying shame he ain't with us today. I loved his company and I think about him a lot. There will never be another Bobby Moore.

Terry O'Neill

Shot to fame in the early 60s as the man who first photographed The Beatles and The Rolling Stones. Terry went to Hollywood where he married his second wife, actress Faye Dunaway. Has photographed many movie actors and actresses over the last three decades and did a famous series of photographs with footballers in the early 70s.

The very first time I met Bobby Moore we were having a kickabout in Chigwell when I was taking pictures for a pre-World Cup shoot. I had a trial for Arsenal myself and was greased lightning over 60 yards, but I was a 'head down' player and didn't make professional level. Bobby's head was always up – the sign of a good player. He said to me: 'You're fast.' So I said to him: 'I could easily get past you.' That's how much bloody front I had. So we were mucking about and I tried to take him on and I found I couldn't because he channelled me over a few yards and blocked me. He explained afterwards how he dealt with fast players. I felt such a fool saying to the England captain that I could get past him. Later, whenever we played in charity games, he was always the hardest bloke to beat.

We instantly became friends. He didn't say much, but he didn't have to. You sensed this tower of strength and felt automatic respect. I was older than him but he had such authority, you felt like his kid brother.

On the surface, he had simple but important characteristics: He was courteous, well-mannered, always considerate to others. But there was something else. If you felt comfortable, so did he, almost out of relief to be treated as a person.

I often thought there was a lot more going on inside him but he would never talk about it. In some ways, he would take on the persona of the people he was with. Or, at least, the persona they deserved. Such character was especially unusual in a footballer.

He was a very generous man. If you lunched with him the only way you could pay the bill was to outwit him by ordering the bill when he went to the toilet.

He loved a good time. I've even seen a picture of him dancing with Eric

MOORE **than a legend**

Morecombe. When you bumped into him you were always really glad to see him. You would say 'hello' and his face would light up. The last time I saw him he was having dinner with Jeff Powell in a restaurant. He had been ill but he looked well.

Bobby really did stand out, but all of Alf Ramsey's team were brimming with honest Englishness. They were pure England and they made us proud. That final was the height of a very special time.

Those of us at the core of the changing scene in the 60s never thought it would last, or at least, it's impact would last. We all thought one day we would have to get proper jobs. You could have bet a million quid that Mick Jagger wouldn't still be singing at 50. None of us knew we were making history or changing the future.

It was an explosion. A time of great opportunity. Something new was happening every day. There would be a new Beatles song, Mary Quant invented the mini skirt, there were blue jeans, always something new. If I wasn't born when I was, I would've missed it and I wouldn't be where I am today. At 22-23, I was in Hollywood and everyone wanted to know about England and when I came back we won the World Cup. It was the best decade of anyone's life.

There was a spell where rock stars started to give movie stars a run for their money. And footballers like George Best and Bobby Moore were equally sought-after. Gangs of us used to go to watch football each week, all the people who were on the London scene: Vidal Sassoon, actors like Tom Courtney, Doug Hayward, the tailor, a friend of ours called Alvaro. There was a huge network of people and everyone knew each other.

During the 60s, I shot film and rock stars, then in about 1970 I started shooting footballers in all sorts of fancy situations.

With Bobby Moore, though, you didn't need that. The respect I had for him meant I just wanted to shoot him straight, with no gimmicks. To be honest, I would have liked to have X-rayed his mind, let alone photographed his face. In the end, I did the shot of him playing chess with Franz Beckenbauer. Two great minds pitting their wits against each other. Just like they were on the pitch in those World Cup matches.

Bobby was a fabulous sight moving forward. Upright, like a lion in the jungle. I have an image in my mind of him on that left side of the field and it's his kingdom. He didn't need anyone backing him up.

Judith Hurst

The wife of Geoff Hurst and a friend of Bobby's first wife, Tina.

Very few people knew about Bobby's illness. Tina swore me to secrecy and I didn't even tell Geoff. The way Bobby handled the illness was typical of the man. He was marvellous, so in control, and he didn't let anything show, working right to the end and carrying on as though there was nothing wrong.

We lived round the corner to the Moores and the kids used to play together. Whenever I popped into their house, we would often stand around in the kitchen

186

and share a joke. Bobby used to pull Tina's leg and he did it to me as well. He was very good at keeping a straight face.

All the wives were excited for the '66 final. We got ourselves done up and we sat together in the stadium. It was a bit tense because Geoff didn't know if he was going to be in. My father sat near me and somewhat prophetically he said: 'Geoff will get three today,' and I replied: 'Don't be daft!' But my father was sure and he was proved right.

It was a bit disappointing because we'd seen very little of them in the build-up. Sir Alf was quite strict about that, but they respected him for it and they knew where they stood. After one of the matches Alf allowed us to go to the hotel for a drink with the boys. We'd only just walked in and had one drink when Alf marched in and said: 'Goodnight ladies, goodnight gentlemen!' One of the lads said: 'Goodnight Alf,' but Alf answered: 'I'm not going to bed, you are!' Someone else said: 'But Alf, we've only just got our drink!' Alf said: 'Goodnight ladies, goodnight gentlemen!' That was it, our cue to buzz off.

It changed our lives very quickly. Our first house was on a small housing estate in Hornchurch, Essex and forty-eight hours after the final, on the Monday lunchtime, the organisers sent this huge chauffeur-driven Rolls Royce to take us to a lunch where Geoff was to be presented with the top goalscorers' award. The neighbours were hanging out of the windows wondering what the hell was happening.

It's so sad Bobby is not around anymore. When he died, I came in from somewhere, heard the news, and I still had my coat on hours later. Even though I'd known about the illness, I was still in shock. Press people were on the phone, at the door, it was bedlam. Geoff was away but he didn't feel he could talk to anyone anyway. We were both stunned. Bobby had always been around. Whenever you went to football things, you'd see him. Then, suddenly, he's not there. It was just awful when the press took the photo of him at the end at Wembley, that was disgraceful.

Geoff was absolutely devastated when Bobby died – I don't think I've seen him so upset. We went down to the ground a few days after he died. Geoff just wanted to go there and have a few quiet moments but press people were trying to take his photograph and he said: 'Please, not now.'

Moore tributes

I didn't know Bobby well. I had a few suppers with him and his wife. He had that glow of the archetype who carries the hopes and identification of the masses, when it goes well. He was also puzzled, no doubt wondering 'Who am I?' in the midst of the mass projections.
Terence Stamp

MOORE **than a legend**

The day they won the World Cup I was a teenager playing in a band and I lived in a bed-sit in Earls Court. Coming from West Ham and being lucky enough to play in the junior team, football was my life until music took precedence. As the big day came I was feeling isolated, surrounded by musicians who wouldn't get up in time. So I decided to return to my father's house in the East End. Because we were playing the Germans, my dad was so wound up – he hated them more than Spurs! We lived every second of the match, mum included. I don't think we sat down once. When the last two goals went in we danced and sang and the council flat shook. That night I took my parents to a pub in Bermondsey where I was playing and celebrations carried on 'till 3am.
David Essex

I was at Chichester at a matinee performance of The Cherry Orchard. I came off stage with Celia Johnson and we were just in time to see the Germans equalise, on a little black and white TV in the costume room. We were able to watch the extra time period, so it was wonderfully exciting and quite unforgettable. I could not believe there was anyone in the audience – 'How can you be here?' I was thinking. The cast had to be. I had no respect for the audience that day.
Tom Courtney

When Bobby died, one of the lights of the world went out. I knew him very well, particularly in the later years when we played golf. He never changed, he was always fit and lively and looked as well as ever, right up to the final weeks. He was a man I never knew to be unfair, bad-tempered or ill-mannered.
Ronnie Corbett

There was an expectant air in the East End of London that day. Our three heroes saw off West Germany – with help from the other eight players. I worked at Brown's supermarket in East Ham and we got the afternoon off because no one was about. We had only a small screen at home so I watched it around my friend's house in Woolwich. Afterwards I had to catch a 101 bus back to East Ham. Car horns were hooting and claret and blue scarves hung from all the windows. Everybody waved at everybody else and street parties loomed. Complete strangers were even linking arms and singing 'Bubbles'. In the evening I went to the Hammers pub to toast Moore, Hurst and Peters.
Richard Digance

In 1966 I was in Wormwood Scrubs. I was in the prison hospital with a .45 bullet wound to the thigh bone; it was hanging off my leg really. So I listened to the game on the radio – I went mad when we won. My only disappointment was there were no Arsenal players in the side.
'Mad' Frankie Fraser, ex-Richardson gang member

Chapter 13
Commercial break

David Walker

Met Bobby when he was organising the World Cup Willie merchandising for the 1966 World Cup. David and Bobby formed a shirt business in 1971. He is now the manager of rock band Status Quo.

It wasn't a case of everything Bobby touched in business failing. In truth, his involvement was either minimal or more often in name only. Bobby had to seek a future beyond football and he experimented with different things. In 1971, I started a business with him called Bobby Moore Shirts and Ties. We found we could make the business pay, but there was no great fortune to be made. Maybe the most honest thing I can say is we were the wrong people and it was the people who failed rather than Bobby.

Bobby and I opened a shop in Upper Montague Street in London. Customers were measured up there and Mike Summerbee's shirt factory made the garments to order. A year later we moved premises, changed the name to The Shirt Maker, installed a workshop, employed a cutter and switched markets to more exclusive shirts. Our first shirt was a disaster. We measured Bobby up and arranged for a photographer to shoot Bobby's fitting to use in some displays. The photographer arrived, Bobby tried it on and the shirt was about six sizes too small. He looked ridiculous!

Bobby was very meticulous in his work, totally professional. It was a very competitive market and it wasn't as easy as we expected. In the end, we licensed out Bobby's name to a conglomerate to mass produce shirts Bobby and I designed. It went on for a couple of years. We often made shirts for Bobby's friends Jimmy Tarbuck and Jimmy Greaves and I knew when we were short of our targets because Bob would ring up and say 'Make a few more for Tarby!'

After the shirts, I went into the music business and ended up managing Status Quo, the rock band. The singer, Francis Rossi, is a very shy person but on stage he can have thousands of people eating out of his hand and Bobby was the same. He wasn't an easy mixer either, quite shy, but out on the pitch Bobby could control the world. You get the impression they are big shots, unapproachable, but the truth is the complete opposite.

I met Bobby at the '66 World Cup tournament. A lion character called World Cup Willie had been created as a mascot for England. I was a sales manager responsible for the merchandising and Bobby helped promote it. They built a Willie village at Wembley and they sold everything: records, stickers, coins, dolls, there was even a World Cup Willie shove ha'penny game that Bobby invented. I swopped a ticket for the final with a spiv for a couple of World Cup Willie dolls. I got inside the stadium five minutes after kick-off and I had a fantastic seat right where they came up to collect the trophy.

Mark McCormack, the golf agent, once wanted Bobby on his books but he was worried because McCormack wanted 25% of everything Bobby earned. 'I don't mind giving him 50% of everything he gets me,' said Bobby. 'But 25% of everything is too much, especially as there is a natural demand anyway, people offer work already.' Personally, I felt it was mistake for Bobby to turn the guy down because

McCormack was the best and he would have got Bobby a lot of work. I think I said something like 'Maybe you're being a bit short-sighted, Bob?'

People talk of George Best and Stanley Matthews, but Bobby Moore was the first real star of football. He even looked like a star. He was one of the nicest guys you could ever meet.

Morris Keston

An England follower for many years, Morris built up a friendship with Bobby, and together they formed a leather business.

I followed Tottenham and England everywhere. In early '66 Bobby played for England against Poland at Goodison Park and we came back on the train together the next morning. We said hello before then, but the train journey forged the friendship. I was chairman of Bobby's testimonial comittee.

During the World Cup in '66, the England lads were staying at the Hendon Hall Hotel and my house was just round the corner. Bobby used to visit and have a cup of tea and a sandwich with my wife Sylvia and I. He used to bring Geoff Hurst or Jimmy Greaves with him. I think they were rather bored at the hotel.

When Bobby had the problem with the bracelet in Colombia we phoned his wife Tina and she came over for dinner a few times and we took her out there. I got a telegram from him in Mexico thanking us for looking after her, which I thought was wonderful in view of the ordeal he had just been through.

My wife is on the committee for handicapped children's aid and Bobby did a lot of work for us. Every year he came to a function at The Grosvenor House Hotel and raised large sums of money. When my wife had a day at Barking Town Hall for handicapped children he came and spent the whole day there just looking after them.

I was in the ladies fashion business and eventually I joined up with Freddie Harrison who was in the suede and leather side. I introduced Freddie to Bobby and we started this suede and leather business and all became good friends. I remember the whole Manchester City team coming down to London about 1969. Some 15 players all got fixed up with leather coats. City were playing in London and they came down to the factory on the Friday afternoon.

We had a show at the Hilton Park Lane leather fair and Sugar Ray Robinson was over in England and he tried on one of our coats. He had his photograph taken with him and said what a charming man Bobby was. He was really excited about meeting Bobby, bearing in mind that Sugar Ray was a star himself.

My friendship with Bobby grew and through the 70s and 80s we went to functions and saw each other at different things. I organised quite a few testimonials for players in those days, like Geoff Hurst and Pat Holland, and Bobby was always the first one to volunteer. 'Do you want any help?' he would say, or 'Can I do anything?' I didn't run them as businesses and take a rake-off, like people do these days.

The 1970 World Cup was Bobby's best as far as any individual performance goes. I watched the draw with Czechoslovakia at the Sporting Club in Tottenham Court Road and as England were through to the quarter-finals, I flew out the next morning to Mexico City and had a five hour drive across the desert to Leon. When we reached the hotel Bobby made us very welcome. 'Everything alright? Have you got your tickets and everything?' he asked. They were always his first thoughts.

I arranged a charity match, at Edgware, a few days before the '70 World Cup. Bobby had promised to play but he didn't have permission from the Football Association so he played in goal. He said 'I can't go out on the pitch, I'll get recognised, so I'll just play in goal. No one will recognise me in a tracksuit!' It was just before they flew out to Mexico.

We had a testimonial dinner and dance for Bobby at The Hilton about 1971 and we had about 1100 crammed in there. Danny la Rue, Ronnie Corbett, Tarby and Lynchy gave their services free, because they thought so much of Bobby.

Jerry Stevens

Tournament and Events Director, Variety Club of Britain Golf Society

Bobby was a member of the Variety Club Golf Society and I used to see him at events. He was a super guy and great to deal with. We organised one big event together in 1990 and it was a joy to work with him. I was amazed by his professionalism - he ran things like he would a defence, covering every point, every eventuality, and he was very precise, thorough and dependable. People talk about his orderliness and that was reflected in the way he wanted everything covered and just right.

We didn't spend a lot of time together because Bobby was heavily involved in business and only attended the events he was able to. But whenever I did meet him or spend any time with him, he was a delight to be with.

Danny Desmond

Chairman of Bride Hall Developments Plc

I can talk about Bob anytime. I didn't meet him until he retired from football – naturally I'd seen him play over the years. I couldn't say I'm a West Ham fan but I'm certainly a Bobby Moore fan. He was one of life's gentlemen and he always had time to smile and make a friendly comment to an admirer.

It always struck me that big business didn't see his enormous potential, especially in an ambassadorial role. I believe many of the top bosses were as awestruck with him as the rest of the nation and it didn't occur to them that Bobby might be interested in using his international status to promote their business or service. They must have decided it was beneath Bobby to get involved. For example, the first time I met him he came up to my office and when the secretary buzzed through that Bobby Moore was there to see me, it caused me a real flutter, I can tell you. But there was this guy with a lovely smile, who said: 'Hello, Mr. Desmond, very pleased to meet you.' We had an absolutely great lunch, such a laugh, and that was Bobby all over. There was never an ounce of arrogance in him. But from a business point of view, he had the best possible calling card: he was, after all, *the* captain of England.

It was such a shame that, as a footballing nation, we failed our top man. He never failed us but we certainly failed him. He was the finest captain we've ever had, and among the top sportsmen ever, the only man to lift the World Cup for England. I can't answer the question as to why the FA ignored him – only they can answer that. We can merely speculate. It has been suggested to me that perhaps Bobby's style in TV interviews, during his playing days, wasn't as polished as some players who made the media arena, and that his true character didn't come across in interviews. I'm not sure if that's the case but, certainly in later years, his relaxed way with the media grew with his exposure – his Capital Radio work and appearances on Sky TV were refreshingly informative. In the days when Bobby played, TV interviews were much less frequent. Bobby would probably have done a post-match interview on *The Big Match* twice a season, if he was lucky. Nowadays the media have a microphone under players' noses the moment they come off the pitch. Like everything, the more you do it, the better you become. Despite that, I personally remain unconvinced it was a factor in the FA's reasoning why they failed to exploit his vast potential off the pitch.

Bobby was always pulling my leg about something. I'd played non-League football in my time and once, at a meal, Bobby asked me, very seriously, to talk about my playing days. I was embarrassed to discuss it but he insisted. So I mentioned I'd played in Manchester United's youth side and for Hitchin, St. Albans and Enfield; that I'd played in the semi-final of the Amateur Cup and had been an England amateur trialist. To be honest, I was stretching it out to make it sound impressive. I added: 'But that's not playing football, is it?' He looked at me with that glint in his eye and said: 'No, know what you mean.' He laughed in that infectious way of his and I realised he'd been winding me up yet again. But that was Bob.

In life, at social gatherings, some people you gel with and you enjoy talking to, others not so much. So in certain situations you might duck those you don't and move on. Bobby would do that but only in the same way we all do. And he certainly wouldn't do it in a way that caused embarrassment or was a huge put-down for someone. He cared about people's feelings. He was such a nice guy.

Looking the part, as usual

Chapter 14
Press call

Jonathan Pearce

With Capital Radio since September 1987, Jonathan has commentated on nine FA Cup finals, three European finals, three European Championships and at two World Cup tournaments.

I was due to see Bobby on the Monday before he died but he was too ill and I flew out to Goa in India for a holiday on the Wednesday and Bobby passed away that morning. When I got to Goa there was a message from the Capital offices to say Bobby had died and to call them, but I was in the back of beyond and I couldn't phone out from the hotel. So I called a taxi and asked the driver to take me to a phone and he drove me into the jungle to the nearest post office.

On the way there the taxi driver said: 'You look upset?'

I replied: 'Yes, someone very special to me has died.'

He asked: 'Was it your father?'

'No,' I responded, 'but in lots of ways he was closer than my dad. He was like the close uncle and brother I never had. Actually, you may have heard of him. His name was Bobby Moore'

The taxi driver drove me to this post office, which was no more than a hut literally in a clearing in the middle of the jungle. It had three walls, no front door and a phone box in the corner with a little geezer who cranked up the phone. I was on the phone to London asking what happened when I turned around to find the entire village had gathered outside the post office. There must have been 500 people milling around in the middle of the Goan jungle. 10,000 miles away they knew who Bobby Moore was. It really hit me how much he meant to the world.

I didn't know he was ill until very late. I phoned him up one Saturday we were due to go to Arsenal. I said: 'You should know the tabloids are after you or one of your family.' He replied: 'I'd heard that so I'm going to make a statement.' I feared the worst and when he said his cancer was terminal I just broke down completely and burst out crying on the other end of the phone. Later, when he arrived at Arsenal, we gave each other a hug.

On the Monday I went to his house in Putney. I arranged a statement for TV and radio and Jeff Powell did one for the written media. Soon after the release of the statement there was an England home game and the TV monitors zoomed in on him and it became a bit of a circus. A few days later he was due at West Ham and the toughest thing I've ever had to do in my life was phone Bob and say: 'I don't think you really want to go.' He said: 'I desperately want to be there.' I suggested: 'It

> "When England were knocked out on penalties, we were so crestfallen. I turned around and Bobby, the man who had lifted the World Cup for England, had tears streaming down his face"

will be like a zoo: TV cameras, zoom lenses, all that stuff.' 'Well,' he said, 'It's your decision.' Thankfully, he agreed not to go.

People didn't realise he was one of the funniest guys you could meet, he had a very witty, dry sense of humour. We were commentating on the England v Republic of Ireland game for Capital in Italia '90. All the way through he kept mentioning the bathroom tap not having a very good game. I didn't understand and was thinking what on earth is Bobby on until I realised the linesman was a Japanese fellow and bathroom tap is, of course, Cockney rhyming slang for Jap.

About '91, Bobby and I answered calls on a live phone-in for Capital radio and a caller, Billy from Balham, asked Bobby about '66. 'Yes, Billy,' said Bobby, 'I remember it like it was yesterday.'

'Do you remember going up the steps to collect the World Cup?' asked Billy.

'Yes, I do,' said Bobby.

'And you took the Cup from the Queen and turned to the crowd?' said Billy.

'Yes,' said Bobby.

'Well, Bobby, while you were doing that, I was seeing your missus!'

I had apoplexy, chest pains, and quickly cut in with: 'Ah, time for a commercial break.'

After we were off the air I said to the producer: 'How on earth did this joker get through?' but Bobby was tugging on my sleeve. 'You've got to vet these bogus callers,' I was saying to the producer. Bobby was still pulling on me. 'Yes, Bobby, what is it?' I asked. 'I want to know what my wife did with those two complimentary tickets I gave her!' he joked.

On the eve of Italia '90, Bobby had to go to a reception and asked me along as his guest. The reception was in a huge hotel overlooking Rome with all the big stars in attendance: Pele, Beckenbauer, Dino Zoff. 'Who do you want to interview?' asked Bobby, ' I'll see what I can do for you.' I said, 'Pele, get me Pele!' So Bobby walked over to him. 'Edson, can you do an interview for Capital Radio in London?' and Pele said: 'No problem.' It was the first time I was star struck in my life. I looked at him and said: 'Er...Mr. Pele...are you enjoying it in Italy?' and he said: 'Yes, it is a beautiful country.' Tongue-tied I couldn't think of anything else to say except: 'Thank you, Mr. Pele.' When I turned back, Bobby was laughing at me. 'You prat, Pearco!' he said.

Bobby, Terry Venables, myself and another reporter were doing the commentary on the England v Germany semi-final. There were only three seats in our box but next door was this big, fat German spread over four seats. I politely asked if Bobby could use one and he said: 'Nein, Nein! I haf paid for all zees seats! I need zem all!' So Bobby stood at the back, behind us. When Germany scored with the free-kick the German was bouncing up and down, and we went potty when England equalised. At the end, when England were knocked out on penalties, we were so crestfallen, I was gutted and when I turned round to look at Bobby, the man who had lifted the World Cup for England had tears streaming down his face.

On a trip to Russia, we were delayed from getting into the press booth by a Russian press officer who claimed we didn't exist. In the end, they let me up to the box and the producer said: Where have you been? We're on the air in two minutes!' Bobby was still 400 feet below by the side of the pitch. Finally, we got through to Bobby on the phone and he made his way up the steps. England kicked off, attacked down the right and Lineker scored. I said: 'Yes, here we are in Russia, England 1-0, blah, blah,' by which time Bobby was sitting next to me and I said: 'Bobby, your reaction to the England goal?' and he replied: 'Oh, have we scored then, Pearco?'

When we did commentary on games in the north of England, he would always insist on doing the driving because he reckoned I had to work harder than him during the game with on-going commentary. I wanted to do my stint, but he wouldn't let me, even when he was ill.

Bobby would ring up most days of the week. He'd chat away to my wife, her mother – he had the ability to make a pauper think he was a prince. He made everyone's opinion as valid as his own. But because of the respect Bobby had from everyone, he got some amazing interviews. Bobby did a very good one with Gary Lineker after he was substituted by Graham Taylor in the European Championship and he got the greatest interview I've ever seen with Paul Gascoigne. Gazza was so awe-struck with Mooro he told Bobby stuff he wouldn't tell anyone else.

We had great fun with him at Capital. When we won a Sony award he was so chuffed he took the whole Capital team to Scribes for a night out. The award seemed as precious to him as winning the World Cup itself.

He was late arriving to commentate on a League match at Oxford, so we rang Stephanie and she explained he'd been to a function. Bobby arrived later, a bit worse for wear, and he said: 'Alright, Pearco?' I pointed to the mike to show it was live and I couldn't talk. I was saying: 'West Ham are on the attack, and in a few minutes we'll have commentary from Bobby Moore who has just joined me having been held up in a traffic jam.' I looked around at Bobby and he was fast asleep. It got to half-time and I dug him in the ribs to wake him up. I said : 'So, Bobby? half-time, 0-0, your thoughts on the first half?' and he replied: 'Well, Pearco, even stevens,' shut his eyes , and went back to sleep!

Martin Tyler

Started out as a TV commentator and reporter for ITV in the 70s and is now working for Sky Sports

I've been lucky enough to commentate in all the continents. Lots of times I've had linguistic difficulties, but mention the name Bobby Moore and there's a friendship there straight away. People want to talk about him in any language.

Bobby had class in everything he did. He'd dress well, his hair was always in place, he was always the embodiment of vigour and good health. It's a cruelty of life, even though he wasn't the youngest of the '66 boys, that he should be stricken in such a way. I saw him at Wembley a week before he died. I was in the sponsors lounge when he spoke and with his illness that took a lot of courage. It was the saddest thing I have ever seen.

My first reaction when I saw Bobby was why on earth had he gone there? I was with Richard Keys, our presenter at Sky Sports whose father died of cancer. Richard said: 'It's obviously something very serious.' We'd heard various rumours about his health but you didn't want to believe them. I realise now it was his opportunity to say goodbye to a lot of people.

I was heartbroken when I came home. It was about 1.30 in the morning and my wife was asleep. Normally, I never wake her. If we start talking then neither of us get to sleep. We've got young children we're invariably up at 6.30am. But that night I said to her: 'I've got to tell you this'. And I explained what had happened. Seeing him did prepare me for the shock of worse news a week later. I've never been affected like that before. It was like a member of my family. I'm very glad I saw him that night and I was one of those he said goodbye to.

I think he went out of his way to see as many people as he could. Maybe he hoped that the worst wouldn't occur and that he would be able to soldier on, but if he knew, and I suspect he did, it must have been the bravest thing he had ever done. He insisted on making the speech and it was terribly moving. He scaled the peaks and then had it cut short. A wonderful, but terribly short life.

Bobby was always such great fun. You'd be at a midweek game somewhere and he and Jonathan Pearce would have driven up. He really loved it. There are some players, or ex-players, who are doing media work because they have to. Bobby was never in that category. He really enjoyed the game. He loved talking about it. Criticising players and managers didn't come easy to him. He was very sympathetic to their difficulties and he became a master at deflecting those sort of questions on the phone-ins. He'd always see the other side of the story, saying: 'That's an interesting point of view, but it's not as easy as you think.' The broadcasting kept him in touch with the game and the people he loved. I always say if a former player is not going to be a manager, it's the next best thing.

Another vivid memory is of *The Big Match Christmas Show* which, in the 70s was presented by players like Rodney Marsh, Terry Mancini, Peter Taylor and Bobby. He was still perceived as being somewhat distant and it was a great coup to get Bobby Moore to say: 'Hello and welcome to the programme...' It was hard, so I was told, to ever get Bobby out of the diplomatic art of archetypical post-match quotes, but in one five second glimpse later in that show we captured the real Bobby Moore.

The first part of the programme had been recorded and he was to do the opening link for the second part. Just to clear his throat, Bobby picked up a glass of water as the red light on the camera came on. He realised it was actually a take and as he was sipping the water he said: 'Excuse me, it's just a gin and tonic...', put the glass down and carried on reading the auto-cue. It was wonderful.

Around 1975, when he was at Craven Cottage, ITV were going to do a *This Is Your Life* for Alan Mullery. We pretended to cover Fulham playing a team of schoolboys and in the middle of the game Eamonn Andrews walked on to the pitch and presented him with the red book. Bobby's *Life* had been done in 1971.

In the car park after the match Bobby said to me. 'Are you going up to the studios? Would you like a lift?' It was unbelievable for me. It was a bit like the Queen saying: 'Pop into the limo for a ride'. He had such impeccable manners, such a sense of dignity. It wasn't done for effect.

The story of why he wiped his muddy hands on the cloth of the Royal box. Bobby told me when he got to top of the stairs all he could visualise was the Queen in pure white gloves. 'We'd been playing on a wet pitch,' he said to me. 'So with such dirty, muddy hands I couldn't possibly shake hands with her and the only thing I could think of was to wipe my hands clean, first on my shirt, then on the velvet of the table.' It showed the instinct of the man.

People will tell you he loved a beer but he was always out the next day, sweating it out of his system. Even at the end you could spot him jogging around Battersea Park and Putney where he lived. He could drink almost as well as he played

but, importantly, he had the capacity to cope with it because he always paid his dues for any excesses. That night on the train coming back from the Fulham v. Birmingham City FA Cup semi-final, he kept going on the beers, saying: 'The hair of the dog and have another tipple,' but there was never any disgraceful behaviour, never any loss of control. Only drunks lose control and fall over. But not Bobby. Nothing like that at all.

Before the '75 FA Cup final Fulham were in dispute over which brand of boots they were supposed to wear and they were served with a writ the day before the final. The players were sitting watching television and drinking tea in the West Lodge Park hotel near Cockfosters and a bailiff marched in and said: 'I'm serving you a writ on behalf of so and so boots.' The room went quiet and Bobby said: 'That's it! We've got a writ-back, a writ-half and an inside-writ.' It was silly, but it just lightened the whole business and everybody laughed.

For so many of my generation, the '66 World Cup started a love affair, and we're still obsessed with it today. I believe if England won it again it would be a tonic for another 30 years. The ageing process is something we'd all choose to stop if we could but I'm very pleased I had my formative years at the time. Everything was optimistic and fresh and free, if you like, and the football success was part of that.

In his heyday, people saw Bobby as a cool, calm customer who could see off the Germans, the Brazilian attack and the Bogota mafia on his afternoon off without batting an eyelid.

He was the golden boy in English football. He looked golden, he played in a golden way and he won golden trophies. The Bobby Moore I knew never boasted about any of that. He really enjoyed other people's company and was happiest of all being one of the boys.

Michael Hart

Began as a messenger with Reg Hayter's agency in 1965. Michael has been with the Evening Standard since 1969.

From the moment I saw Bobby Moore play, he had for me, simply, a style about him. Even the way he carried the ball out of the tunnel was stylish. No one does that now. Bobby Moore and Bobby Charlton were from a time when the game had a bit more style and certainly a bit more dignity. It is gross in some respects today.

I first met Moore in person in 1968 when I worked for Reg Hayter's sports agency. Reg had a contract with Shoot! magazine, to provide a column with the England captain. I was 17 and he chose me to write it. I was very flattered.

I was a West Ham fan and Bobby was one of my heroes, so the thought of being in the presence of Bobby Moore was quite something for a young reporter of my age.

I would get a bus to the training ground to meet him and after training we would get in his Jaguar car and he would almost always drive to his clothing factory in Bethnal Green. During the journey, which lasted 30 minutes, I sat in the passenger seat with a tape recorder on my lap, a microphone in my hand and I would ask him questions for the column. Sometimes he had an idea, but more often than not, he had to be prompted. He would drop me at Mile End and I'd take the tube to Blackfriars, go into the agency office in Shoe Lane and write it up. It was a great honour and it was almost impossible to convince my friends I was actually interviewing Bobby Moore.

I was from a very ordinary background and when I was writing his column, I only had one jacket – my school blazer with the badge taken off! One day when I got in the car Bobby asked: 'Don't you have another jacket?' and I replied: 'No, I don't.' Two weeks later I got in the Jag and laying on the back seat was a mohair suit. He said it was a gift from him and if it didn't fit, he'd get me one that did. I was thrilled. I kept that suit for 20 years. It was a very kind gesture and it meant a lot to me.

> **"I got in the Jag and laying on the back seat was a mohair suit. It was a gift from him"**

I wouldn't describe myself as Bobby's friend. I believe he had very few really close friends who he confided in. He kept his own counsel pretty largely, but we got on well and I liked him as a person and admired the way he appeared never to let the storms in his life get on top of him.

Shortly after the bracelet affair, in August '70, someone sent a three-page anonymous letter, posted in Birmingham, to the Evening Standard saying that, 'Five men, two of them armed, would go ahead with a plan to kidnap Mrs Tina Moore and would only release her if Bobby paid them £10,000.' The police were informed, Bobby dropped out of a pre-season trip to Bournemouth to stay at home while detectives kept a round-the-clock guard on his family for several days. I remember

I went round to his house with the letter later that week and The Evening Standard ran a picture of Mooro with detectives and another of his house with his white Cadillac parked outside next to a police Morris Minor. Bobby and I joked about the whole thing afterwards but the police certainly treated it seriously. I recall Bobby himself was not in the least bit phased by it all.

I got quite close to him when he was at Fulham and did a few interviews with him during the '75 FA Cup run. Bobby was pleased to get away from West Ham when he did and he enjoyed his time at Fulham and began to mellow. His experiences later as a manager broadened his outlook on football further still and he was a better person for it.

After the announcement saying he was ill. I saw him in a corridor at the England v. San Marino match. He was visibly ill. It was a bit uncomfortable although we spent perhaps two minutes talking about nothing in particular, but I was really pleased I'd seen him and we'd talked. He died a week later and I was staggered. It really upset me.

Bobby was an icon and he's recognised as one of the key personalities of a very exciting era. In London, he was probably the most significant sporting personality of that time. There was Terry Downes and Henry Cooper, but somehow Bobby seemed to embrace the mood of the moment, good-looking, tall, golden hair – I wouldn't have minded being him, I must say!

Brian Glanville

The Sunday Times football correspondent for 33 years until 1992. After a spell with The People he now writes for The Times.

I had known Bobby for many years, but yet, I realised I didn't know him at all. I was asked to write a profile on Moore and was horrified to discover I knew so little about him. Bobby was very hard to get close to. Always to me, extremely courteous, genial and pleasant, but I never really got near him and I don't think many others did either.

He had a certain dry, East-London humour. He wasn't a natural comedian in the way Jimmy Greaves was, but I recall Bobby had the occasional dry aside. But he was such an introverted person, not expansive at all, with a reputation of answering a question with question. You would say: 'Hello Bobby, everything alright?' and he would answer: 'Yeah, alright? Sleep well?'

He probably was a great player, although he wasn't a great natural talent, more a triumph of mind over matter because he made himself into a great player. A bit like Kevin Keegan. Bobby was certainly an encouraging example to young players because you can make it if you have the willpower.

The most extraordinary example of his coolness under pressure was the Green Fire affair in Bogota - the bracelet business. I don't think there is any doubt that he was completely innocent of taking it and a story has since been circulated that he took the rap for a younger player. I'm not sure that was true, either, but I'm quite sure Bobby Moore didn't take the thing.

Bobby wasn't the white hen who never laid astray. He liked a drink. I remember before a match against Portugal in 1964, Bobby and six others broke curfew for a meal and a drink and then came back and found Alf Ramsey had put their passports on their beds as a warning. Apparently, as the story goes, Alf said nothing and let them squirm for two days then at the training session on the morning of the match he said to the squad: 'Out you go then. Except the seven. They know who they are.' When the seven were left behind he said: 'Let's make sure this doesn't happen again.'

To be fair, the rest of his career after West Ham was an anti-climax. I think perhaps he could have been a bit shrewder about what he got involved in. I remember there was a choice remark in Hunter Davies's *The Glory Game* saying: 'Everyone you met seemed to be a business partner of Bobby Moore'.

I liked him very much and I was disappointed things went so wrong for him.

Kenneth Wolstenholme

Started commentating for the BBC in 1947 and covered the '66 World Cup final saying those immortal words: 'They think it's all over....it is now!' He left the BBC in 1971 and now works for Channel 4.

I first became aware of Bobby Moore when he was an ever-improving member of the West Ham team, and then in 1962 he was something of a surprise choice for the England World Cup squad for Chile. It was believed he would just be a member of the squad rather than first choice, but his international debut in the warm-up game against Peru was the making of him. He was outstanding and from that day onwards his international career blossomed.

Bobby was a quiet individual but he didn't suffer fools gladly and he was quick to give a tongue-lashing to a team-mate who put his side in trouble.

He was an outstanding player because he was not the usual stopper-type centre-half. Instead he was a creative defender, rather in the manner of Neil Franklin. The nearest modern example of him, in my opinion, is Celtic's Alan Stubbs. Whenever Bobby won possession, which he invariably did thanks to his incredible powers of anticipation, he always wanted to use the ball. True, sometimes like everyone else, he had to boot the ball into row Z of the stand, but Bobby liked to make the pass which would turn defence into attack.

A great example was the brilliant pass he made to Geoff Hurst in the 120th minute of the '66 final. I knew there was hardly any time to go and I noticed the referee had put his whistle in his mouth so some fans thought he was going to blow and they started to climb over the barrier and run onto the pitch. So I said: 'Some people are on the pitch, they think it's all over...' Just then, Geoff hit the ball and the words just came: '...It is now!' Actually, I said: 'It is now' before the ball hit the back of the net, because it wouldn't have mattered if it had gone wide. The referee restarted the game, but blew up straight away.

It was a magical final, England v West Germany. There was no bad feeling evident even though a lot of people thought there would be. There was no segregation and Germans stood next to Englishmen with banners and hunting horns and goodness knows what. It was friendly occasion, like a carnival. The game was not the greatest football you've ever seen in your life, but it had all the tension and excitement simply because England were in the final. They won, and of course, Bobby lifted the World Cup.

Ken Jones

Sportswriter for the Daily Mirror for 14 years, the Sunday Mirror for 14 years and has worked for The Independent since it was launched.

I don't think any of us can say we really knew him. He was slightly introspective and a terrible insomniac too. He'd go walkabout in the early hours if he couldn't sleep. I remember coming across him on a park bench in Moscow at three in the morning. He wasn't drunk or anything, just sitting there resting, trying to get some kip. Bob wouldn't advertise the fact he was an insomniac. I think I said: 'How are you, Bob?' and he replied: 'Yes, alright, thanks,' as though it was totally normal to find the captain of England sitting on a park bench at three in the morning in the middle of Moscow!

On the eve of West Ham's European Cup Winners' Cup match in Zaragoza in '65, I was in a bar very late, one-thirty in the morning - and the curtains parted behind us and there was Bob Moore. I said: 'For Christ sake, Bob, what are you doing here?' I knew he couldn't sleep but there a few West Ham punters on the other side of the bar. I said: 'Look, do yourself a favour, get back to your room,' and he answered: 'I know what you're saying, Ken,' finished his drink and left. Thankfully, nobody else saw him. You couldn't do that these days, of course, there would be headlines everywhere. The next day, though, he was magnificent, even playing in an unfamiliar straight centre-half position.

He was hard though. Bob could hurt people on the field if he was provoked and you wouldn't see it happen. He wasn't an intimidator, but if there was trouble from the opposition – you know, bully-boy tactics – Bob could handle it. Some players were vindictive. I know one West Ham player who would wait three seasons to get revenge on someone who had done him, but Bob wasn't like that. Sometimes you'd see someone kick Moore and later the fellow would be on the deck and Bob would be thirty yards away, looking at the sky!

In the dressing room, he wouldn't say much, he wasn't a ranter. But when the buzzer went, he just picked up the ball and said: 'Come on, let's go to work!' Apparently, that's exactly what he said before the '66 World Cup final.

After the '70 World Cup game between Brazil and Czechoslovakia finished 4-1, everyone was buzzing about Pele, but what bothered Alf Ramsey most was the free-kicks. Jairzinho would stand in the wall and disrupt it, Rivelino would run at the ball, twist and hit it with his left peg, Jairzinho would duck and the ball would fly into the net. In training Alf was very concerned and Bob said: 'It's not a problem. I'll stand behind the wall.' In the game, the Brazilians did get a free-kick in the same area, so Bob stood behind the wall. Rivelino whacked it, but Bob killed it on his chest, let it drop, hit Geoff Hurst with a thirty-five yard pass and jogged away in that nonchalant way of his as if to say: 'What's all the fuss about?'

Nigel Clarke

Joined the Daily Mirror in 1965 and was responsible for 'The Bobby Moore Column' in the Mirror for two years. Joined the Daily Mail in 1997

Brian Clough tried to sign Bobby Moore. Cloughie turned up by chance at the Wimbledon tennis championships one year and asked me about Bobby moving to Derby County. The place was full of people dressed in posh outfits and Cloughie wandered through the gates wearing an England top with the badge hanging off, a pair of shorts, no socks and tennis shoes.

'I want your mate,' he said to me. 'You sound like you want to do some serious business?' I replied. 'I want your mate,' he repeated. 'Fine,' I said, 'here's his number, you'd better do something about it.' I rang Bob immediately and told him to expect a phone call and, sure enough, Cloughie rang and they arranged to meet at Churchills for a drink and a chat. I wrote a story on it in the paper saying Cloughie wanted Moore to play for Derby, it was quite sensational at the time, they put it on the front page. Ron Greenwood, the West Ham manager, dropped Bobby and was none too happy about the whole thing - everyone blamed me. In the end they had to call the deal off because Greenwood was determined not to let Bobby go. So Bob stayed and realised he had to keep doing his best for West Ham and his England captaincy. It wasn't Bobby's nature not to try.

Later, towards the end of Bobby's playing career when Cloughie was managing Brighton and Hove Albion for a very short period of time, he again asked me if Bobby would be interested in coming to play for him. Bobby was at Fulham at the time and he didn't want to let them down after just getting to the 1975 FA Cup final.

For two years I used to write Bob's column in the Daily Mirror and it usually took us all day. We would either meet at Bob's factory or we'd meet at places like the Old Globe in Bow about 11.30am. I'd stay with Bob 'till about six-thirty and the column would take in about six other watering holes. Sometimes Bobby would be doing a personal appearance somewhere, opening a store or doing a presentation and I'd go with him. It was easy to do because we were firm friends. Much of the time, I'd have an idea about a subject and he'd be more than happy. Bob made sure he contributed because he was very conscious of his image but he invariably trusted me to expand on an agreed theme. It was a total labour of love for me. I noticed Bob's preferred drink was light ale and he rarely seemed to eat - if he did, it would just be a cold plate of meat. I tried matching him beer for beer but I almost drowned in a sea of light ale and lager!

Around '73, before the tour that took in matches against Czechoslovakia, Russia and Poland, the squad was staying in a London hotel and I was invited up to Bobby's room: 'Quick, quick, Come in! I've got something to show you!' said Bob, gesturing for me to enter. Remember that Alf Ramsey was very strict with the players and I couldn't work out what was going on. Bob ushered me into the bathroom, closed the door and pointed to the bath. Submerged under the water in the bath were about two dozen cans of light ale. He was so delighted with this little stash of beers he had smuggled in that he kept running the cold tap to keep them cool.

Bobby was one of the only men I knew who could say 'No!' to a gorgeous woman. We would be in a country like Italy and sitting in a bar having a quiet chat and a beer and locals would spot him and gather round - he was adored by the Italians. And there would be real stunning women, birds who other blokes would be drooling over, and they would be flocking around Bob making it very clear they wanted him, but Bob was so nonplussed by it all. He'd say: 'Look, darlin', you're beautiful, but I'm married and I'm having a nice talk about football with my mate, thanks.' He could've pulled women all over the world, but he just wasn't interested, even in the incredible women. I don't care what you say, most blokes are hot-blooded and all that and it takes a special kind of guy to be a world-renowned celebrity and have beautiful women throwing themselves at them and still be able to resist.

> **"Bob ushered me into the bathroom, closed the door and pointed to the bath. Submerged under the water in the bath were about two dozen cans of light ale."**

There was a different kind of relationship then between press and players. We were genuine friends and we'd talk football, you'd never dream of breaking a confidence or writing anything that wasn't football. The relationship has altered because the press has changed. With football being such big business, news reporters cover games. They don't have to build relationships with anyone, just report what they're asked for, then the next day they're assigned another job. When players get stitched up the trust goes and players can't distinguish between sports reporters and news hounds. We would go out as a foursome with the wives and there was never any question of me writing Bobby Moore was drinking. Trust was a two-way thing. If I ever said to him: 'Have a good drink last night?' He'd invariably reply: 'Well, Nige, a car needs petrol, old son!'

He was hard to get to know but when you did get to know him, he was a good, solid friend. He also loved his country. If ever a man was born to be captain of England it was him. The best moment of his playing career was walking out wearing that captain's jersey for England and the worst was when Alf dropped him for the Poland game and played Norman Hunter instead. Bob was really hurt, crushed, by the decision to drop him.

Pele used to study tapes of Bobby's defending because he knew he would have to be extra special to get by him. Pele thought Bob was a genius. Funnily enough, Bob thought

Bobby making a young footballer's day as he presents the prizes at Wembley.

the same of Pele. The first time Bob played against him he realised he had a subconscious fear of Pele because for years he'd read about how the Brazilian was a superman who could run, jump and shoot faster and harder than anyone in the world. Bob said when the game started he trapped Pele on the by-line and went to put his tackle in but by the time his foot got there, Pele was two yards away. It was, Bob said, the most convincing feint he'd ever seen because Pele dropped his shoulder, sent Bobby the wrong way and it let the Brazilian slip past. And not many players got a ball past Bobby Moore.

The only time Bobby lost his temper and snapped at me was, believe it or not, over a can of lager. We were returning from Norwich by train early one season and it was a boiling hot day. In those days, travelling journalists often joined the teams on the trains and I had been invited to have some dinner at a players' table. I was sitting with Bobby, Clyde Best and Frank Lampard and there was a journalist pal of mine sitting behind us. For some reason, there weren't enough beers on board and we only had a few on the table and I passed one to the journalist. Bobby whirled around on me and said: 'What are you doing?' I said: 'Giving a beer to my pal.' Bobby's eyes were flashing and his nostrils flared and he snapped: 'Don't you ever give my beers away!' He meant it. He was really cross because I'd given away one of his beloved lagers. But that was the only time we ever had a cross word.

I don't know the whole reason for the country's reaction to Bobby's death. All the obvious things were true: he was brilliant at what he did, a great ambassador, proud to be an Englishman, had great style, clean cut, there was nothing ever dodgy about him. Bobby was respected everywhere, even by Northerners and the Scots, who hated the English. I remember at Hampden Park one year a big Jock leapt out of the crowd and ran towards Bobby - for a second people thought he might attack him but he handed Bobby a bunch of daffodils. Bob just smiled, smelled them then calmly presented them to someone in the crowd. He personified the football hero: blond, good-looking, pretty wife, expensive car, big house, the lot. I went to Upton Park after Bobby died and the tributes were incredible, especially as it was all for just one man.

Like so many people who'd followed his career from the press box, I saw him at Wembley for the San Marino match for the last time. He looked dreadfully ill and he came up and said: 'Hello old son, how are you?' I shuddered and I couldn't continue the conversation and when I walked out of the press Room I had an awful tightness in my chest and I felt sick. When the news came in of his death I cried at my desk in the office. I just couldn't help it.

David Miller

Until 1997, David was a football writer for The Times. He now writes for The Daily Telegraph. He has written many books, including 'The Boys of '66 - England's last glory'

Prior to Alf Ramsey becoming manager, England used an international selection committee to pick the team, which meant there was a high turnover and the England team were often like strangers to each other.

When Alf came along, he picked the team. There were fewer changes, less turnover in personnel, and the changes he did make were gradual. Alf chose 'team' players to fit the system, not necessarily the best in the country. He understood the importance of character just as much as ability, he wanted blokes who were entirely reliable and everyone in that team who won the World Cup came under that scrutiny.

Alf created a 'club' at England level. A squad ethic. There was competitive training but little rivalry within the squad. Bobby Moore talked about the team having units within it that functioned together. There was Moore, Hurst and Peters from West Ham and Bobby Charlton and Nobby Stiles from Manchester United, which was half the team straight away. It was a coincidental by-product of the selection but something Alf was happy to exploit.

He was a very loyal man, not a shallow person. He was an exemplary professional. Last out of the bar, maybe, but always first on the training ground.

For all nations, yearning for success in sport is a spontaneous, natural emotion. It is collectively reassuring and gives pride and pleasure in a subjective way, especially with team events, where we feel the team is representing us. At such moments, the team become brothers. The affection in which Moore and his colleagues were held continued long after the impact of their triumph. Bobby's passing touched the nation and many people suddenly realised they had not appreciated him sufficiently when he was alive.

For me, his ability to retain quietly responsible bearing in all circumstances were never more apparent than when he was held under arrest in Bogota for five days in 1970, falsely accused of stealing the bracelet. Of the six sets of fingerprints found on the jeweller's glass cabinet from where the bracelet was allegedly removed, none were Moore's. A fact known by the Bogota police from the outset. He came back to play with such authority that drew even more admiration than four years previously.

Trevor Smith

Sports Editor at the Newham Recorder, where he has worked for 49 years.

Bobby didn't say much. I remember one of his first games for West Ham when they'd lost. I went into the dressing room – Ted Fenton gave me a lot of freedom in those days – and the players were having a heated examination of why they'd lost. Bobby was sitting in between Noel Cantwell and John Bond, he was about 18 then. Players were chipping in all sorts of things yet Bobby was just sitting there, sweat pouring down his face, listening intently to what was being said. He didn't miss a word but volunteered nothing himself.

In one match, I was up in the crowd in the main stand and sitting near me was Bobby's mum, Doris. Somebody in the crowd started having a go at Bobby so she stood up and had a right go at him. 'Don't you speak to my son like that!' she was saying.

Just before Bobby went off to his first World Cup in Chile in '62, he got engaged to Tina. We did a nice engagement picture for *The Recorder* of the two of them, I did an interview with Bobby, said goodbye and wished him luck – he was leaving for Chile the following evening. The next day I was walking my dog in the park when it ran off to investigate amongst some long grass and disturbed a couple having an innocent kiss. When I went over to collect the dog, they stood up. It was Bobby and Tina, saying their goodbyes. They were only having a cuddle because they weren't going to see each other for a month. Bobby looked very embarrassed – but I was more embarrassed than him!

This may sound strange, but he was God-like. He looked like we imagine God to be: upright, broad, blond hair – I think that scared the hell out of the opposition for a start. It's hard to accept he's gone, even after all this time.

Dave Hill

Author of 'England's Glory: 1966 and all that'

Bobby Moore was imperial at the back for England. He covered, organised, took the ball away from the danger men with assurance and style. I was particularly impressed with Bobby's quick free-kick against West Germany in the '66 final. With those little steps, he chipped the ball directly in the space in front of Tilkowski, their keeper, apparently towards no one in particular – until, of course, Hurst arrived in mid-air and nodded the ball into the bottom of the net. In the second it took to create the goal, no one except Moore and Hurst appeared to be playing. Tilkowski stood and pointed, Hottges was miles away. None of the Germans had ever been to West Ham's Chadwell Heath training ground. It had been the same in the game against Argentina. Hurst scored a similar headed goal and proved that none of the Argentinians had been to Chadwell Heath either.

The tournament in '66 generated enormous public interest. On the day of the final, nothing else mattered in England. Not the public spending cuts, not the run of the pound, the war in Vietnam, the Rolling Stones, Twiggy or LSD. It's absurd, but there it is. Only Alf Ramsey, a fierce patriot, and his brave England team were important.

By '66 the social status of footballers was gathering pace. Footballers had experienced the end of the maximum wage, a few had judged beauty contests and most had bought upmarket motor cars. But they were still youth-culture virgins, they all still had short haircuts. They were touched by the emerging mood but did not represent it.

However, some of them had already begun to think: 'I'll have a piece of that.' It was certainly beginning to happen to George Best. He had been dubbed 'El Beatle' by the Portuguese press after his performance at the Stadium of Light for Manchester United and I remember seeing a TV clip where Dave Mackay was showing a camera crew over his house – it was about 1963 – and it was a house with all mod cons. When you look back, Bobby Moore certainly had more potential than most to become a swinging footballer. He was handsome, blond hair, although he never really behaved like a member of The Who, did he?

Eventually many of the players became part of the youth boom – certainly by '70, many of them were sporting long hair and were wearing flares. Out of Ramsey's team, Moore and Alan Ball were the two, weren't they? By 1970, they'd caught up with the 60s. John Connelly told me that Alan Ball had visited him after the '66 World Cup and pulled up John's drive in a Lotus Elite. This was at a time when ordinary people were driving Morris Oxfords.

Bobby was very aware of who he was. Bobby seemed to have a very elegant look about his play, and yet he sometimes looked awkward, too, like when his little legs had to rush to reach a loose ball. He wasn't a particularly graceful player nor a gifted athlete but he did have an imperial way of carrying himself. In truth, he was able to look awkward and elegant at the same time, if that makes sense?

There was one moment in the Mexican match which was priceless Moore. It was 0-0 and the crowd had been impatiently chanting: 'We want goals!' England's defence was virtually redundant and Cohen sent a long cross over. On the end of it was Moore, in the box, who outjumped the Mexican defenders and headed just over the bar. One for the scrapbook that: a header at goal by Bobby Moore. It wasn't typical Moore, but then again, it was very Moore.

He went forward much more than people imagined.

Dennis Signy

A respected journalist, Dennis also wrote several books on West Ham.

I spent a lot of time at West Ham United in the 50s and 60s when I did a book with Ted Fenton, the manager, titled *At Home with the Hammers*. I knew Bobby before he became famous. He was a polite, pleasant lad and, unlike some people, the fame didn't change him through his career – he was always courteous.

There was a fellow at West Ham called Jack Turner – his title was Property Manager, and he dealt with players' problems, advice on insurance and houses. One day he said: 'There's a promising lad called Bobby Moore. He's going to develop into something big and I'm taking him under my wing and I'd like you to help in any journalistic matters.' So Jack and I decided to act for Bobby. I'd hate to use the word 'agent' but we guided him along.

In his early days in the first team, Bobby got sent off against Manchester City. There was a certain amount of naivety about him because he rang me on the Sunday and asked me to keep it out of the papers. Of course, they were already printed.

I had a ticket with my wife for all the England games in the '66 tournament and two years before that for the FA Cup final between West Ham and Preston North End I had a seat where the players came down after collecting their medals. I've got a photograph of Bobby holding the cup up and me congratulating him. Nice memories.

As secretary of the Football Writers' Association, I was delighted when Bobby won the Footballer of the Year award. His speech of acceptance was very dignified. At one of the dinners Bobby was sitting with Alan Mullery and George Best, who arrived late. After a while I looked up and George wasn't there. I said to Bobby: 'Where's George?' He had drunk a little too much wine so Bobby had quietly helped him out, led him to a cab and got him home without anyone realising he had left. No fuss. Bobby took responsibility, dealt with any crisis. That was typical of his thoughtfulness.

I don't think Bobby let too many people down during his lifetime.

Joe Lovejoy

Football correspondent at The Sunday Times

I had good cause to remember Bobby Moore when I was a kid. I was a Tottenham punter and one of my early heroes was Jimmy Robertson, the winger. I went to watch him play West Ham one day, quite excited about the problems he would cause down the wing, and I recall Alan Mullery played him inside the full-back and Jimmy was in on goal. They said Bobby Moore had no pace, but he materialised from nowhere, took the ball off Jimmy's toe and I thought: 'You bastard!' He made up so much ground to sneak the ball away, Bobby made it look as easy as shelling peas.

My other love was the Middlesex cricket team and one of my heroes was Alan Moss, the England fast bowler. He turned out for the Seconds – I think he was coming back from injury – and Bobby Moore, who was a fair cricketer, was playing for the Essex Second XI – a common occurrence in those days. Anyway, Moss was bowling at Mooro and the first three balls – all mean balls – were hit by Bobby for fours. I thought: 'You bastard!' Everywhere I looked, he was spanking my heroes.

MOORE **than a legend**

There didn't seem any limit to his ability.

The contrast between him and some of the current players and ex-players was immense. Take Michael Hart's story: when interviewing Mooro as a young lad, he had given Michael a suit to make him look smarter. Today's players would have sold him the suit and charged him for the interview!

Hugh McIlvanney

An award-winning journalist who was a sports writer with The Observer for 30 years. He has been at The Sunday Times for four years.

A lot of people were taken unawares by their feelings over Bobby Moore's death. The romance of sport can still move people and it got to them in a very special way with Moore. He had an understated quality, a straightforward manliness about him. That term embarrasses people but you've got to reach for special words when you're trying to describe him. It was infinitely more poignant because it was Bobby Moore who died. The nation would have been sorry to lose any of the '66 fellows, but I doubt any would have provoked the same reaction.

After the war, football took a wee time to recover. I don't believe in peddling nostalgia for the sake of it, but 50s football was exceptional, there were some gods playing: Matthews, Kopa, Di Stefano, Puskas, Wright and Edwards. The 60s were remarkable for football but as a decade it kidded itself it was wonderful when much of what was going on was self-delusion. But the good football spilled over into the 70s. To my mind, the serious decline in the English game began around the mid-70s.

Bobby was a great player throughout a period filled with some pretty remarkable players and to make himself such an attractive and heroic figure when he was a defender was some achievement.

Jock Stein watched Bobby play for Fulham in the twilight of his playing career in an Anglo-Scottish tournament up in Motherwell. Jock said to me: 'I saw that Moore play - there should be a law against him, he knows what's happening twenty minutes before anyone else.' It was a serious tribute from a great manager.

I was a big fan of Jimmy Greaves and I'd rather have played the World Cup with Jimmy than without him. There was even a school of thought that would rather have lost it with Jimmy than won it without him, but maybe that was rubbish. Bobby and Jimmy were good friends but Jimmy was a bit mischievous. He probably sensed he was drifting out of favour with Alf and got a bit more cheeky because of it. He was liable to be singing *'What's it all about, Alfie?'* in the back of the bus, things like that. Moore was linked with Jimmy because they were mates, from the same part of London.

For all his quietness, he took great joy in showing what he could do. You got the impression that normal pressure wasn't enough to bring out the best in Moore, he actually needed a crisis. When you see footage of the '70 World Cup match with

Serving in his sports shop

Brazil, you realise people didn't get carried away at the time with his performance. All those one-footed tackles, some of them looking very ungainly, tackling with the wrong foot, facing the wrong way, not textbook tackles, but Bobby is getting the ball off some pretty serious company. His timing of the moment to challenge was as vital as the timing of the tackle itself.

Brotherhood in sport really happened for Pele and Bobby Moore. Years after they stopped playing, Pele came to Wembley with a Brazilian film crew and Bobby set up an interview for me. Pele didn't arrive because the filming had been cancelled, but Bobby did. He drove all the way from Surrey to ensure the interview went ahead. I can't think of anyone else who would have taken so much trouble. When he found out Pele hadn't arrived he fixed it up for the next day. Eventually we had a long interview, at the end of which Pele explained he had never scored a goal at Wembley. He was wearing his street shoes and a leather jacket but he ran out on to the pitch with a ball, dribbled from the half-way line to six yards out and belted the ball into the net. Twice!

The greatest players have humility. They don't play the game to be flash or draw attention to themselves. The most effective thing they do is the simple, apparently dull things. If they need to tap it short, they'll do it. If there is something extravagant required, then they'll attempt it, but only when it's necessary. Football is not there for people to exhibit how smart they are. It's a team game and you get the job done. Bobby was very much like that. He said to me: 'If I've got to practice passing a ball from A to B ten times, I might be bored by it but I'll do it because that's what it takes to be a real player.' He had assurance, but he wasn't flash. He never took things for granted.

When I mentioned Bobby's slowness to him once he was quite sharp with me. He said: 'Speed means very little. A lot of players who thought they were fast achieved nothing because they didn't know where they were going.'

Most of the conversations I had with Bobby consisted of him asking questions. If some of them were mundane, it was to keep you from getting too close. When you knew him better, he was more expansive, but if somebody got a wee bit interrogative he would go back to the old question routine. He wasn't one for long monologues about how he did things. There was always a distance. You felt there was always another door inside him you could never reach.

Bobby wasn't the most eloquent guy in the world, but he was blessed with a presence that enabled him to convey what he wanted without saying much.

I know a lot of performers in sport but there aren't many I admired more than Moore. He was so utterly exceptional that you couldn't shout it from the rooftops loud enough.

Peter Stewart

As managing editor of Shoot! for many years, Peter compiled the 'Bobby Moore writes for you.' column. He is now editor of the West Ham United programme.

When *Shoot!* magazine was launched, Bobby was the magazine's first columnist. For me, being a West Ham supporter, the chance to see Bobby once a week for a chat was a dream come true. I would go down to Upton Park, where they used to do much of the training in those days, and sit in his car or I'd sometimes go to Rob Jenkins' physio room and ask Bobby questions while he was having treatment. Occasionally we would go to Cassettari's cafe and have a cup of tea. Once or twice I had to do interviews with him when Bobby was staying with the Engalnd squad at Hendon Hall and places like that. I felt very privileged when he would break training, walk over and sit on the grass with me.

On one occasion I did six interviews with him in one go because he was going away to Mexico for the 1970 World Cup. When I got home and replayed the tape, it was blank. I actually caught him at the airport in time and we found a little room in the VIP lounge, sat down and he went through the whole thing again. It shows what a true professional he was – it's bad enough getting players to sit down once, but to do a monster session like that twice is something else.

We arranged to do a 'My treasured possessions' column one week. I went to his house, Morlands, in Chigwell, with a photographer and when we arrived there was police everywhere, with reporters and cameramen, all parked on his front drive. We marched up to the front door and a policeman answered. Bob saw us and said: 'Its okay, let them in.' I asked what was going on and he explained they'd received a kidnap threat. But as tense as he must have been, he did the piece, answered questions, posed for pictures. As we left we were surrounded by English paparazzi and newsmen, all wanting to know who we were, what we were doing at the house and what was going on. Of course, we didn't say anything. He was a true professional and even under those circumstances, he fulfilled his obligation to the magazine.

One day outside his sports shop, it was teaming with rain and there were two small boys standing outside waiting for his autograph. Bobby turned up with some other players who refused to give them autographs yet Bob took the kids into the shop, dried them off, gave them an autograph and had a little chat with them. They came out like they had just seen Father Christmas.

I never found him anything less than cooperative, helpful and polite. If he said he would turn up for functions or meetings, he always did – even if he was occassionally late because he tried to cram so much in. Also, he never mentioned money. He was paid for the column, but it wasn't a great deal by today's standards. I think he appreciated the magazine taking him on and sticking with him – he became very much part of Shoot!. Not only did he never moan about money, but when the contract was up we seemed to continue on a verbal arrangement.

Invariably, he took any rare stick with a bit of fun. At Coventry once the fans were chanting 'Where's your bracelet Bobby Moore?' and he patted the back of his shorts as though it was safe in a pocket! I only saw Bobby lose his temper once during a match and retaliate to the crowd. In one of his rare mistakes he fluffed a backpass, the 'keeper was slow in coming out and got injured by the incoming striker, who had nipped in to get the ball. It was unusual because if Bobby got fouled he would just get up and dust himself down without a murmur but one of the fans in the Chicken Run shouted out: 'That was your fault, Moore!' Bobby whirled around and told the bloke where to go.

I used to see a fair bit of Bobby, what with doing the interviews, but didn't socialise with him as such. Like the rest of the press, I'd seen him at Wembley on his last visit, but a few days after I got a phone call from him, out of the blue. He said: 'I was just ringing to say thank you for all you have done over the years.' Of course, he was ringing to say farewell, wasn't he? I know I am not the only one he phoned.

The evening they announced his death I had just got in from the office and my wife said they had started to decorate the gates. Seeing all the tributes a few days later was very moving, very emotional. Bob would have found all that adulation very embarrassing, you know?

My father died a few years ago and his ashes are buried only a few bushes away from where Bobby is at The City of London cemetery in Wanstead.

Matthew Lorenzo

Sports correspondent with GMTV

My dad Peter was great friends with Bobby Moore. He was a reporter with the Daily Sketch, then he moved to the old-style Sun, which was a broadsheet, and at the same time during the mid-60s he was working for ITV and started 'Star Soccer' which was their first Sunday afternoon football programme. I was very lucky as a kid because dad's job meant I could get close to footballers. I went along with him to matches, knelt in the press box and he'd use me to break the ice when he interviewed them. We would watch West Ham matches even if he wasn't working - only my old man could get in without a pass and take an eight- year-old into the press box and get away with it. Bobby would pop round to our house and see dad about three times a year, usually on a Sunday, and they would have a cup of tea and a natter.

My old man took us on family holidays in the summer and, strangely enough, we always bumped into footballers! Once we went to Portugal and my mum was really looking forward to it. We'd been there only about two hours when she bumped into Kathy Peters, Martin's wife, and her suspicions were aroused straight away. It turned out we were in the same hotel as Martin, Bobby Charlton, Don Revie and Alan Mullery, but my dad swore blind he hadn't done it on purpose. Another time in Spain I was out for a walk along the beach with my dad and who did we find sunbathing 200 yards down the beach? Bobby Moore. He and dad spent the whole day in a bar!

Bobby with Geoff Hurst and former 'Star Soccer' presenter Peter Lorenzo, Matthew's father.

My mum told me about another time they went to Portugal. Dad and her were walking past this bar and through the open window he saw Bobby Moore and some of the lads. He said to mum: 'You walk home to the villa, I'll just have a quick drink with Bob.' She strolled up the road and dad went into the bar. A few minutes later, Bobby came running up the promenade chasing her and said: 'You come back and have a drink with us too, Max.'

The great thing for me was that I was able to follow in my old man's footsteps and work in the same arena.

People are forever using the word dignified to describe Bobby but it is the one word that always comes screaming out.

My experience was that anybody could walk up to Bobby and he would have time for them. You always got a buzz when Bobby shook your hand. You thought Blimey! That's Bobby Moore shaking my hand. I never got over that thrill.

Roger Hutchinson

A journalist and author, Roger wrote 'It Is Now! - the real story of England's '66 World Cup triumph' Living in Skye he writes for the West Highland Free Press.

The '66 final was similar to a Royal wedding in that the whole family watched it. You watched out of a sense of duty. It was what you did because you were English. Grannies and aunts knew that whatever happened it would be something everyone would be talking about for days afterwards. It was an excuse for a family get-together, cakes, buns, the lot. The game itself was comparatively irrelevant. It was the shared national experience.

MOORE than a legend

There were moments in the game that were lost on the uninitiated. When Germany equalised in the last minute I was having hysterics on the floor and I was in no mood to explain to the family what it meant. But Wolstenholme, the BBC commentator, was great for grannies and aunts. His commentatary was of somebody introducing the game to the viewer. He was forever saying: 'Of course, the off-side rule means that...' When he spoke, grannies and aunts paid attention, then went back to the tea and cakes.

There was no doubt in my mind that although British fans loved England for winning the World Cup, Alf's system wasn't popular. Football changed because of Ramsey's style. Work-rate replaced flair and football became more defence orientated. Something was decidedly lost. In fact, the number of goals in the English First Division actually dropped by about 30 to 40 per cent over the suceeding years. Everything was about stopping the opposition, prevention, a perfectly organised defence can stop any goal from happening. It's all absolutely true but its a very sterile view of the game. That's how Ramsey won the World Cup – 'Don't concede any goals and you'll get through.'

The British saw the team as a clean team, possibly a bit dour and stuffy and difficult to beat, but the rest of the world thought we were dirty. Some of the English tackling was disgraceful. Stiles on Simone of France was the worst, but there were others. In his book 'Football against the Enemy' Simon Kuper talks about being brought up in Holland and everybody there wanted Germany to win, even though the Dutch hated the Germans – it was only 20 years after they had been occupied in the war. It was the style England were playing and nobody really liked it.

Moore and Ramsey were similar in that they had both re-made themselves from working-class Essex backgrounds. In the sense that Ramsey went to elocution lessons and ended up talking like Peter Sellars' affected shop steward in 'I'm Alright Jack' – for a working-class boy to speak like that was crazy. For Moore, the equivalent was a flash lifestyle. Most professional footballers, particularly of Moore's era rather than Ramsey's, moved out of their class after the maximum wage restriction was lifted. My feeling is that Moore was quite a Thatcher supporter, frequent visiting Downing Street in the 80s. There was no question, Moore was looking after number one in pay deals. He was famous for being a tough negotiator at West Ham, hanging on for the last minute, probably to keep them waiting and see what everyone else was getting, in order to get the best possible deal. So much so that when the World Cup came around he was out of contract at West Ham and had to sign a temporary one. I have to say I don't honestly know why he stayed at West Ham. I suspect they were possibly dangling a 'stick around, next season we'll be up there challenging' promise in front of him, but, nevertheless, perhaps that's why he fought for a decent deal? It was only right the loyalty of the England captain was rewarded.

Moore certainly had a rapport with Ramsey. He once complained to Alf and the England doctor about the strictness at the squad get-togethers. The feeling among the rest of the players was that if anyone else other than Moore had complained, they would have been dropped. Let's not overlook Ramsey's qualities. He had an intense loyalty to those he put faith in, provided it was reciprocated. Ramsey inspired great confidence and Moore knew where his manager was coming from.

MOORE **than a legend**

If Bobby had asked Ron Greenwood if West Ham were going to win the league he would have probably got:'Well, maybe, there are some good teams out there.'With Ramsey, they got:'Yes, we're going to win the World Cup!'All the England players saw in Alf someone who was determined to win.You may find, of course, that those who weren't picked, tell a different story.

Actually, Ramsey was a manager who concentrated, foremostly, on defence. Moore was a defender, and what does a defender want? A manager who is as obsessed with stopping the opposition from scoring as he is.

Everybody says Moore was the player for the big occasion, but, even so, Moore's performance in that '66 final was just beyond belief.When you watch those takes now with the advantage of a thirty-year absence, the subtlety of the man grows on you.They claim there were three world-class players in that team: Moore, Banks and Bobby Charton, but Moore was the best of the three without question.

On the third viewing of Hurst's equaliser, you realise how utterly remarkable it was. Not only did Moore take the free-kick, but he won it as well. Moore has pushed upfield, he realises that he isn't going to take on Weber for speed because he hasn't got any speed, so he turns and faces his own goal to shield the ball from the German and just goes for the trip, which he gets. He doesn't hardly hit the ground and he's up, grabbing for the ball. He's got his hand on the ball, placing it, and he's up looking for the early cross. He starts to move forward, he's a long way out, and vision is such that he stops because he has seen Hurst's position and he knows that a split second too early and it will be wasted. So he checks the run, waits a second, then floats it over. It's all very well having the vision to see the opportunity but then you've got to have the ability to actually play the ball you need. But he does. The placement is perfect, Hurst has run into the space and doesn't even have to jump, his marker is nowhere and it's on his head and in the goal. 1-1. Moore was playing snooker with a football – he gets the ball to kiss Hurst's head and its in the pocket.You or me or my granny or aunt could've scored that goal if we'd been on the end of Moore's floated cross. England were back in it, thanks to Bobby.

Furthermore, in the dying seconds of extra time, he plays the one-two in his box while the whole world is telling him to boot it – undoubtedly it is what Ramsey would have wanted him to do.As Alan Hansen – one of the players people compare with Moore – says:'Nobody ever scored from row 23 of the stands.' But instead of doing that, Moore chooses to produce the most constructive piece of defending you'll ever see in your life. On receiving his return pass, Moore is looking to play a ball into the German half and it's perfectly flighted into Hurst's path.That was a completely anti-Ramsey footballing statement from Moore. For all the impression that Alf made on him, he was too much of a great footballer to do anything other than play great football when he wanted to, and that included the last minute of extra time in the World Cup final when England were just one goal up and Germany were pressing. Somehow he found space in his own half that was full of nine Germans.What took over was natural footballer's instinct.All the conditioning and responsibility was shrugged off in one moment.

There was so much of his performance that was outstanding that day, it is difficult to detail his contribution thoroughly.Apart from the mundane stuff you take for granted like no mistakes, keeping possession, accurate passing, shrewd positioning, no mistimed tackles, there were more subtle, vital examples of how good he was.

For instance, it was Moore who changed the whole emphasis of the England attack. He realised in the second half that Bobby Charlton was having a quiet game and that Ball was the one who was going to be the main man. Time and time again he ignored Charlton in favour of Ball, which was most unusual. Charlton had been a match-winner all through the tournament and Ball was a newcomer, a kid. He wasn't supposed to be such a major force and take the Germans apart. Bobby Moore saw that Charlton had done a good job in eclipsing Beckenbauer, who was terribly dangerous moving forward, so often scoring for Germany, but it just wasn't happening for Charlton that day. That was the real reason everybody noticed Ball was having such an outstanding second half and extra time period – it was due to the service he was getting from Moore. The captain was finding the time and space in possesion to let Ball get into position and pick him out with a pass. Some of the team took Bobby's lead and began feeding little Ballie. In the end, in extra time, Ball is everywhere, including the left-back position to play a one-two with Moore in the move that led to Hurst's third goal. But the switching of the emphasis from Charlton to Ball was just extraordinary. There probably isn't an accurate modern day comparison.

I've certainly never seen a greater British defender. When I heard Moore had died, it brought back memories. You retain this image of hitched-up shorts, a picture of health, jogging around Wembley holding that trophy with a huge grin on his face. If there was a better defender in the world, he would have to be pretty bloody special to compete with Moore on all the levels he was good at, wouldn't he?

He was genius.

Jeff Randall

Has been City Editor and Sports Editor at the Sunday Times.

I t was 1962 and Bobby Moore had not long made his England debut. I couldn't take my eyes off him. Handsome, outrageously talented and best of all, a local lad. For a kid born in London's East End, Moore was the quintessential hero.

On my ninth birthday, mum and dad took me to Moore's shop in Green Street, directly opposite the ground. They had promised me a West Ham tracksuit, and I was thrilled. But my excitement turned to awe when we arrived and Moore himself was there.

I'll never forget it. He helped me try on my new kit and then came outside for a photograph. I almost burst with pride. Bobby and me, like old mates, his arm round my shoulder, captured on film forever. Boy, did I sicken my school friends with that snap. My mum had it framed and parked it on top of the television.

It never occurred to me that I would meet Moore again. But 27 years after getting that tracksuit, I was invited to a charity golf day in Oxfordshire with Bobby Moore as my playing partner. By then, my passion for football had cooled but I couldn't wait to see the great man again.

Moore had only just got over his first bout of cancer, and I wasn't sure what to expect. But he turned up looking a million dollars, a little thinner than I had remembered, but still unmistakeably England's finest sportsman. On the way round, I told him about my picture and asked him if he would pose for another, just like the first, when we finished.

Ever the gentleman, he agreed. It was a smashing photo, and my mum had it set alongside the old one in a single frame. The juxtaposition of a black and white shot from the 60s with a colour one from the 90s worked beautifully. Bobby didn't look much different; despite his illness he had worn remarkably well. I, of course, had changed but the beaming smile on my face was the same – Bobby and me, well chuffed.

Moore died two years later. His passing unsettled me deeply, much more than I had expected. Sweet memories turned sour. A treasured part of my childhood had been ripped away.

Jeff Powell

Has worked at the Daily Mail for over 30 years. Jeff's biography 'Bobby Moore: the Life and Times of a Sporting Hero' is one of several books he has written.

Bobby Moore represented one of the last great, clean sportsmen. He was a self-made man with tremendous dignity - he could be put on a pedestal without losing the common touch. People felt a huge sense of loss in that respect. He wasn't terribly touched by commercialism either. The most important thing in his life was to play for his country. Putting that shirt on meant so much to him. He always said he never assumed he would be picked, not until that letter from the FA landed on the mat, which was how they did it in those days. Bobby Moore was driven by pride, not ego. I believe the nation felt it had lost an ambassador for the proper way of doing things, the proper way to be a sportsman. A throwback, if you like, to the virtues of life.

Bobby could communicate with a single gesture better than most men could with a thousand words. A classic example of that was when Germany equalised in the final. Bobby wasn't very happy with Jack Charlton's positioning just prior to the goal and he turned around and gave him the most serious glare. Jack says if Bobby had ranted at him he could have ranted back, but the stare from Bobby said two things: it was down to you, but let's get on with the game and don't do it again.

As a boy Bobby was painstakingly neat. Books on the shelves, toys in the box. And this neatness held him in good stead when he made it into a football dressing room. I'm sure everyone will speak of Bobby's tidy clothes, but it does compare with the slob generation of today. It's quite fascinating that his sense of order made history. From tidying toys to chesting down a loose ball and an inch-perfect pass to Geoff Hurst for what was one of the greatest incidents in the history of the world game. I think that's true, don't you? Toys in the box to balls in the box.

The night they won the final in '66, the squad went to the Royal Garden hotel where they waved to cheering crowds packed in the streets below. I remember Bobby told me at midnight, after the squad had attended a banquet in their honour, he wandered out onto the balcony alone to get some air to discover the street outside was still crammed with expectant crowds, waiting for a further glimpse of their heroes. Bobby said it gave him a real lump in the throat and it began to dawn on him how much winning the trophy meant to everyone. Shortly before Bobby died I met him at the same hotel. It turned out to be our last meeting and as we reflected on the 30th July all those years before, Bobby said to me: 'You know, old son, we had the world at our feet that night?'

At that final meeting, Bobby was wearing his best leather coat. After he died, Stephanie gave the coat to Malcolm Allison, one of Bobby's firmest friends. He was the main influence on Bobby in the beginning of his career. Malcolm has a very magnetic personality and he satisfied Bobby's attraction for larger-than-life characters.

Some people claimed Bobby was deliberately aloof. Bobby had no problem presenting a firm exterior when he felt someone fidgeting to get into his company. It was actually his way of being polite. If he sensed someone trying to muscle in he allowed that exterior to prevail so he didn't have to be rude to someone and have to virtually say: 'Sorry, not now.' He disliked declining a handshake or greeting, so it was his way of building a little protection around himself, a diplomatic front, if you like.

Did you know Bobby was taught some very useful things about movement from a ballroom dancer called Lenny Heppell? He had been assisting some of the players at the club with running technique. Even when Bobby had made it to the top of the rung he would still listen and he would reserve judgement on most theories until they were proven or disproven. Heppell told Bobby he ran upright like a coat hanger and it made his running harder and slower, so he talked Bobby into rolling his shoulders, but not his body. Using this technique, Bobby found he could make repeated runs and still feel fresh. Heppell also taught him to turn by moving his head first. Bobby began throwing his head and instead of falling over it helped his balance. Bobby told me it was magic. Something he wished he had heard of years before.

Bobby actually had heroes of his own. Ray Barlow was his first, the West Brom left-half. Bobby admired the calm way he played the ball around. Johnny Haynes' passing inspired him, but Manchester United's Duncan Edwards was the first player in the England team that Bobby identified with: clean-cut, handsome, great presence. Believe it or not, given his disciplined childhood, Bobby even played truant from school to watch Edwards play at White Hart Lane.

The rift that developed in later years between Moore and Ron Greenwood was, I suppose, a difference in style, not lack of professional respect. One example of this was when Ron signed John Cushley from Celtic, who could put it about a bit - exactly what West Ham needed. In his first game, a friendly against Borussia Dortmund, Cushley pursued Siggi Held and kept knocking him over, stopping him dictating play. The players thought he was doing a superb job, but Ron told him to take it easy. The result was Cushley never made another tackle for West Ham. Ironically Ron could turn a blind eye if Bobby whacked someone - and he did it with aplomb, even elegance - but Ron loathed kicking if it was so obvious. Their clash boiled down to Ron's purist ideals versus Bobby's realism. Regardless of the reason, West Ham lost something because of the mutual failure of both of them.

In the year of the Heysel tragedy, I won Sports Writer of the Year and for the presentation meal I was allowed to invite a few people and I invited Bobby and Ron, without telling them the other was coming. When I met them at the bar I said: 'You're both my pals, you've both been involved in my career and as I'm getting this accolade I want you both to share it with me.' Anyway, they shook hands, cuddled, we all had a meal and it was great. Any lingering stiffness in the relationship was disposed of. Bobby felt he had a greater appreciation of Ron's tremendous knowledge as time went by and Ron, on reflection, probably feels he should have compromised a bit. They were very warm to one another and I was overjoyed to have effected their reconciliation.

After the '66 win, Bobby was on show almost every minute of the day. I remember him telling me about how, when he was abroad on holiday, he rose in his hotel room at around six a.m. and opened the curtains to a roar and burst of applause from a Mediterranean crowd gathered beneath his window. It was like a scene out of Monty Python's Life of Brian where the crowd follow their messiah. He could do no wrong. In a restaurant everyone else would be sitting watching him and when he cut his steak a roar would go up like he'd just scored the winning goal.

Bobby was a bit cheesed off about not being used by England in any kind of consultant capacity. He didn't desperately want management of the England set-up necessarily, just to contribute. His great dismay was the state of our defending. I'd watch games with him and he'd say: 'Nobody has taught people to stay on their feet when tackling - you can't defend sitting on your backside.' He felt the art of the tackle was never fully appreciated - to him a clean dispossesion was as wonderful as a bicycle-kick.

He wasn't into lunging, either, not because it was beneath him, but he believed so many other aspects were more crucial, like cutting off angles, shutting off openings and denying space, and making it impossible for attackers to break through without relinquishing the ball. Bobby believed if you have to make a last-ditch lunge to retrieve a situation, something has gone seriously wrong beforehand. Defending, he said, began with your appreciation of the play as it developed in front of you. Only when you understood that, could you interpret it and nip it in the bud. The lunging tactic, Bobby felt, wasn't productive to good defending because you take yourself out of the game - you didn't want to slide tackle a Brazilian and give away free-kicks on the edge of the area or lunge at George Best, it was suicidal. And whacking through the back of forward's legs to get to the ball, in Bobby's eyes, was offensive and ignorant. Bobby's creed was that controlled interception should always be more preferable to a steaming tackle and that you should defend cleanly and correctly. He was terribly saddened that the teaching of the defensive arts was neglected. Any professional defender who wants to learn about their craft should watch a video of Bobby Moore in action.

There was also a feeling at one point that Bobby was giving his all for England, but not for West Ham, although he never subscribed to that and I don't think anyone else seriously did in truth. 'I wanted a League championship medal so badly,' he said to me, 'I would have lifted West Ham to the top single-handedly if it was possible.' I'd be surprised if a man going through the motions with his club football would say that, especially not with such conviction.

I believe Bobby was sold short in management. He wasn't necessarily a great communicator in the public arena but on the training ground had a lot to impart. All the misconceptions about him were a shame. If you talk to Terry Venables about Bobby's brief time at Crystal Palace working with the youth team, he'll tell you that the kids felt they learnt more with Bobby in one week than they had in five years.

Bobby with Franz Beckenbauer and Jeff Powell

The eventual outcome of the situation in Bogota with the accusation of stealing the bracelet showed Bobby's true mettle. They messed with the wrong guy there, didn't they? There was this man arrested at the hotel, imprisoned under house arrest, facing charges of stealing, a World Cup tournament imminent. Not sure what would happen to him, it was a complete nightmare. In the end, the guards, who Bobby called Jose and Pedro, got so used to him, they would happily sleep on in their chairs and let Bobby go out for his early morning run, quite confident he would return. Later, when Bobby secured permission to train on a local park pitch, he found Pedro and Jose and a gaggle of urchins waiting with a football. The guards kept their guns on as they joined in an impromptu kickabout with Bobby Moore and dozens of barefooted Bogota kids. The TV cameras arrived and overnight Bobby was transformed from jailbird into a national hero. When he was cleared and released to leave the country, thousands of Colombians massed at the airport to see him off and Bobby passed through waving to the throng, shaking hands and kissing the foreheads of babies thrust into his face. Only Bobby Moore could win over a country like that - be held under guard and end up leaving like Muhammad Ali or Nelson Mandela.

Although it was a shock to the people of England at the time, others were more aware of some of things that can happen in Colombia. Omar Sivori, the Argentinian midfield veteran, told him that tricks like those were normal in Colombia, they try blackmail, some people worried for their reputation pay a few thousand dollars for whatever it is they are supposed to have stolen; and Joao Saldanha, manager of

Brazil, said that it had happened to him in the same hotel, but with a different shop, so he locked the door, threw away the key and called the police, demanding they find anything missing. Bobby took solace from such support, but I think it always bugged him that there were still people out there who suspected he might be guilty.

Bobby died at a time when men who could attract modest admiration were in desperately dwindling supply. Also, Bobby was the first to go out of the '66 lads and he was the one who looked the most indestructible. That team represented the summit of our achievement in the game that we take our greatest national pride from. We all get vunerable when friends and contempories die, we feel a reminder of our vunerability. I think the nation looked at the indestructible Bobby Moore and decided he'd gone at a seemingly-impossible young age - it gave everybody a sudden awareness of human fragility. In losing him we lost a pillar. That's why it had such a profound effect - the feeling was: If he could go, then it could happen to any one of us.

The truth of the matter is we haven't replaced him either. Tony Adams is a battler, but he doesn't have Bobby's control of the ball or what's around him; Bryan Robson was a similar leader by example, but didn't carry Bobby's presence in the eyes of the nation; Gary Lineker was a nice clean boy and a good goalscorer, but not a leader like Bobby. There's been no Henry at Agincourt. We've never replaced

Bobby and I'm not sure we ever will.

Bobby would want the next great rallying figure to present himself so that England could be great again, so we could beat the Germans instead of narrowly losing to them again. He wouldn't resent the next Bobby Moore at all - in fact, if he was alive, he would even help develop him.

I miss him. Especially the late night phone calls when he had insomnia, he wasn't averse to calling me in the early hours. But there was the flip side to his insomnia problem - if you wanted someone to talk to at three in the morning, you could rely on Bobby to answer the phone.

Bobby would always pick up the phone. He was that sort of man.

MOORE than a legend

Moore tributes

Bobby's second first team appearance was against Nottingham Forest. Johnny Quigley ran him ragged as the Hammers got trounced 4-0. By pure coincidence it was the night of his first date with Tina and he spent it preoccupied with whether or not he would ever play for West Ham again.

The gateway to first-team football was cracked open again when John Smith left for Tottenham. Although he got selected, the results were poor, but things changed for Bobby with the arrival of Ron Greenwood in 1961. In the FA Cup final in '64 against Preston, at 1-0 down, it was Moore's pass that fed John Sissons that eventually created the equaliser. Winning goals from Hurst and Boyce followed. In the European Cup Winners' Cup final against TSV Munich the following year, Moore contributed again in one of his greatest performances. It was his cross from a short free-kick that Alan Sealey tapped in for the second goal.

Even when the battle on the pitch was at its fiercest, Bobby had the calm and serenity of a man fishing in solitude on some faraway river bank.
Steve Curry, Sunday Telegraph

You struggled to find any weakness in Bobby Moore: In only his second game against Hungary in the '62 World Cup, Lajos Tichy sidestepped him to score the opening goal; he let a long ball go over his head for Dzajic to knock us out of the European semi; when Sigi Held ran at him he gave away the penalty to put Germany 2-1 up in Netzer's match; his drag back let Lubanski in for the goal that effectively knocked us out of the '74 finals and he was standing on the line when Anastasi's shot went between his legs . . . but all of this was at the top and tail of his career. From '63 to '71 he was, unanimously, everyone's best defender. He could've kicked pieces out of people but even during the Hunter-Storey era, he kept faith with clean tackling. It's England's loss that his style of play didn't start a trend.
Cris Freddi, *When Saturday Comes*

Bobby Moore had a word in the last tactical master-stroke of the '66 team, which was to bring in West Ham's Geoff Hurst. He rarely spoke of the decision but was deeply sympathetic when his closest friend, Jimmy Greaves, paid the price.
Norman Fox, *Independent on Sunday*

In a sport that has spawned its share of scallywags, Bobby Moore had a stature and a bearing that was never diminished.
Brian Moore, ITV Sports presenter

It never surprised me that he found management was harder than playing for him. 'I'd rather face Pele in a match every day of the week than tell some young player I'd dropped him,' he told me. He once organised a charity match at St.

MOORE than a legend

Albans and managed to get so many star names, including Franz Beckenbauer, who flew in from Germany, that he didnt know who to leave out. At the start of the second half he had 13 players in his team and when the referee pointed it out, he said: 'Well Franz, it looks like you and I are out!'
Brian Madley, *The People*

After his quiet private funeral in Putney, there was a sad, slightly numb, national consensus that there had rarely been such grieving for a sports star. There was an over-powering sense that something had changed, something in ourselves, per-haps even that some of our dreams had shattered. Younger generations could not help but stop and ask: 'Who was this man, this footballer?' Something about Bobby Moore carried him over the decades.
James Lawton, *Daily Express*

A measure of Bobby Moore's greatness was the way his dignity – and his sense of humour - survived the ordeal of falsely being accused of stealing a bracelet in Colombia. He said later: 'I find myself out shopping and looking in jeweller's win-dows with my hands stuck in my pockets, pointing things out to my wife with my nose.' We should have made a better job of celebrating Bobby Moore when he was alive.
Patrick Barclay, *The Observer*

Moore was a man of few unnecessary words, rather like Alf Ramsey. Neither was comfortable with a microphone pushed into his face and television cameras scru-tinising every twitch. Reporters would make a beeline for Nobby Stiles or Jack Charlton if they wanted a racy quote. Ramsey and his captain would only con-cede the obvious, and with no particular fluency. In these days of 20-second soundbites, both would have been left gasping. Bobby was too nice to make it as a manager, his forcefulness on the pitch vanishing once he was in civvies.
Tony Francis, TV presenter, writing in *The Sunday Times*

In 1964, the BBC started a programme to train all our cameramen and techni-cians for the World Cup. We didn't have any crews specialising in covering soc-cer. One day they'd be doing an opera, the next a boxing match. In the end we had 54 people at Wembley and eight cameras. We gave each cameraman photos of each squad and told them to learn the players. Some of the crews were nervous but, in the end, when the goals went in, they were the coolest people around. The heat in the control room was unbearable and we were all exhausted at the end. At 7pm I came out and walked around the pitch. It was deserted and there was just the noise of plastic cups rustling in the breeze. With no-one else about, I wanted to savour the moment. It felt good.
Alec Weeks, producer of the BBC's *Match of the Day* and 1966 World Cup final

Chapter 15
That was then...
Bobby's era

Chris Lightbown

Has worked on The Sunday Times as a football writer for 19 years

There are reasons why Bobby Moore captured the imagination of the nation. Football has always been tapping into something far, far deeper and England's winning the World Cup in 1966 and Bobby's death showed this.

I remember my auntie and her daughter coming to stay and asking if we minded their watching the football that night. I think it was the game against France. Of course, we didn't mind – we were watching it anyway. But it was incredible seeing them watch it, too. Believe me, you could not have two more unlikely football fans than my auntie and cousin.

But that was happening all round the country. People who did not have the slightest interest in football were becoming involved with England and that was how football became a national sport instead of just a sport for a section of the country. The 1966 World Cup is what did that.

At that time, people were desperate for the country to do well in any way and for Englishness to be asserted. But the reaction would not have been so great had the sport not been football or the leader not been Bobby.

There was a specific reason for this and it was because in the mid '60s, we were losing Englishness. Englishness was falling through our hands like mercury and it was all the more frustrating because you couldn't see how it was happening but you knew that it was.

Then that team, led by Bobby, gave us back our Englishness, in a way that even swept up people like my auntie and her daughter who detested football.

I never really understood this until 1988 when I was writing a book about Millwall's involvement with their local community and talking to John Stalker who had become involved with the club. We were talking about why teams have certain colours, when he said: 'The colours go back to the holy wars. Even when people have moved out, and never go to a ground, they still keep the association. It is a love that lasts a lifetime.'

This was almost said as a throwaway in a long interview. But it made a very powerful impression on me and, if you follow it through, it explains why Bobby Moore made such an impact on our country and why football means so much to us.

You have to remember that football began as my village versus your village, when each village had a distinctive identity. Then after a while, the need for a flag would arise as a badge of its identity. That would be a big decision. You might want to commemorate, say, the death by drowning of a well-loved family in a flood in your village, so your flag might include red for blood and blue for water. Or you might want to show that yours was the village of golden wheat, really fine wheat which had given your families a good living and become a source of pride. So you might base your flag on yellow, perhaps adding some green for the earth.

Eventually, that village would join up with the others to go and fight in the holy wars, which were the medieval version of the World Cup. They actually thought the holy grail – the cup Christ drank from at the last supper – was in Jerusalem and they were going to win it and bring it back to Europe for our reli-

*Prime Minister
Harold Wilson*

gion. So the Lord of your manor kitted out the village's men in the colours of your flag and the different villages joined together and out of their coming together, there became an Englishness.

So look at football again. Look at 90 or so clubs, each having a distinctive identity, even if it is only a mile away from another club. The clubs are the villages by another name, tapping into very deep senses of identity. The same deep lying folklore lingers on in other ways, in some pubs and churches, in bits of handicraft and music and in certain local traditions and language. But nothing retains the connection back to the times of local identity as vividly as football does.

That is the deeper level the game has always been tapping into. It is the reason why the feelings about football run so strong, it is why the game will periodically take hold of people who hold no brief for football and it is the underlying cause of hooliganism. The villages were the strands of our national identity for thousands of years and strands which have been woven over such time do not disappear. They just submerge and then surface in things like football.

But the Englishness that bound these strands together was coming apart in the mid 60s. That is why Bobby had such an impact on people who had no interest in football. For Bobby was really a person of the 50s and in the turmoil of the 60s, that made him a symbol of more secure times. He was certainly a great player, but it was the state of the national stage when Bobby arrived on it that made him so important to the country as a whole, as opposed to the football fans.

This needs explaining because in the national memory the 60s were a vibrant time, with British ideas and personalities taking the world by storm and Bobby playing a part in that process. But that was not the whole picture and the bit that is missing shows why Bobby had such a stunning effect on the country.

At the time, things like Mary Quant's fashions, the Minicar and the Carnaby Street stuff were seen for what they were – good fun and great morale boosters – but trivial things we were turning to because everthing else was going wrong.

In the mid 60s, Britain and England – few people made a distinction at that time – were in dreadful trouble. Anyone of that generation will remember the Prime Minister, Harold Wilson, repeatedly making ministerial broadcasts about the latest financial crisis. He was always saying all of us had to tighten our belts. One crisis led to the amount of money anybody could take out of the country being restricted to £40. It was really serious stuff. My family were quite frightened and that was not unusual. There was crisis after crisis, with no sign of things getting any better.

Other factors made it worse. Labour's election in 1964 had seemed to be the solution to our decline. We had had a Tory government for 13 years and people felt immense frustration with it. They were old-style Tories who were wrong for the new era. Not just politically wrong, but culturally wrong, like parents who forced you to stay at home too long. They had kept the country within its limits and there was a yearning to break out, even if the result was unclear.

Then Labour won the election. All hopes were raised and it looked as if everything which had been held up for 13 years was finally going to be sorted out, or at least addressed. But when they got into office, Labour found that the balance of payments deficit was much greater than they had been led to believe by the Tory treasury and we faced a national emergency. It got worse because the institutions that kept their money in sterling did not want a socialist government and did everything possible to undermine it. So trying to run the country became like trying to complete a Rubik cube while others were trying to undo every move you made. It was impossible.

By 1966, faith in Labour was wavering and people were getting confused. Wilson had called an election earlier that year, and turned a small majority into one of nearly 100. But it was seen as his last chance because the hopes he had raised hadn't been satisfied.

Ask anybody now, and they will remember that year for the World Cup, and rightfully so. But underneath the enthusiasm, there was an underlying realisation that this was froth on top of beer which was turning sour and soon, all we were going to be left with, wonderful as it was, was the froth. I think that is one of the reasons why there was so much hysteria about '66, hysteria which repeats itself on major football occasions to this day.

Wilson got to the game by flying through the night from America. He landed at 1.30pm and was driven straight to Wembley. In the aftermath of winning the World Cup, people have forgotten why he had gone to America in the first place. But he had gone for emergency talks with President Johnson about Britain's near-bankruptcy. We were right on the edge.

The feeling of security we had taken for granted, even through the war, was slipping away, almost by the day at that stage, and the English aren't very good at feeling uneasy in circumstances like these. Not in circumstances of realising we hadn't really won the war and that Germany and Japan, of all countries, were overtaking us.

This mocked what we had endured during the war and the insecurity was undermining the unity which had helped us to win and then continued into our consensus politics. We had taken a stab at what we thought was a radical government with Labour, and that was not working, either. So we were entering uncharted waters and people wanted to run back to their villages and bury their heads under the pillow or – depending on their temperament – blame the village down the road for the crisis.

Usually, this works in England. There is no such place as London, it's a vast collection of little villages that have got joined up and the same applies to the other cities because the tendency to live in small communities which bicker with the one next door is extremely strong in England.

But in the mid '60s, when the country needed a form of social ease to fall back on because of its economic unease, the village mentality that had always sustained us, was slipping away.

This had begun in the war. Not because of the war, but because of the way the city children had been evacuated. When it seemed that the Germans were about to bomb the cities, the children were evacuated to the country en masse. That undoubtedly saved many of their lives. But the way it was done had unforeseen consequences. The kids were used to a way of life that had been going on for generations, with families spending their lives in the same area.

If your parents drove you up the wall you could spend time with an auntie or grandmother round the corner. If you were ill and had no money for the doctor, you could get weird old remedies only your grandmother knew, and had been handed down over centuries.

The Beatles

If someone a bit strange lived in your road, you could persecute them, but if someone from the next street persecuted them, your street would join up to protect them and batter the next street. Things like young, old, black, Jew, gypsy, retard, whatever, were subordinate to your street, never mind your area. Again, the life of the village was being led in the city.

But when the kids were evacuated, they were literally labelled with their name and age and sent out in trains, with the last carriage being arbitrarily lopped off at a point deep in the countryside. So your brother or your best mate could end up hundreds of miles away. Then you were taken to the local hall and whoever picked you out, kept you for the duration of the war.

Some kids freaked out, some integrated and never went back. Some went abroad, some later returned to brothers and sisters they did not know or to families which didn't want them or had been killed. So for the first time, instead of kids defining themselves by their streets and by lore which had accumulated over generations, they identified with each other's experiences. That was the basis of youth cults and, as it happened, one of the first was to do with football.

The generation whose lives had been disrupted by the blitz fastened onto Manchester United in the late 40s. Kids picked up on this young team of home-grown players, many of whom had gone through the same traumas, and had an avuncular father figure, Matt Busby, for a manager. The generation who were distributed around the country by the evacuation is what gave Manchester United the national following that continues to this day. Not the reaction to the Munich disaster. That accentuated something which was already underway.

By the mid-60s, this was happening across the board. People were getting drawn into categories like young and old which were displacing the traditional roots.

Then, as the country reeled under the awful economic news and started to realise how little England counted for, people instinctively turned to their roots but found they were withering.

The Church was losing credibility, pubs were getting invaded by the young for the first time, football was getting more violent and drugs had gone from being a strange habit of the avant garde to being widely available to the young. Black immigrants were appearing in most big cities for the first time. The sexual revolution was beginning and anti-establishment comment of a sort that even the most anti-establishment figures would never utter in public, was being uttered on the BBC, still seen as a pillar of English values and integrity.

Above all, there was the music. The revolution launched by The Beatles had satisfied the frustrations of many young people, but worried a lot of older people who might have been exasperated by the Tories but liked the traditional values and felt threatened by a Socialist government.

But The Beatles shook the house and nothing stayed up. They threatened every known taboo about sex, religion, relationships, everything. There had never been pop stars like these and all our social liberation movements began with The Beatles. Even if parents became comfortable with The Beatles, they didn't feel comfortable with many of the groups that followed in their wake, particularly those with a clear connection to drugs. The revolutions that The Beatles unleashed bothered a lot of people who had never bothered about much before.

US President John F Kennedy

But suddenly, amidst this sea of confusion and uncertainty that was smashing against us from every direction, came the sight of England taking on the rest of the world and winning. England actually winning. If you designed a scenario for football to become a national obsession built out of elements of religion, love, passion and national pride, you couldn't have concocted a more potent scenario than 1966.

The country had lost its bearings and eleven men in red shirts were righting the ship in one go and at the centre of it, stood a rock of certainty, a man who effortlessly personified all the Englishness we were losing. The country stood still, watched, applauded and eventually, shouted itself hoarse.

They were, by comparison to most, a clean team. People thought Nobby Stiles was just enthusiastic, that Jack Charlton was a lovable rogue who only succeeded in making brother Bobby look even more saintly and nobody dreamt of Bobby Moore kicking anybody. Nobody realised Jack stood on the 'keeper's toes to stop him jumping or that Bobby Moore settled scores off the ball. Neither did it matter. England were winning and doing it in an English way that did not seem to work in any other context.

The defeat of Argentina in the quarter-final was very important because they were seen as cheats and we had come to realise that in the real world, cheats prospered. The Japs had cheated by copying ideas from others, the Germans cheated by recovering from the war with American money and when we finally got a government that wanted to catch up, the international bankers cheated by taking their money out of the country. But suddenly, we were beating the cheats.

At that point, anybody who wasn't taking notice, started taking notice. That was the moment the roll really began to gather momentum and rolled to its ultimate conclusion. It was an incredible time.

People talk about feelgood factors now and believe that saving 25p a month on their mortgage makes them feel good. Unbelievable. The difference is on another scale in another world in another universe.

The final *had* to be England v. Germany. That was written in the stars. Some of the football people never quite understood this. I remember Ron Greenwood saying to Dave Sexton that every time he saw a film of the final, he increasingly expected Germany to win, as they were technically superior to England. But he was missing the point. Some of the people from the continent I have spoken to have said that when the referee went to the Russian linesman to ask if the Hurst goal was a goal, they knew everything was up for the Germans.

Somehow, it was known around parts of Europe, but not in England, that Tafik Bakramhov, the linesman, had fought the Germans in the war. Did anybody believe that a man who had seen the sort of things he would have seen on the Eastern front was going to get the Germans off the hook? Once the referee started walking over to consult Bakramhow, the Germans might as well have packed up and gone home.

So the final, the competition and our reaction to Bobby were about much more than football. By the end, Harold Wilson had cottoned on to what was happening. 18 months before the competition began, Dennis Howell, the Sports Minister had asked Wilson for £500,000 to get facilities ready and Wilson had said: 'What's the World Cup?'

But on the night of the final, Wilson tried to follow Bobby onto the balcony of the Royal Garden Hotel when he went to show the crowd the cup. Howell had to restrain him. In subsequent years, people came to believe Wilson pulled off his big election victory on the back of the World Cup win, a folk memory he never discouraged. In fact, the election had been four months before. But that shows how much the game and the state of the country were intertwined.

Which is the echo we picked up when Bobby died. That week, I spoke to Ken Bates and he made an interesting observation. Bates said that this had a parallel with President Kennedy's death, because both of them would always be remembered as young men.

It is a very shrewd point. While Kennedy is remembered for dying before he could fulfill his potential, Bobby was seen as fulfilling his potential by leading England to victory in the World Cup.

But Bates is right. Bobby was frozen in time by the World Cup victory, almost as if people wanted to remember him at that glorious moment.

In the week of Bobby's death, I also talked to Reg Burr, and he said this: 'Bobby's type of Englishness drew on the better side of our national character, on our sense of fair play and of dignity and determination in the face of overwhelming odds. He reminded people of an era when, by and large, they were better behaved towards each other.

'The 1940s and 1950s may not have been wholly like that, but it didn't matter; Bobby Moore showed us that football could be like that and if football could, then so could life.

'What has stunned me is the reaction of younger people. Our players are very upset. Some great footballers have died recently and you might expect our lads to say: 'Oh yeah, Bobby Moore's dead,' but they are treating this very seriously. People of all ages feel we have lost a link to a better, more decent time and I think they are right.'

Chapter 16

We'll support you ever Moore

I first started going to Upton Park with my dad in the mid-50s and saw Bobby play for the reserves. I used to make up scrap books of cuttings and statistics. When Bobby made his 600th appearance, Everton made a big presentation to him at Goodison Park – he got a glass decanter. Curious, I checked my own records and I discovered it was only his 599th game. West Ham had got it wrong. I rang Trevor Smith at the *Ilford Recorder* to tell him and they called at my house, took photographs and interviewed me. It made the front page of the *Newham Recorder* and the sports page of the *Ilford Recorder*. So Bobby Moore's 600th was only his 599th. Quite amusing really.

Some of the United yobs used to spit at him where the players disembark from the coach at Old Trafford. There was never any reaction from him. I remember another story about a Scottish player spitting in his face during a Home International. Bobby wiped it off, offered it back and said: 'I believe this is yours?' Then he got his own back in the only way Bobby knew how - by playing a blinder, winning the match, thereby ramming it down the bloke's throat.

The Stretford End's favourite song to try and wind him up was: 'Where's your handbag, Bobby Moore?' After the '70 World Cup, it changed to: 'Where's your

Bobby Moore O.B.E.

bracelet, Bobby Moore?' In one game, play had stopped for an injury and they started singing it and he turned around and started conducting them like Henry Mancini at the Royal Albert Hall. It was so funny. Even the old Mancs appreciated it, and they clapped him. I guess they thought he 'aint so bad after all.

At the semi-final at Hillsborough in '64 against Manchester United, he made our third goal for Geoff Hurst and, to my mind, it was actually a better goal than the one he set up for Hurst in the World Cup final. There were about ten minutes to go, it was

peeing down with rain, West Ham were 2-1 up and United had just pulled one back. He went down the touchline out of defence with the ball, and got closed down by three United players. They didn't think he would get past but he went down the touchline in that quagmire, kept the ball in play, looked up and pumped a ball down that inside left channel where Hurst was already galloping, just as he did in the Wembley final. He ran on a few strides and let fly with a screamer with his left foot - the only difference was it went low in the near corner, to the keeper's right, instead of the roof of the net. That, to me, was the moment of all moments. It was better worked than the goal in '66 because of the awful conditions and the way Bobby evaded three players.

After that, with about five minutes to go, Bobby went down with cramp. The West Ham end had been outsinging United throughout the match. United were 3-1 down, but they had been in the same position to Sunderland in the 6th round and had won. Suddenly, from being coasting at 3-1, our rock, Bobby Moore, was down and didn't look like he was getting up. The massive West Ham kop went silent. Literally, it was like walking into a church. For the two minutes he was on the floor we all held our breath. If he doesn't get up, we thought, we could lose. But he did get back up and everything was all right again.

This might sound silly, but when Bobby was around, as fans, you felt safe. You felt that everything would be okay. Strangely enough, it was the same in life. When he passed away I think many people thought we'd lost our protector. The sensation was if something like that can happen to him, what chance do I stand?

Richard Miller

I was shocked when I heard Bobby was dead. I got the train home about ten 0'clock and there was a person sitting opposite reading the *Evening Standard* and the headline said: 'Moore Dead!' I just couldn't believe it.

My best memory was winning a Sunday newspaper competition where I got to have dinner at the 25th anniversary of '66. It was a big function at Wembley where I sat at the same table as the newspaper editor, Trevor Brooking and his wife, my wife and a couple of other winners. On the head table were Moore, Hurst and Peters. I arranged to get a photo taken with me in the middle of them, my arms around their shoulders, which is probably my proudest possession.

That night, I'd gone to Wembley, dickie bow and all the rest of it, and the first thing I did was go to the loo. I was in there and who was standing next to me, but Mooro. I couldn't think of anything to say to him in there but I certainly talked to him quite a lot over the evening. He was always very chatty.

I went to the memorial service at Westminster Abbey. There was an inner sanctum, where all the celebrities sat and all the fans were sitting in the big outer section. The turnout was very impressive and the service rather moving. A lot of people wrote off for tickets and many people didn't get them. To me, attending the service was the one way I could actually show my respect. I'm not a church goer, nor am I religious in any way, but to go along and reflect on him was something I needed to do. A lot of people turned out.

Stuart Allen

I worked for William and Warne Rubber Company in Barking and Bobby Moore came to work there during the summers of '56 and '57. We had a few of the boys down for work and they did general labouring, helping out in the yard, sweeping. I first went to see West Ham as a kid after the war. I went to the Preston and Munich finals but the match that sticks in my mind is the Manchester United semi-final - the finest game I ever saw West Ham play. Magnificent match.

At one time, Bobby never drank. One of the players, a guy called Ken Tucker, used to have a lot of parties and I remember him saying Bobby would never touch alcohol. Bobby must have changed his ways!

Ted Ellis

Even with people not interested in football, the topic of conversation in Britain was the World Cup and whether England could win. The possibility of winning was, in a way, like an accolade for winning the Second World war. An uneasy feeling hung around that we had won the war, but we were beginning to lose the peace.

People were binding up their wounds during the late 40s and 50s and there was a very strange mood. Even the dimmest person realised that things could never be the same after the bombs at Hiroshima and Nagasaki, but there was a feeling of unease, almost a threat hanging over everybody. The war was over, but something far worse might have taken place.

The war had left deep scars and in the decades afterwards there was a lot of grief about, but there were the beginnings of optimism, that England had turned a corner. By the time we reached '66 there was a chance, a strong hope, we could win - football was, after all, our national game. When we did win, it was like: 'Oh my God! We've won! Nothing else matters now.' It was a big lift for the country in so many ways. It was almost as if there was a collective grin on everybody's face. Even if you couldn't see it, you could certainly feel it.

Everyone was taken up with it all. I remember there was a television rental shop around the corner and there was a huge crowd swarming round it earlier in the day, long before the match started.

People talk about the Queen's white gloves and Moore wiping his hands, but after he had been passed the Jules Rimet Trophy, he showed his manners yet further when he continued shaking hands down the line of VIPs, before he faced the crowd and held up the trophy. He must have been bursting to turn around the moment she handed him the Cup. Most captains would have snatched it out of her hands and not wasted a second to show it off. Good manners indeed!
Rose Robertson

I am part of the generation of West Ham fans who never saw Moore play in person. What I knew of him was gleaned from images such as the embrace with Pele after the England v Brazil game that told you everything about him, and yet hardly anything at all.

Of course, some of my older friends talked about him. He was precious. It was inconceivable to think of him not being around - in the same way that you never imagine your mum or dad not being around. He was a constant in West Ham fans' lives, a reassurance, somebody that represented them.

Before he died, I remember seeing him on the *Footballers' Football Show* picking a best-ever eleven with Denis Law and George Best. They got to right-back and Law suggested Breitner and Best suggested Wilson. Moore sat there with a serious face and said: 'One we shouldn't leave out of consideration is Fulham's Les Strong.' Then he broke into a smile and everybody fell about laughing. I knew then that there was more to Moore than the usual soundbites trundled out by the media.

People's reaction to his death was so strong that I was intrigued to find out more about him. He was one of the first footballers to cross the class barriers and show them for what they were - ridiculous. He did it by being himself - it was as if one of 'Us' was not just holding his own with 'Them' but outshining 'Them' to boot. He was what he was because of his background and not despite it. I think he realised that to deny where you came from was to deny a part of yourself.

I always say that Moore was West Ham's Shankly. Both of them realised what a massive part football played in people's lives and that it was a humbling experience rather than an excuse for grandeur and aloofness. They came from places where how you treated others was far more important than things like how much money you earned. To see Moore on the world stage with the same values and principles as normal people, gave a lot of validity and hope to the man in the street.

While people mourned, I was reading about Moore. I understood then what people mean when they say you should celebrate somebody's life when they pass away. I wish I'd found out about him while he was still with us.
Dave Thomas

When I was seven I was living in Harlow, Essex, and Bobby Moore was the guest of honour at our town show. I didn't know him from a bar of soap then but my dad told me all about him. When the show started Bobby came riding in on this pony and trap. My excitement got the better of me and I ran out in front of the pony to get his autograph. Bobby got down off his seat, smiled at me, picked me up and sat me on his seat and promptly signed my autograph book. That was the start of my hero worship of him and West Ham.
Steve Wells

I will never forget the game after Bobby died. I was selling fanzines outside Roker Park. The snow was coming down fiercely, the wind was in our faces, it was bitterly cold, but the atmosphere was, strangely, very warming. I couldn't believe how many Sunderland fans, both young and old, came up and shook my hand; some even gave me a hug – complete strangers; and one or two even had tears in their eyes. Everyone was united in grief over Bobby Moore. This was followed by the quietest minute's silence I had ever heard. It doesn't matter where you are, somebody usually hasn't the sense to stay quiet for 60 seconds, but I know it was common that week that the silences up and down the country were impeccably observed. Bobby's death started a new trend – minute's silences that were actually silent. The Sunderland fans did us proud.

A story I heard about the time Bobby died is worth recounting. There was a racehorse called Bobby Moore. The owner, a bloke called Henry Alper, who lived near Upton Park, changed his racing colours to claret and blue and wanted to name a horse after Bobby. Mooro agreed on the condition that he let Bobby know when the horse was running. Bobby wasn't much of a gambler, but the first few times out Bobby bet on the horse and it came nowhere. It ran when Bobby was playing abroad for England and romped home at 10-1. Then when Bobby came back and started betting on it again, Bobby Moore, the horse, didn't bloody win again!
Gary Firmager - Editor, Over Land and Sea - West Ham United fanzine

My first football memory was Manchester United beating Benfica in the European Cup final. A lot of kids my age became Cockney Reds but that summer my mum took me into Bobby Moore's sports shop to buy my first pair of football boots. Tina served us and Bobby said: 'Hello.' My mum said: 'You know who that is, don't you?' I'd heard people speak of Bobby Moore but I never appreciated who he was.

Bobby ran the game. He had magnetism, an aura. If you were watching the match your eyes drifted towards him, no matter where play was at the time.

I'll never forget the night he died. I came home from work and a mate rang to tell me Moore had passed away. Then I saw it on the news and I burst into tears. I couldn't believe it. I don't know what made me go down to the gates, but different people rang and we all decided to go. We all had the same feeling. I think we were the first to arrive. I stayed till about 1am. It was cold.

In the morning I went to work and someone said: 'Shame about Bobby Moore.' I just welled up again and had to walk out. I went to the gates every night until they took the tributes away. It was unbelievable. People were turning up and laying wreaths and crying. It was such a sad occasion. I took my mum over there to see it. She died of cancer a year later.

Moore's death threw me. One night, going over to see the tributes, I had an accident in the car because I wasn't concentrating properly.

The first game after he died was up at Sunderland and a group of us went up on the coach and there was a camera crew following one of my mates for a TV documentary. It was snowing a blizzard. They put World Cup commentary over the tannoy before the minute's silence and the Sunderland fans were absolutely silent. It was a really nice gesture.
Alex Sorenson

I never saw Bobby play. I was too young. But I was named after Geoff Hurst and my middle name is Robert, after Bobby Moore. My family agreed to name me after the next player to score for West Ham. Luckily enough it was Hurst and Moore, the week before it had been Ade Coker!

The day he died I came home and saw the news on Teletext. I was balling my eyes out when a few mates rang and we all agreed to go down to the gates. We had to take something down there so I dug out that number six shirt from the wardrobe. I had no idea of the impact it would have. I put it on the centre of the railings and everyone photographed it for days afterwards. It was all in the papers and on the news.

The shirt belonged to one of my junior school teachers and I won it in a school raffle. He knew I was mad on West Ham so he fixed it for me to win by letting me buy about 50 tickets more than the other kids. I'm not sure if it was an actual team shirt of Bobby's and I don't know where my teacher got it from. I'm only sorry I didn't see Bobby actually play to appreciate him more.
Geoff Marling

My dad took me to see my first West Ham games in 1968. I remember Bobby because he stood out with his curly hair. I recall him moving on to Fulham. Kevin Lock, his replacement, was described as 'the new Moore.' Poor kid never had a chance of living up to that tag. No-one ever has.
Graham Salter

Looking at the tributes at the gates, I felt a strange mixture of sadness but also one of great pride at the way one of our players pulled everyone together, not just our own fans, but people everywhere.
Tony Pearce

I sat through 'Escape to Victory' with my mum not so long ago, where the Germans play the Allied prisoners of war. With Germany leading the Allies 4-0, I still get a lump in my throat when old Mooro makes that run to the far side of the area. He calls out: 'Far post, Eric!' and when it comes over, he volleys it into the net. It was like watching him for real. Me and my mum leapt off the sofa and cheered as if we'd won the World Cup all over again. Silly, but fun.
Lee Phillips - Over Land and Sea – West Ham United Fanzine

Bobby loved West Ham and we loved him. Even during the scrappy years of the late 60s and early 70s we seemed to stave off the constant threat of relegation merely on the strength of his leadership.
Jim Munro

I ran a football team out of a pub in East London which then changed hands. I wrote to Bobby Moore because he was about to open a new bar called Mooro's in Stratford. I asked if he would be interested in sponsoring our team. I thought no more of it until one Sunday when there was a knock at the door. My wife answered it and came back into the room saying: 'It's Bobby Moore at the front door!' I said: 'Don't be stupid, woman!' and she said: 'Well, go look for yourself.' When I went into the hall I could see Bobby Moore standing on my doorstep. I was amazed. I asked him in but he couldn't stop because he was going somewhere. He said I should call into Mooro's to discuss the team. Later that week I did and he was really hospitable. He gave money for the kit and we had a good few years playing under the name of 'Mooro's.'

> **"My wife said: 'It's Bobby Moore at the front door.' 'Don't be stupid woman!' I replied"**

I frequented the bar occasionally and he would often go out of his way to come over and drink with me and my wife, and despite what some fans say about him being tight with money, he always insisted in paying for our drinks. He was very generous. On one of these occasions, we were chatting and I said to him that I had been a West Ham schoolboys player and that I'd always wanted to be a professional footballer and to my surprise, Bobby said that he didn't particularly like playing football. I said I was shocked and asked him why. He replied that it was the only thing he was good at. Yet, years later, when I saw him interviewed after he had stopped playing, he said he missed playing and that he didn't appreciate it during the time he did.

He was always jingling change in his trouser pocket. He hated loose ends and whenever he had amassed enough coins he would call the barmaid over and swop them into a note. Bobby always maintained that he didn't really have many true friends. In fact, he virtually admitted he was quite a lonely man.
Colin Morris

Despite the fact I never met Bobby Moore, despite the fact I never saw him play, I loved him and I mourned his loss as deeply as if he were a close relative. Enough

to travel to the gates of Upton Park and tie a scarf to the railings the day he died, and wear a black tie to work for a week.
Robert Banks - author of 'An Irrational Hatred of Luton'

Bobby Moore had just been a face on an Esso World Cup coin. At least that was the case until October 1970 when his Jaguar cruised through the gates of Romford's Brooklands Road ground for Harry Obeney's Testimonial. By the time he had killed the engine and stepped out of the car, a scrum of biro wielding nine-year-olds had ambushed his car. Buttoning his leather coat, he raised his arm with the authority of a thousand dinner ladies. Instantly, an orderly queue of excited youngsters snaked the length of the car park. Even now, when I look at that crisp, yet yellowing signature, I still vividly remember my heart pounding into my ribs as I waited for the moment when, at last, I would meet the man on that Esso coin.
Steve Blowers, *Hammers News Magazine*

Being too young to have seen Bobby Moore play live, my only experiences of his playing career have come through watching videos and from what my father has told me. As a young child, I remember watching a video of the 1964 FA Cup Final and for some reason thinking it was a rule that West Ham's blond number six didn't give the ball away to the opposition, because he only seemed to make good passes to his own team mates. We all dream of having Bobby Moore's footballing skills, but he was also the type of human being we all want to be, and that is the biggest tribute I can pay him.
Danny Francis, *Hammers News Magazine*

In 1964, I was just 12-years-old and made up my mind to buy a claret and blue bobble hat from Bobby Moore's sports shop opposite the ground. I walked in and there in front of me was Bobby. Stuttering, I asked him for the hat on display and he contracted the sale himself. I'll never forget that moment.
Bill Williams, South Woodham Ferrers

One of my friends was due to play in a corporate golf day. Bobby, who was changing beforehand, dropped his shirt and my friend quipped: 'Good job you weren't a 'keeper!'
David Prudames, Hoddesdon.

It was my ninth birthday on 30 July 1966, my friends got train sets but I got a unique present - my heroes scored the goals and everyone's hero collected the World Cup. A fantastic birthday…and 50 million went to the party!
Jonathan Bill, Belfast

In 1971, me and my dad found the West Ham team sitting in one of the carriages of the Darlington train. Immediately my eyes found Bobby Moore but my legs just wouldn't move as Dad put the programme in my hand so I could get his autograph. All I could whimper was: 'You go.' He gripped my hand and led me on a white knuckle ride. I froze again as Dad asked him to sign. 'Certainly Guv'nor,' he smiled,

but it was too much for me as I hurried back down the train. Twenty six years on, that programme still hangs on my wall.
Mark Pickering, Redcar.

I have a tattoo on my right leg. Surrounding the club crest is written: 'Bobby No Moore but Here Forever.' Fitting words indeed.
D. King, London, N12

I met Bobby Moore at East Ham Town Hall during a special dinner to celebrate the great 1965 Cup Winners Cup win. He had a quick word with as many people as possible including myself and my wife Joan. He sank a few jars but came away from the celebration as sober as a judge which was more than could be said of me! Football will be hard pressed to see his like again.
Gerry Warner, East Ham.

I saw Bobby standing inside the main gates at West Ham before a game in 1991. People were just walking by and nobody appeared to recognise him. 'Don't these people know who he is?' I thought as I stood watching. 'This is BOBBY MOORE - the greatest footballer this country has ever produced.' I told my workmates the

next day but they just laughed. They didn't understand.
Keith Mullem, Witham

My uncle and I met Bobby on Southampton station after a game in 1969. He was sitting alone and we sat and discussed the game with him. As we left, he wished us well. We could not believe he had taken the time to speak to us.
C. Hunter, East Ham.

During the late 60s I delivered evening newspapers from Goddards at Woodford Station. Bobby used to come into the shop to pick up a classified results edition of the 'Evening News' and 'Evening Standard.' The man was famous, but he carried on like any other customer. The only difference was that he'd been playing in front of forty-thousand people an hour-and-a-half earlier.
P. Morten, Harold Wood.

My husband Joe is still embarrassed by the fact that as an eight-year-old he wrote a letter to Bobby Moore inviting him to tea! He

still has the signed photo and letter from Bobby thanking him for his kind invitation but politely declining. It says a lot about the man that he took the time and trouble to write.
Hazel Wildash, Peterborough.

Bobby Moore gave so much inspiration to others.
Len Anderson, Hornchurch.

Bobby Moore O.B.E. – One Beautiful Englishman – by S. Hammond.
    A gentleman, a World class act, impossible to follow.
    His death at such an early age was very hard to swallow.
    Bob didn't need to knock on heaven's door - no fears.
    Because you see he'd held the key for 27 years.
This is an extract from a poem written by my father just after Bobby's death.
J. Hammond, Corringham

As a teenager, I went to most of West Ham's away games on the football special. The team were usually on the train, too and on the return journey we were allowed in their carriage after they had eaten. I obtained Bobby's autograph many times. I was proud that England's finest wore claret and blue.
John Northcutt, Great Baddow

I met Bobby many years ago when he visited my boss. He shook my hand and asked me if I used to stand in the Chicken Run. I don't need his autograph, the memory of those few words and a handshake will live forever in my memory.
Marcus Hamilton, Teddington.

I saw Bobby make his debut against Manchester United in September 1958 and I still have the programme with his name pencilled in as a team

change.
D.T. Monk, Winsford.

Bobby Moore always had time for people who approached him in the right way. and shortly before his illness was announced I sent several photos to his home. Within a week he signed and returned them all and even included a coloured 1966 World Cup shot of himself with his compliments. Even with his awful illness he found time for me. You just can't buy memories like those.
Terry Connelly, Collier Row

I'm told that Ron Greenwood kept a post-match crate of beers in the dressing room. After one game when West Ham had played badly, the team were apparently supping their bottles when Ron came in and read the riot act. He started arguing with one of his younger players who, it's been alleged, might even have been Harry Redknapp. As tempers flared the manager ducked just in time to see a flying bottle smash on the wall. Greenwood supposedly stormed out, fuming:'Be in my office at 9 o'clock sharp on Monday morning.'The dressing room fell silent for a while before Bobby Moore said:'You shouldn't have done that!'The youngster replied:'Well, he singled me out when we all played badly.'
Mooro interrupted:'No, I meant it was a full bottle of lager!'
Jack Forsey, Buckhurst Hill

On a grey East End morning in 1964, I was on my dad's shoulders waiting to see the FA Cup paraded through Stratford. Everyone was wearing colourless overcoats against a backdrop of dirty buildings but when the open-topped bus turned the corner a burst of colour unfolded and there was Bobby with the cleanest face I'd ever seen, holding the huge, shiny Cup like a morning star.
Stephen Benham, Hook

During school holidays, there were over 100 of us who would simultaneously thrust our autograph books under the players' noses as they left Upton Park. Bobby Moore would always take time to speak to you and make you feel important.
Kevin Jenkins, East Ham

I once spent an entire 90 minutes plucking up the courage to ask Bobby Moore for his signature and during all that time it never occurred to me that I didn't have a pen! To this day, that very first autograph I so nervously asked for remains the only one signed in pencil - albeit a pencil owned by the great man.
Stephen Marsh, West Ham United Autograph Society

Bobby had been so unassuming when we spoke, but just weeks later we were there at Upton Park crying at the gates, only briefly cheering up when we read the message amongst the flowers:

'West Ham, England, now the Heaven eleven.'
Guy Nash, London W14
Bobby Moore - A Tribute (an extract)
At West Ham we so admired you
You could open Heaven's door
A legend in our lifetime
Remembered ever Moore.
Paul Wray, Witham

Who could forget that stout, balding referee's funny little run?
Bobby copied it and got a good ticking off!
Fred Lee, Sutton Coldfield

Being a cheeky 12-year-old, after a game in 1972 I asked Bobby Moore if I could open the door of his red Jaguar for him. It made my day when he agreed. If that wasn't enough, at the following home game I was waiting at the barrier again, when Bobby spotted me and threw me his car keys!
R. Laverty, Wickford.

Despite being a Chelsea fan, my all-time hero was Bobby Moore. In 1972, I stood in the Shed and saw him in the flesh for the very first time. I didn't take my eyes off him and he even scored in West Ham's 3-1 win. Afterwards I tried, unsuccessfully, to get his autograph as the players raced to their coach. I was disappointed but just to see him that day was an unforgettable experience for me. He lives on in my heart and I'll never forget him.
Debbie Medcalfe, Paddock Wood.

In 1969 while I was waiting at Wolverhampton for my train, Bobby was signing autographs. I joined a lengthening queue and by the time I reached him there were more fans behind me. He signed the portrait of himself in the programme, but politely refused to do the team picture as well due to the queue. He signed 50 or 60 autographs, but the quality of his signature on the programme - which I still have - remains with me to this day.
Grant Bargh, Rochdale

My friend Geoff Lee and I were lost on our way home from my first-ever Hammers game at Crystal Palace in 1971. Then, we saw the team coach in a jam and Bobby Moore was looking out. I managed to stand on Geoff's shoulders and passed our programmes through the window. Bobby signed one before saying: 'Sorry mate, your pen's run out.' That autograph still remains one of my most prized possessions ... but I don't think I've seen Geoff Lee since that day!
Peter Day, Baldock.

MOORE than a legend

On a cold day in 1987, I called into a petrol garage in Silvertown and as I went in to pay, a man coming out of the shop held the door open for me. It was Bobby Moore. I told him how pleased I was to meet him and he returned the compliment before getting into his car and driving away.
Gary Hayes, London E16

It was raining heavily at the 1964 FA Cup semi-final. Our rosettes had run and the colours from our freshly painted pith helmets had dripped down our faces. We were 2-1 up but United were coming back strongly until Bobby Moore picked the ball up and threaded it through to Geoff Hurst who cracked it in.
I'll never forget the next morning's headlines: 'Moore's Muddy Marvels.'
Doug Bauckham, Benfleet.

In October 1966, this football mad youngster pestered his parents for a new pair of boots. They took me to Bobby Moore's shop where I was served by the great man who even fitted them onto my feet. Bobby could have got an assistant to do it, but he knew it would give me such a thrill. Those boots were the most comfortable pair I ever had but sadly I grew out of them within 12-18 months - in fact I think it was that long, too, before I washed my feet again!
Colin Thompson, Shefford.

Any team comprising Lev Yashin, Pele, Bobby Moore and any eight others would have been unbeatable!
S.P.A. Smith, Basildon

During the minute's silence at the Wolverhampton Wanderers match I had tears flowing down my cheeks. 15 years of my life flashed before me during those sixty seconds and I'll never experience such emotion again. I remembered the banter I'd had over the years with my uncle - a Spurs fan - who also died young, but from the age of ten Bobby could do no wrong in my eyes.
Chris Phillips, Newmarket

I lived in Manchester and my dad, a United fan, took me to watch them play West Ham. With Law, Best and Charlton they won 5-2. But the man who stood out was Bobby Moore. He led his team off proudly, head up, like they had just thrashed United. I had a No. 6 West Ham jersey for my next birthday and my dad was upset. He wanted me to support United. Moore was brilliant. I loved him. In fact, some of his greatest performances came on my Subbuteo table.
There was no mistaking him – the black paint scraped off his head to expose white

plastic (obviously, a mop of blond hair). Somebody stood on him once and the glue repairs around his broken ankles were a bit messy, but that made him more special. He took all the penalties in my team.

For years, a photograph of England's captain was on the ceiling directly above my bed. Every night it was the last thing I saw. 'Goodnight Bobby!' I'd say. Most of us are destined to lead dull lives without ever tasting real success but, for a while in 1966, we were all winners. He made his country's dreams come true. Goodnight, Bobby.

Jamie, West Ham fan

I would like to see the Bobby Moore memorial match played every year. Bobby Moore is not somebody who can just be remembered by one game.

G. Hartmore, Billericay

He was my world. I couldn't stop crying on the bus all the way down to the gates. I watched him when I was small and used to jump up and down on my bed when West Ham won. I couldn't believe he'd gone and I still can't.

Jackie Dyer

Yours is a name I have been proud to carry all my life.

Bobby Moore, Spurs fan

When Kenneth Wolstenholme said: 'Some of the crowd are on the pitch', I was one of them. At the time I was a drummer with the band Gullivers People. I bought a ticket for a fiver off the band's keyboard player – I don't think he could be bothered to go. I clambered on to the pitch in all the excitement. It was sheer elation. I wasn't a hooligan or anything. I didn't get very far, no farther than the touchline, before I was dragged off by six policemen. They didn't get heavy, they just dropped me back in the crowd. There was a real carnival atmosphere.

Michael Richardson, backing musician to Elkie Brooks and others.

Bobby Moore actually scored in the '66 final. Hurst went up for a challenge with Tilkowski, the ball bounced loose to the edge of the area, Bobby came in and drilled a low shot past all the Germans into the net. Unfortunately, Hurst was adjudged to have fouled Tilkowski and it wasn't allowed. That would have been something – all three West Ham players scoring!

Dave Rose, Blackburn fan

Just after Moore died Chelsea were at home to Arsenal. There was a minute's silence and I didn't hold out much hope for quiet. But Bobby Moore silenced the crowd like I'd never seen before. Lads not even born in '66 had their heads bowed. It was the most amazing gesture I had ever seen towards an opponent.

Peter Watts, Chelsea fan, Sutton, Surrey

In '66 I was eight years old and lived in Germiston, South Africa. My family and I listened to the World Cup final on the radio – there was no television. The government of the time believed it was evil and would corrupt people's minds. I first saw Bobby a year later when he came to South Africa on a coaching tour with Terry Venables, Geoff Hurst and Gordon Banks. The four stars played in a match between the local club's youth and reserve teams. Bobby controlled the game from the back, hardly breaking sweat, passing the ball about, barking orders and giving encouragement to the young players. The opposition couldn't get past him.

Greg Struthers, Norwich fan

When the Fulham squad went to go up for their losers' medals in 1975, Moore stood aside at the foot of the stairs and, one by one, he patted each of his players on the back as they trooped past. He was the very last to go up. When he did get to the top of the steps, you really felt for him. Beaten by his old team, it was obvious this was his last hurrah, with all those years of winning cups, all the glory, long behind him - he must have felt lousy - yet the smile he gave when he shook hands with the dignitaries and accepted his loser's medal was never more broader or more genuine. The man was undeniably gracious. That's rare.

Simon Thomas, Bedford

Most of the kids in our block of flats supported Arsenal or Tottenham. I remember one kid would always want to be Alan Gilzean when we had kickabouts over the park. The Alan Gilzean at Spurs was a pretty tasty player and a Scottish international but the Alan Gilzean in Barmy Park used run home crying after getting his arse kicked by Bobby Moore and Geoff Hurst (me and my big brother).

Lol Scofield

I am very proud that my dad, Terry, played with Bobby in the same West Ham youth team, and one of my most treasured possessions is a large, framed photo of Bobby, taken in about '70, which dad asked him to sign for me. It is a giant portrait of Mooro looking typically classy in a green-and-white striped Ben Sherman shirt The main reason I have supported West Ham since the age of eight is due to Moore, Hurst and Peters and that entertaining team of the 60s. Those of us who were honoured to have seen the Hammers stars of that era will inevitably keep comparing them to the players who have followed, which is unfair on those who can never hope to emulate the real West Ham greats. Who can possibly achieve that distinction now? Football has changed so much since then. To most kids of the 60s, Moore, Hurst and Peters were West Ham United – the reason, above all, that we wore our claret and blue with pride, and I'm very lucky to have seen them in their prime.

Tony McDonald, _Hammers News_ magazine

MOORE than a legend

Surely anyone who enjoys football, whatever their allegiance, would recognise this man for what he is - more than a legend.
Martin Sampson, Romford

Presentation copies

POPPY MOORE	STEPHANIE MOORE
FREDERICK HOBBIS	IMPERIAL CANCER RESEARCH FUND
ROBERTA MOORE	FULHAM FC
DEAN MOORE	SOUTHEND UNITED FC
TINA MOORE	OXFORD CITY FC
JO DANIELS	CAPITAL GOLD SPORT
LEN DANIELS	FOOTBALL FOOTBALL
FOOTBALL ASSOCIATION	PELE
WEST HAM UNITED FC	FRANZ BECKENBAUER
	MICHAEL CAINE

Subscribers

BILL WILLIAMS	KEVIN BRADBROOK	JACK FORSEY	BRIAN TURNER
CLIFF LARKIN	T.M.WEST	DUNCAN K. SMITH	RICHARD WALSH
GARY BUSH	P.M. DODD	GRAHAM MACKENZIE	FRED LEE
SEAN TYRELL	D. J. KING	TERRY CONNELLY	JEREMY S. FISHER
LIAM TYRELL	C. R. LAKER	NIGEL LAWRENCE	DAVID HERBERT
MARK PICKERING	G.W. HALFFMAN	KEVIN BARRETT	C. D. CORDERY
PAUL BIRD	MARTIN BASS	PAUL BLUNDELL	PAUL BOUNDEN
CHRIS BRADLEY	IAN HENDERSON	KEVIN UREN	STEVE SMITH
KEB BRADLEY	C. E. CASEY	PAUL WHITEMAN	DON ROBERTS
KEVIN PAUL	MISS J.A. HAMMOND	SUE & DAVID THOMAS	DAVE SATCHELL
KEITH MULLEM	IAIN HARVEY	ANTONY BEAMAN	DANIEL STANDING
TREVOR WISDOM	PAUL A. F. CLARKE	NOEL CRAIG	JACK MARKS
C HUNTER	KEVIN PENDERGRASS	STEVE TIPPLE	R. LAVERTY
JON WHITTLE	DAVE ANTHONY	STEPHEN J.T. BENHAM	SHARON PEARCE
P. I. CHAMBERS	JOHN HELLIAR	JIMMY BEAN	BILL HINKEN
KEITH KNIGHT	DON HARRISON	IAN NELSON-HARRIS	PAUL B.WRAY
ANDY K. CARR	JOHN NORTHCUTT	PETER HARRIS	J. POSTLETHWAITE
TERENCE M JONAS	U A PRESTON	BARRY NORWIN	P. M.WISBY
COLIN DAVIS	DAVID PRUDAMES	TONY BARRITT	TONY FOSTER
ANDREW GREEN	JONATHAN P. BILL	RON DALE	TREV PAUL
HARRY J DOYLE	REG E. MARSH	C. G.ASHBY	GEOFF WALKER
KEITH MEREDITH	MARK BERG	SCOTT ROUSE	G. E. McGREGOR
JOHN WHITE	DANIEL JOHN BORLEY	ANDY ROUSE	JOHN CURRY KEANE
GERRY G.WARNER	PHILIP W. BLEWETT	ANDY FLECKNEY	SEAN NEWLAND
P MORTEN	GRETA BRYAN	LAWRENCE EASTON	ALAN DOUGHTY
LAURIE EDMANS	D.T. MONK	DAVID HEDGE	MICHAEL OLIVER
ALEXANDRA EDMANS	MARCUS HAMILTON	NIGEL STOCK	SIMON J. BREMNER
MARK BROWN	STEVE CHANDLER	JOHN REYNOLDS	LAWRENCE TURNER
JOE WILDASH	PAUL HOLMES	BEN JENKINS	MICK BRIDGE
LEN ANDERSON	S. BULL	SIMON GOODLEY	ANTONY POTTER

MOORE than a legend

DEREK MALONE
MICHAEL TOMS
GARETH LESLIE JONES
PETER DAY
ANDY CAMPEN
KEVIN McBIRNEY
M. EAGLESTONE
CRIS JONES
DAVID A. WEST
PATRICK SMYTH
TOM WOODALL
P. YOUNG
A. E. THAIN
MARIA FITZGERALD
DANIEL KERR
ROB SHAW JNR
I. W. SCOTT
DAVID RODDY
GEOFFREY WOOD
F. P. FLYNN
STEPHEN JONES
D. R. DRURY
S. P.A. SMITH
PHIL S. LATCHFORD
ALAN CHAPMAN
KEVIN CALAZ
COLIN THOMPSON
DOUG BAUCKHAM
CHRIS PHILLIPS
GARY HAYES
GUY NASH
BILLY PEGG
MARTYN G. WOOD
SUSAN HART
N. S. KING
RICHARD SLATER
HELEN WATTS
MRS W. McCOY
PETER HAWKINS
JOY BRYANT

BRYN BIGGS
P. M. BURCH
GEORGIE BAKER
PETER TREVILLION
ANTONY PEREIRA
CAMERON EVANS
DANNY SHEA
JENNIFER HARDING
BARRY J. QUIGLEY
DENNIS J. CURTIN
STEPHEN PELLICCI
E. R. BOWLER
W. F. BOWLER
JOHN 'B' DISCOMBE
GRANT BARGH
DAVID BARGH
ANDREW BARGH
JON VINTON
NICOLE VINTON
AIMEE VINTON
MARK CORNISH
STEVE CORNER
IAN YUILL
JOHN KEYS
COLIN FLACK
ESTHER RIXON
CHRIS O'NEILL
STEVE O'NEILL
ANTHONY HALE
STEPHEN MARSH
EDDIE CORNISH
KEVIN COUTTS
ALAN LAMING
BETTY & JIMMY WEBB
STELLA & SID ABBOTT
HOPE MIDDLETON
JOHN BANKES
MIKE CLARK
M MIROSEVIC-SORGO
MARILYN STOLLER

TONY HOGG
CHRISTOPHER HOGG
GEOFF THOMPSON
TED TARRANT
BILL WILLIS
ANTONY HALE
ROBERT BANKS
ROY FRANCIS
SCOTT FRANCIS
ROSS FRANCIS
KEN GOODMAN
GEORGE WEBBER
SAMANTHA WEBBER
LISA COSBURN
RICHARD KREIDER
FRED JEAPES
CHRIS DEERE
DEBBIE MEDCALFE
STEVE HARDING
PAUL WEBB
SAM BLOWERS
HARRIET BLOWERS
WILLIAM SALMONS
JOHN SIGGINS
ANTHONY GALE
MICHAEL J. HUTTON
STEVE ZYSS
MICHAEL TRUNDLEY
KEITH D. LOWE
ALAN PICKWELL
ALAN KENNELLY
STEVE SHULVER
MARTIN HARRIS
LEE MAJOR
NORMAN EWEN
JOHN SEAL
MALCOLM ANDERSON
MARTIN SAVAGE
DARRON POLYBLANK
ROBERT STONE

JACK POLYBLANK
JIM NIXON
DEREK BALL
DES BUTTERWORTH
GLENN PHILLIPS
ALAN PHILLIPS
KEN PHILLIPS
SHARON PHILLIPS
LINDA WOOLLEY
RAY PHILLIPS
DEREK EADY
SUE JANEWAY
MATTHEW HOBBIS
DEBBIE LAMBERT
MARK SMITH
DEAN HEAD
LUCY DUPUIS
LISA WHITEHEAD
KAREN LEEKS
NICK MacFARLANE
PAUL BARCLAY
STEVE JONES
JASON CHRISTENSEN
SARA DEDMAN
LES GARNHAM
ROBERT SEELEY
GRAHAM SALTER
PAUL MANKTELOW
TRACY RUFFELL
MIA McDONALD
GEORGE McDONALD
JACK McDONALD
PETER GARNHAM
STAN CLARKE
JAMES HARRISON
JOHN PEACOCK
JENIFER SALMONS
ELIZABETH SALMONS
RON JONES
EDD HOLLINGSWORTH

Chapter 17
Career record & statistics

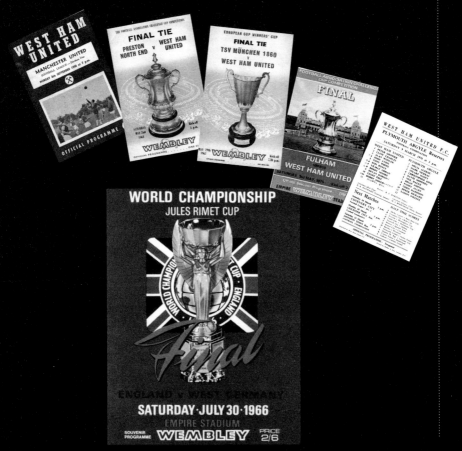

Bobby Moore: the facts

Born April 12, 1941, Robert Frederick Chelsea Moore was the only child of
Robert and Doris Moore, who lived in Waverley Gardens, Barking, Essex. He
attended Westbury primary school. Bobby played for South Park Boys in the
Ilford League and was a winning captain as Barking Primary Schools won the
Crisp Shield. He then attended Tom Hood Technical High School in Leyton and
represented both Leyton Schools and Essex Schoolboys. Showing promise, he
was invited to train with West Ham Colts and signed amateur forms for West
Ham United in August 1956 before leaving school on July 19, 1957.

Honours
Awarded Order of the British Empire 1967; World Cup winners' medal 1966;
European Cup Winners Cup winners' medal 1965; FA Cup winners' medal 1964;
League Cup runners-up medal 1966; FA Cup final runners-up medal1975;
Footballer of the Year 1964; Hammer of the year:Winner: 1961, 1963, 1968,
1970; Runner-up: 1964, 1967, 1971.

West Ham United debuts
Colts   QPR (away) – Oct 6, 1956
Reserves   Birmingham (home) – Dec 7, 1957
League   Man.United (home) – Sept 8, 1958
League Cup   Charlton Ath. (home) –Sept 26, 1960
FA Cup   Stoke City (home) – Jan 7, 1961

Bobby's final League match for West Ham was on New Year's Day 1974 against
Norwich City. His last-ever game for the club was against Plymouth Argyle
Reserves on March 9, 1974.

International appearances
108 Full England caps; 8 England Under-23 caps; 18 England Youth caps; Peter
Shilton made 125 appearances but Bobby's 108 full caps are the most ever won
by an English outfield player. Also played 12 League representative matches.

	League		FA Cup		League Cup	
	Apps	Goals	Apps	Goals	Apps	Goals
West Ham United	544	24	36	0	49	3
Fulham	124	1	15	0	11	0
Total	668	25	51	0	60	3

October 2, 1957 – *England Youth team debut against Holland in Amsterdam.*
December 7, 1957 – *Makes debut for West Ham Reserves against Birmingham.*
Easter 1958 –*Captains England to runners-up spot in the European Youth*
  Championships
May 1958 –*Signs professional forms for West Ham.*
September 8, 1958 –*First team debut against Manchester United at Upton Park.*

254

September 21, 1960 – *Selected for England Under-23 but misses out as East Germany fail to obtain visas.*

November 2, 1960 – *Wins first cap for the Under-23s.*

May 20, 1962 – *Awarded first full England cap in win over Peru in Lima. Selected for World Cup squad.*

June 30, 1962 –*Marries Tina Dean in Ilford.*

May 20, 1963 – *Handed 12th cap and captaincy against Czechoslovakia.*

May 2, 1964 – *Captain of West Ham as they beat Preston North End 3-2 in the FA Cup final*

May 1964 –*Elected Footballer of the Year.*

September 23, 1964 – *Leads the first West Ham team to appear in Europe as Hammers win 1-0 in La Gantoise, Belgium.*

January 24, 1965 – *Moore's first child, Roberta Christina is born.*

May 19, 1965 –*Captains West Ham to a 2-0 victory over TSV Munich 1860 at Wembley in the European Cup Winners' Cup final. Alan Sealey scores both goals.*

March 1966 – *West Ham reach the League Cup final for the first time but lose to West Bromwich Albion 5-3 on aggregate.*

July 30, 1966 – *Collects the World Cup from Her Majesty the Queen after England defeat West Germany in the final, 4-2 after extra-time.*

January 1, 1967 – *Awarded the OBE in the New Year's Honours list.*

March 24, 1968 – *Moore's second child, Dean Anthony, is born.*

May/June 1970 – *Falsely accused of stealing a bracelet from a jewellers in Bogota, Colombia, but released on the eve of the tournament.*

August 10, 1970 – *Receives a kidnap threat to his wife Tina and children.*

November 14, 1970 – *Accidentally knocks out referee J. G. Lewis during a match against Wolves before retrieving the whistle and stopping play!*

November 16, 1970 – *A crowd of 24,448 pay £19,793 and seven shillings to watch a 3-3 draw with Celtic in Bobby's Testimonial .*

January 3, 1971 – *Following Hammers 4-0 FA Cup defeat against Blackpool, Moore is reported to have been seen in a nightclub on the eve of the game. He is left out of the next two games and then – for the only time – is put on the bench against Derby County.*

January 26, 1972 – *Takes over in goal in the 3-2 League Cup semi-final defeat against Stoke City. He saves a penalty but is beaten by the rebound.*

February 14, 1972 – *Wins his 100th cap against Scotland at Hampden Park.*

February 17, 1973 – *Passes Jimmy Ruffell's West Ham United record of 509 league appearances against West Bromwich Albion at Upton Park.*

November 14, 1973 – *Plays his 108th and final game for England against Italy.*

January 5, 1974 – *Bobby is carried off with twisted knee ligaments in what proves to be his last senior game for West Ham against Hereford in the FA Cup.*

March 9, 1974 – *Plays his last game for Hammers reserves in front of a few hundred spectators at Upton Park against Plymouth Argyle.*

March 14, 1974 – *Joins Fulham for £25,000.*

March 19, 1974 – *Makes his Fulham debut against Middlesbrough.*

October 8, 1974 – *Fulham beat West Ham 2-1 in a League Cup third round tie.*

May 3, 1975 – *Fulham lose 2-0 to Hammers in the FA Cup final.*

MOORE than a legend

Summer 1976 – *Plays for San Antonio Thunder in the North American League.*
May 14, 1977 – *Plays his final game for Fulham against Blackburn Rovers.*
Spring 1978 – *Becomes mentor to Danish Third Division side Herning.*
Summer 1978 – *Again plays in the NASL, for Seattle Sounders.*
December 12, 1979 – *Becomes manager of Oxford City until 1981.*
1983 – *Coaches Team Eastern Athletic in Hong Kong.*
March 1984 – *Becomes manager of Southend United, but leaves in May 1986.*
January 6, 1986 – *Divorces first wife Tina.*
1990 – *Becomes a football analyst and commentator for Capital Gold radio.*
April 22, 1991 – *Undergoes an operation for suspected cancer of the colon.*
August 5, 1991 – *Poppy Grace Moore, Bobby's first grandchild is born.*
December 4, 1991 – *Marries Stephanie Moore – by remarkable coincidence,
Stephanie's parents are Peter and Vera Moore – at Chelsea Registry Office.*
February 15, 1993 – *Makes his illness public.*
February 17, 1993 – *As radio analyst, appears at Wembley for the final time.*
February 24, 1993 – *Bobby Moore dies at home in Putney, aged 51.*
April 28, 1996 – *Frederick Robert Hobbis, Bobby's second grandchild, is born.*

Statistics compiled by Stuart Allen

The
Bobby Moore
Testimonial